Birds of The Bahamas and the Turks and Caicos Islands

Bruce Hallett

MACMILLAN
CARIBBEAN

Macmillan Education
Between Towns Road, Oxford OX4 3PP
A division of Macmillan Publishers Limited
Companies and representatives throughout the world

www.macmillan-caribbean.com

ISBN-13: 978–0333–937–44–0

ISBN-10: 0–333–93744–9

First published 2006

Typeset by CjB Editorial Plus
Illustrated by John Sill
Bahamas Archipelago map by Virginia Maynard
Cover design by Gary Fielder at AC Design
Cover photographs by Bruce Hallett
    Front cover: male Western Spindalis – Grand Bahama
    Back cover: male Bahama Yellowthroat – Abaco

Dedicated to Sheryl with love and gratitude

Printed and bound in Thailand

2010 2009 2008 2007 2006
10 9 8 7 6 5 4 3 2 1

Contents

Quick Reference Guide	*v*
Acknowledgements	*vii*
Map of The Bahamas and the Turks	
and Caicos Islands	*x*
Introduction	1
The region	2
Habitats	5
Taxonomy and bird names	8
The American Ornithologist's Union	9
Subspecies	9
Migration	10
Molt and plumage	13
Outline and plan of the species accounts	15
Bird topography	23
Species accounts	
Water Birds	25
Ducks and Geese	26
Grebes	35
Shearwaters	37
Storm-Petrels	38
Tropicbirds	39
Boobies	40
Pelicans	43
Cormorants	44
Frigatebirds	46
Herons, Egrets and Bitterns	47
Ibises and Spoonbills	60
Flamingos	63
Rails, Gallinules and Coots	65
Limpkin	70
Plovers	72
Oystercatchers	78
Stilts and Avocets	79
Sandpipers	80
Gulls, Terns and Skimmers	96

Land Birds 117

New World Quail 118
New World Vultures 119
Hawks 120
Falcons 122
Pigeons and Doves 125
Parrots 134
Cuckoos and Anis 135
Barn Owls and Typical Owls 138
Nighthawks and Nightjars 140
Hummingbirds 143
Kingfishers 147
Woodpeckers 148
Tyrant Flycatchers 151
Vireos 157
Crows 160
Swallows and Martins 161
Nuthatches 166
Gnatcatchers 167
Thrushes 168
Mockingbirds and Thrashers 169
Starlings 173
Pipits 174
Waxwings 175
Wood Warblers 176
Bananaquit 199
Tanagers 200
Grassquits and Sparrows 203
Grosbeaks and Buntings 208
Blackbirds and Orioles 211
Old World Sparrows 217

Appendix 218

Glossary of Selected Terms 218
Endemic Species (E) with Subspecies (e) 222
Photography Notes 224
Checklist of the Birds of The Bahamas
  and the Turks and Caicos Islands 227
Bibliography 232

Index 237

Quick reference guide

Ani	137	Nightjars	140–142
Bananaquit	199	Night-Herons	58, 59
Bittern	48	Nuthatch	166
Blackbirds	211–216	Orioles	214–216
Boobies	40	Owls	138, 139
Bullfinch	205	Oystercatcher	78
Buntings	208, 209	Parrot	134
Coot	68	Pelican	43
Cormorants	44	Pewees	151, 152
Cowbirds	212, 213	Pigeons	125, 126
Crow	160	Pipit	174
Cuckoos	135, 136	Plovers	72–77
Doves	127–133	Quail	118
Ducks	26–34	Rails	65, 66
Egrets	50, 51, 54	Sandpipers	80–95
Falcons	122–124	Shearwaters	37
Flamingo	63	Shorebirds	71–95
Flycatchers	151–156	Skimmer	116
Frigatebird	46	Sparrows	206, 207
Gallinule	69	Spindalis	200
Gnatcatcher	167	Spoonbill	60
Grassquits	203, 204	Starling	173
Grebes	35	Stilt	79
Grosbeaks	210	Storm-Petrels	38
Gulls	96–102	Swallows	161–165
Hawks	120, 121	Tanagors	202
Herons	49, 52, 53	Terns	103–116
Hummingbirds	143–146	Thrasher	171, 172
Ibises	61, 62	Thrushes	168
Kingbirds	154–156	Tropicbird	39
Kingfisher	147	Vireos	157–159
Limpkin	70	Vultures	119
Martin	164	Warblers	176–198
Mockingbirds	169, 170	Waxwing	175
Moorhen	67	Woodpeckers	148–150

Acknowledgements

It would have been impossible to undertake a task like this without help from other people. Not only did I rely on others for information and knowledge, but I also greatly appreciated their support and encouragement. The key players were: **Ailene Bainton** (Nassau and Long Island, NY) read the whole manuscript and provided many helpful comments at each stage of the process, as well as giving me a consistent dose of support and encouragement. I first met Ailene on a mattress on the back of a pick-up truck while birding Great Inagua in 1993 and since then, her friendship and the good laughs have been a vital link in this whole endeavor. **Tony White** (Nassau and Bethesda, MD) is responsible for having introduced me to The Bahamas in 1993. Since then, we have shared not only a friendship but also many terrific trips to the region investigating various old and new locations. He is the author of an excellent bird-finding guide to the region but, most important for me, his meticulous research on the records, status and range of birds from his book, made it possible for me to include that information, and more, in this book. He also had a major hand in getting this project started and helped write the first draft, for which I am very grateful. **Paul Dean** (Nassau) is the bedrock of knowledge and experience for the birds of The Bahamas, especially New Providence. He is an outstanding field man and has been recognized for many years as the key guy in the region. Paul reviewed all the species accounts and gave me invaluable advice and information about distribution, plumage, arrival and departure times, and vocalizations. I have benefited greatly from discussions and birding trips with him and I can't thank him enough for his input. **Woody Bracey** (Treasure Cay, Abaco) read much of the manuscript and contributed many helpful insights and suggestions. I relied on him on many occasions for information on status and records from Abaco. It has also helped that he is a great pal and birding companion with an infectious brand of enthusiasm and energy that helped me keep the fire within. **Giff Beaton** (Marietta, GA) is my local authority, cheering section and good friend. He read the whole text – some sections several times – and I could always count on him to provide me with helpful comments and suggestions. Being a published author himself, he was also sympathetic to my gripes and patiently listened to whatever I had to say. I also relied on Giff to make sure that the descriptions and statements about the birds with which he was familiar were accurate, so I will look to blame him if it later turns out there are any inaccuracies! **John Sill** (Franklin, NC) produced the black and white illustrations for the bird topography section and several of the species accounts and I heartily thank him for his efforts. He graciously made himself available for the projects I proposed and was always amenable to any changes. I have always admired and respected his skills as an artist and appreciate his ability to get the correct 'look' or 'feel' of a bird. My gratitude is also extended to the other **photographers** who contributed their photographs to fill in the many voids in my own library. Their names and their individual photographs are listed in the appendix.

There were others whose opinion I valued and who made their contribution. **Patricia Bradley** (Georgetown, Grand Cayman), author of two excellent bird books on the Cayman Islands, read portions of the manuscript and quickly homed in on what she felt could be improved. **Eric Carey** (Nassau, New Providence) who has done so much in drawing attention and awareness to birds and conservation in The Bahamas, was always available for comments and encouragement. **Audrey Davis** (Atlanta) took on the task of organizing and word processing the whole project, so she deserves considerable thanks and appreciation. **Erika M. Gates** (Freeport, Grand Bahama) was very helpful in both sorting out bird records from her island and in giving me my only opportunity to photograph a Key-West Quail Dove. She also deserves a lot of credit for her work promoting appreciation of birds through her business and through the media. **John Kricher** (Cape Cod, M.A.) and his most delightful wife, **Martha Vaughan**, read an earlier draft and were positive about proceeding. **Nancy E. Norman** (San Antonio, TX) took me on several field trips in the Cayman Islands to track down certain birds and their vocalizations and gave me several suggestions for the manuscript. **Neil Sealey** (Nassau, New Providence) helped me with a couple of the introductory sections and always made himself available for my phone calls or visits. **Bailey Smith** (Great Exuma) was responsible for guiding and assisting me to take photos of breeding terns on an offshore cay outside Georgetown Harbor and for providing valuable information about the local Roseate Terns.

Another group of people assisted my efforts in a variety of ways. Whether it was their hospitality, a birding trip, comments or new information, I want to acknowledge them for their contributions: Michael Baltz, Sheryl Bear, Betsy Bracey, Jon Dunn, Ruth and Walter Gander, Lynn Gape, Judy and Tom Gire, Chris Haney, Tony Hepburn, Steve Howell, Linda Huber, Andy Kratter, Dave Lee, Lionel Levine, Pericles Maillis, D. Moore, Caroline and Bart Milligan, Mark Oberle, Kathy and Rick Oliver, Freddie Schaller, Carolyn Wardle and Trina White.

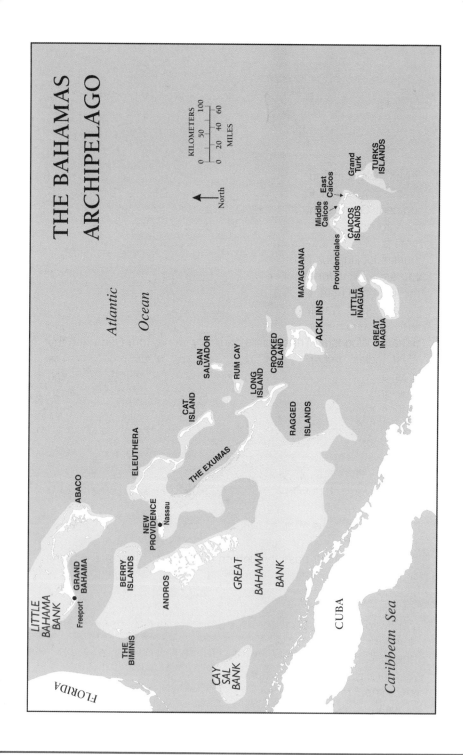

THE BAHAMAS ARCHIPELAGO

FLORIDA

Atlantic

Ocean

LITTLE
BAHAMA
BANK

Freeport •
GRAND
BAHAMA

ABACO

THE
BIMINIS

BERRY
ISLANDS

ANDROS

NEW
PROVIDENCE
Nassau •

ELEUTHERA

CAT
ISLAND

SAN
SALVADOR

RUM CAY

THE EXUMAS

CAY
SAL
BANK

GREAT
BAHAMA
BANK

LONG
ISLAND

CROOKED
ISLAND

RAGGED
ISLANDS

ACKLINS

MAYAGUANA

Providenciales

Middle
Caicos

East
Caicos

CAICOS
ISLANDS

Grand
Turk

TURKS
ISLANDS

LITTLE
INAGUA

GREAT
INAGUA

CUBA

Caribbean Sea

North

KILOMETERS
0   50   100
0 20 40 60
MILES

Introduction

It has always intrigued me that, less than 70 miles off the coast of West Palm Beach, Florida, there exists a very different birding environment. Grand Bahama Island has clear waters, pleasant beaches, mangroves, hardwoods (called coppice) and pinewoods – very similar to parts of South Florida. There are resort hotels, 'fast food joints', tourists looking for 'fun 'n sun' – also similar to Florida. However, if you are looking for Cardinals, Blue Jays or Carolina Wrens, you will not find them here. Instead, Loggerhead Kingbirds, Cuban Pewees, Olive-capped Warblers, and Bahama Yellowthroats are what you'll find – even two new species of hummingbirds, Cuban Emerald and Bahama Woodstar. These birds originally came from Cuba and the West Indies, rather than Florida and North America. There are 'crossover' birds such as Laughing Gulls, Northern Mockingbirds and Blue-gray Gnatcatchers which also exist in Grand Bahama, so there is some evidence of the influence from Florida but, for the most part, you will find a distinctly separate avian community.

The objective of this book is to introduce both visitors and residents to the bird life of not only Grand Bahama but also the other islands in The Bahamas and the Turks and Caicos. Currently, there is no one reference or field guide that is devoted entirely to the birds of just this region.

The text contains photographs and information on all of the breeding birds of the region, together with the most commonly recorded migrants that either pass through on their way to other destinations or that stay for the winter season. Not every bird that has been recorded in the region is discussed, because that would go beyond the intent of the book. In the species accounts, the emphasis is on how to recognize or identify the various species and the various plumages they acquire. Not surprisingly, some birds are easier than others. Additionally, there is information on how the birds are distributed throughout the islands and whether or not they are common, uncommon, rare, etc. Behavior and habitat preferences are covered as well as calls and songs. There are also comments about the region's subspecies especially those that are endemic to the area.

The region

The Bahamas Archipelago in the western tropical Atlantic Ocean consists of a varied range of hundreds of large and small islands and many smaller cays (pronounced 'keys') and exposed rocks. These islands lie in a north-west to south-east direction for over 600 miles (1,000 km) from the northern Bahama islands of Grand Bahama and Abaco to the southernmost island of Grand Turk in the Turks and Caicos Islands. The whole area covers over 100,000 square miles (260,000 sq km) of which only 5,500 square miles (14,000 sq km) is land. (The main islands are illustrated on the map on page x). The western end of Grand Bahama is less than 60 miles (100 km) from West Palm Beach, Florida and the southern tip of Great Inagua is less than 80 miles (130 km) east of Cuba. The Turks and Caicos Islands are less than 80 miles (130 km) from Hispaniola.

The archipelago consists of two political entities – the Commonwealth of The Bahamas and the Turks and Caicos Islands. The Bahamas became an independent nation in July 1973 after 250 years as a colony of Great Britain. In 2000, there were 305,000 people, of which 70 per cent (or over 200,000 people) live on New Providence, where the historic capital of Nassau is located. Nassau is the main business center and commercial port catering for both hotel and cruise ship tourists. Another 50,000 people live in and around the town of Freeport on Grand Bahama, the other main destination for tourists. The rest of the population and tourist destinations are spread throughout the towns and settlements on the other islands of The Bahamas (mostly Abaco, Andros, Eleuthera and Great Exuma) which are known collectively as the Family Islands or the Out Islands.

Although administered by both Jamaica and The Bahamas in the past, since 1973, the Turks and Caicos Islands have been a self-governing British Crown Colony. Of the approximately 25,000 residents in 2000, 18,000 live on the island of Providenciales (often referred to as 'Provo') in the Caicos Islands. Provo is by far the most developed island in the Turks and Caicos and is the principal site for tourism. The capital and seat of government is Cockburn Town (pronounced 'Ko' burn') on the island of Grand Turk.

Geologically, The Bahamas Archipelago should be looked at as a series of submerged platforms that rise from the sea floor with the exposed parts creating the islands of The Bahamas and Turks and

Caicos. The islands average only 50 feet (15 m) above sea level, with Mount Alvernia on Cat Island being the highest point at 209 feet (64 m). Eons ago, the formation of The Bahamas platform started with the skeletal remains of countless millions of sea creatures piling up in layer upon layer of sediment over millions of years. This sediment, consisting mainly of calcium carbonate, consolidated to form the limestone rock – the exclusive bedrock of the islands. During sedimentation, the platform broke up in places, and deep troughs and canyons developed in and around the platforms of the northern and central Bahamas. Examples include the Providence Channel, between Little Bahama Bank and Great Bahama Bank, which is 10,000–13,000 feet (3,000–3,900 m) deep and the Tongue of the Ocean between Andros and New Providence at 3,000–6,000 feet (1,000–1,800 m) deep. The southern Bahamas and the Turks and Caicos Islands are positioned like isolated pinnacles, surrounded by much smaller banks than are the northern islands. In turn, deep ocean waters surround each bank. It is believed that this part of the archipelago may have a different foundation and more recent origin compared to the sedimentary building process of the northern and central Bahamas.

More recently, during the last ice age, which ended roughly 16,000 years ago, the region was affected by changes in sea level, due to the large volumes of water trapped on land in the form of snow and ice much further north. It is thought that the sea level dropped several times to a maximum of 400 feet (120 m) below present levels, creating large areas of land. On the map on page x, the outlines show what the land masses of the Little Bahama Bank and the much larger Great Bahama Bank would have looked like at that time. When the ice melted, the sea levels rose again, flooding the banks and islands to the present levels. Shallow water over the banks averages about 20 feet (6 m) deep. Thus, The Bahamas and the Turks and Caicos Islands look today very similar to what they did 16,000 years ago.

Throughout the book there are a number of references to various locations in The Bahamas Archipelago, the West Indies and the Americas. The Bahamas and the Turks and Caicos Islands, while technically not part of the West Indies because they do not border the Caribbean Sea, are considered part of the West Indies because the plant and animal life are so similar. The following explains what these locations include. References to 'the region' include all of the islands of The Bahamas and the Turks and Caicos Islands (abbreviated as TCI).

The Bahamas Archipelago

Northern Bahamas: Grand Bahama, Abaco, the Biminis, Berry Islands, Andros (north, central and south), Cay Sal Bank, New Providence and Eleuthera.
Central Bahamas: The Exumas, Cat Island, Ragged Islands, Long Island, Rum Cay and San Salvador.
Southern Bahamas: Crooked and Acklins Islands, Samana Cay, Great and Little Inagua and Mayaguana.
Caicos Islands: West Caicos, Providenciales, North, Middle and East Caicos.
Turks Islands: Grand Turk and Salt Cay.

The Antillean West Indies

The Greater Antilles: The group of islands which lie in a general west to east direction and which consist of Cuba, The Cayman Islands, Jamaica, Hispaniola (Haiti and the Dominican Republic), Puerto Rico and the Virgin Islands.
The Lesser Antilles: The group of islands which lie in a general north/south direction, ranging from Anguilla in the north to Grenada in the south and which include major islands such as Montserrat, Guadeloupe, Dominica, St. Lucia and Barbados.

The Americas

North America includes Canada and the United States of America abbreviated as USA. South Florida refers to the southern tip of Florida from Fort Lauderdale through Everglades National Park. The Florida Keys from Key Largo to Key West.
Middle America includes Mexico and the Yucatan Peninsula through Panama.
South America mainly includes just the northern countries of Colombia and Venezuela.

Habitats

Habitats are the places where birds feed, breed, nest, roost, etc. and generally make their living. Some resident birds stay in the same habitat year round, while others may move to a different one, depending upon the season or the food supply. Winter residents may spend the non-breeding season in a different habitat from that of their breeding season. Gaining familiarity with birds and their preferred habitats helps anticipate what species to look for and may help with identification. The following five general categories cover the main habitats in The Bahamas and Turks and Caicos Islands and include examples of species typical of that habitat. More detailed information about each species and their habitat preferences occurs in the species accounts.

1 *Uninhabited offshore islands and cays relatively close to deep oceanic water.* Audubon's Shearwater, Brown Booby, Magnificent Frigatebird and several tern species use these islands for breeding. Cays with vegetation or trees may also attract White-crowned Pigeon, Zenaida Dove or Yellow Warbler.

Offshore cays: Acklins

2 *Fresh, salt or brackish water environments found either along the coast or inland.* These areas include beaches, tidal flats, estuaries and lagoons, ponds and lakes, shallow saline ponds, marshy spots with reeds or cattails and mangrove marshes. Salt evaporation ponds and golf course ponds, although man-made, are included. Some shorebirds will make use of puddles created by rainfall. Water birds include grebes, cormorants, herons, egrets, ducks, rails and shorebirds. Land birds that use the vegetation or mangroves surrounding a wet area include Antillean Nighthawk, Belted Kingfisher, flycatchers, vireos, swallows, warblers and bananaquits.

3 *Pinewoods:* The Bahamian variety of the Caribbean Pine (*Pinus caribea*) grows only on Grand Bahama, Abaco, North Andros and New Providence in the northern Bahamas. If allowed to mature,

Freshwater pond: Abaco   Shallow saline pond: Ragged Islands

these pines can grow to 80–90 feet (24–27 m) but, today, most of the pines are shorter. The understorey, which may be either dense or sparse, consists of thatch palms, ferns and grasses. The pinewoods depend upon occasional fires to burn out the understorey and allow new seedlings to grow. (The indiscriminate lighting of fires by people for their own purposes without regard to the larger picture is destructive and not beneficial to the pinewoods.) Pinewoods are the preferred habitat of Cuban Pewee, Loggerhead Kingbird and Bahama Swallow and is the only habitat in which to find Brown-headed Nuthatch and three species of warblers – Pine, Olive-capped, and Yellow-throated (Pine and Yellow-throated Warblers are resident endemic subspecies). Another Bahamian variety of the Caribbean Pine grows in the Caicos Islands on Pine Cay and on North and Middle Caicos, but these pinewoods are more sparse and do not cover as much of an area as those in the northern Bahamas. The bird life on these islands has no particular preference for pinewoods as they do in the northern Bahamas. The native Caribbean Pine

Pinewoods: Grand Bahama   Pocket of coppice in pinewoods: Abaco

should not be confused with the introduced Australian Pine or Casuarina (*Casuarina litorea*) which occurs throughout the more developed islands.

4 *Coppice*: A mix of native hardwoods or broadleaf trees is known as coppice in the region. Visitors would call it 'woods' or 'woodland' and locals often refer to it as 'the bush'. Coppice can grow high or low, thick or sparse and is found on all the islands, including those with pinewoods. In some cases, small coppice stands are found within, or along the edges of, pinewoods. In the northern and central Bahamas, where it is relatively cooler and wetter, the coppice is generally taller and thicker than coppice in the southern Bahamas where the vegetation is lower, more scrub-like, and includes more cactus plants. The Turks and Caicos Islands are similar to the southern Bahamas where the seasons range from warm to hot and dry to arid. Rainfall averages between 20–30 inches (50–75 cm) per year. The islands of North, Middle and East Caicos receive relatively more rain than do the others, so the coppice is relatively more lush. Birds associated with coppice include doves, cuckoos, vireos, Red-legged Thrush, Bahama Mockingbird, certain species of warblers and Greater Antillean Bullfinch.

Tall coppice: Great Exuma   Low coppice scrub: Provo

5 *Human altered habitats*: Any area that has been changed or altered by humans. The list covers a wide range and includes gardens, ornamental trees, flowers and shrubs, grass lawns, hummingbird and seed feeders all of which may be found around houses, settlements, parks and hotel or resort grounds. Often there is a mix of taller, native and non-native trees and plants around these areas, which can be good for attracting birds. Other human habi-

tats include golf courses, harbors and marinas, farms (livestock, crops or fruit) and garbage dumps or landfill sites. Associated birds are Cattle Egret, Ruddy Turnstone, Killdeer, gulls, doves, Smooth-billed Ani, hummingbirds, Red-legged Thrush, Northern Mockingbird, starlings, bananaquit and House Sparrow.

It should be noted that all the environments or habitats of The Bahamas and Turks and Caicos Islands have been affected or altered by humans in one way or another. The pinewoods were heavily cut and logged during the 1950s and 1960s and the coppice has been heavily cut or cleared in the past. The areas that we see today are not the original vegetation, although they may look relatively untouched.

Taxonomy and bird names

There are thousands of bird species throughout the world and there is a scientific system that arranges and classifies all these birds based on their evolutionary history and the relationships (similarities and differences) between them. Relationships include physical features, body structure, physiology, behavior, etc. The science of dividing and grouping these classifications and naming them is called **taxonomy**. All the names are in Latin and the same system is applied to all other plants and animals. The names of the categories range from the general to the specific with one building upon the previous one: Kingdom, Phylum, Class, Order, Family, Genus and Species. In some cases, further divisions are required and suborders, subfamilies or subspecies are created. For this book, classification includes only the family, genus and species. The family is a group of genera (plural of genus) that share related characteristics, while the genus is a group of species that share related characteristics. The species is the basic unit of the system upon which higher classifications are built. Subfamilies and subspecies are mentioned or described in the appropriate species account.

All birds have a common name followed by a scientific name, such as the Loggerhead Kingbird: *Tyrannus caudifasciatus*. The common name is given in English for this text, although names vary between countries or languages and are therefore not universal. The two-part scientific name is always in Latin and usually italicized. That name is recognized world-wide and is not shared with any other two-part name. The first name, *Tyrannus*, refers to the genus that the bird belongs to and is always capitalized. The second name, *caudifasciatus*, refers to the species and is not capitalized. If there is a subspecies (also called race), as there is for the Loggerhead Kingbird in The Bahamas, then a third Latin name is added *Tyrannus caudifasciatus bahamensis* which may be abbreviated as *T. c. bahamensis*.

The American Ornithologist's Union

The American Ornithologist's Union (AOU), founded in 1884, is the governing organization for the classification and naming of the birds of North America, which includes Middle America and the West Indies. A committee within the AOU reviews the research and makes decisions about changes, additions and deletions to the list of birds. These decisions include redefining family or genus classifications as well as accepting and naming new species. The AOU publishes a checklist of North American birds and revises it periodically. The order, or sequence of the listings, is based upon their evolutionary history: the oldest birds being placed first and the most recently evolved being placed last. The list of birds described in this text generally follows the sequence and specifically follows the names of species of the AOU's most recent publication *The AOU Checklist of North American Birds* (7th ed, 1998). Supplements, which update changes since 1998, were published periodically but now come out annually and information from them is also included up through 2005. For instance, the AOU in 2003 rearranged the order of bird families by placing whistling ducks, geese and ducks ahead of grebes. The main deviation from the AOU checklist in this book takes the quails, vultures, hawks and falcons out of sequence and places them at the beginning of the Land Birds section for convenience. There is also some slight sequence juggling with several of the families in order to present resident breeding species first followed by migrants. A checklist of the birds of The Bahamas and the Turks and Caicos Islands, in correct order, is given on page 227.

Subspecies

Many of the species described in the text have one or more subspecies (also referred to as race) in the region. Some are recognized as an endemic subspecies, unique because they breed only in the region and are not found in any other locations – anywhere. A subspecies is defined as part of a population of a species where individuals show some variation, or distinctness, which is unlike any other population of that same species. For example, part of the overall population of Bahama Yellowthroats is a subspecies, *G. r. coryi*, on Eleuthera and Cat Island, which is unlike any of the other subspecies on the other islands where Bahama Yellowthroats occur. Subspecies usually occupy a distinct geographical area, such as an island, where they evolve in isolation from other groups of the same species. Some of these variations may include plumage, song type, size, behavior, etc., but most of the time, these variations are slight and are not always distinguishable in the field. Subspecies are important because they show geographical variation within a species, they test birding skills, and they may, eventually, become a full species. Also, they are included because people whose opinion and mentoring I value, would physically harm me if they were not.

Recognition of a subspecies, however, may be overdone in some instances as the validity of some recognized subspecies is questioned by taxonomists. Since subspecies are essentially created by scientists, there is always considerable debate over the methods or techniques used and the conclusions reached. With this in mind, arguments over the validity of a subspecies in this book are not discussed. Going back to the Bahama Yellowthroat, for example, some authorities (scientists) recognize three subspecies for the region while others recognize four (see species account).

All endemic subspecies and some of the other subspecies which have a restricted or particular range in the West Indies, are noted in the species accounts. The AOU does not publish subspecies in its most recent (1998) checklist. The Howard and Moore *Complete Checklist of the Birds of the World* (3rd ed, 2003) does, however, publish the subspecies of each species, along with its range, and has been chosen as the source for any subspecies listed in this book.

Migration

Migration refers to the regular movement of birds between their breeding and non-breeding (or wintering) grounds. Distances vary dramatically. Black-bellied Plovers, for example, make long-distance migrations from the arctic tundra of North America to the region, while some populations of White-crowned Pigeons make short migratory flights between their breeding areas in the Florida Keys and their non-breeding areas on Andros. The time spent on the wintering grounds, for many species, is six months or more, which makes it a critical part of their life cycle. Between 65 per cent and 70 per cent of the species in The Bahamas and TCI are considered migrants and nearly all of them are from breeding areas of North America. Furthermore, close to 50 per cent of the total land bird population in winter on some of the northern islands, will be migrants. Some migrants reach the region in fall, spend the winter and leave in spring. Others stay for a period of time before continuing on their migration, or simply overfly the region and do not stop. A few migrate to the region to breed. Migrating birds move across a broad front, rather than through narrow corridors and many travel at night, when atmospheric conditions are more suitable than during the day. Favorable winds are a key component to their travels, but strong headwinds, rain or storms may force them to land which would be fatal for some species if over water.

Birds are not considered to be migrating in the region when they move back and forth between the islands or disperse to other areas after breeding. Lesser Yellowlegs that move from Long Island to Great Inagua during the winter season to find better food resources are only making movements not migrations. Similarly, after the breeding season, when a juvenal Little Blue Heron from New Providence moves to the Exumas to start a new life, this movement is based on post-breeding dispersal and is not considered migratory behavior.

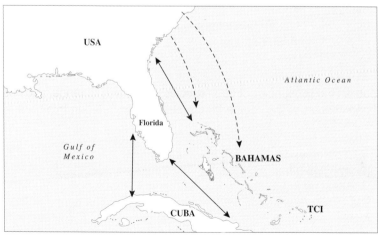

Map shows general routes for migration between The Bahamas and TCI and North America. Solid lines with arrows in both directions represent spring and fall migration. Broken lines are additional routes for fall migration.

General orientation for migratory birds is north/south. However, in the region, it is believed that birds in spring migration follow a general northwest route towards Florida. Migrants from other parts of the West Indies also take this northwesterly direction towards Florida (although birds from western Cuba would head on a more northerly course). Futhermore, birds from Grand Bahama and Abaco and some of the easterly islands, like Eleuthera and Cat Island, are also thought to head northwest, but this route takes them over open water, usually missing Florida completely, and reaching land further along the southeast coast of the USA. Spring migration begins in March and continues through April and most of May. Herons and ducks are usually the first birds to leave in March and Blackpoll Warblers, Bobolinks and a few shorebirds from outside the region are usually the last species to pass through in May. Spring migration for Antillean Nighthawks, Gray Kingbirds and Black-whiskered Vireos, which migrate from northern South America to breed in the region, starts with their arrival, mostly in April and, most likely, completing their migrations by mid-May. Spring migration, when birds try to reach their breeding destinations as quickly as possible, involves a relatively short time period. Given good fat reserves and favorable winds, migrants will infrequently stop along their route and will overfly most areas in the region.

Fall migration (late July/early August to November) involves a longer period of time and happens at a relatively more leisurely pace. Some shorebirds and warblers, for instance, start their fall migration in July and August and, while a few trickle down to the region at that time, the main thrust of fall migration occurs between mid-September and mid-October. Birds continue to move late into November and early December but not in such great numbers. The arrival of ducks, gulls and sparrows in November usually indicates the final touches to fall migration, but there are always a few lingerers regardless of species. The fall is the best time of year to encounter rarer species. The routes for fall migration are similar to those for spring migration but in fall, there are significantly more birds and species. There are two reasons for this: first, more birds have shifted their fall migration easterly and, second, there are additional numbers of juveniles and immatures. Birds that migrated to eastern North America in the spring, through Middle America or across the Gulf of Mexico, well west of the region, move more easterly for the start of the fall migration. For many birds, the easterly shift takes them to the east coast of the USA and from there they are thought to move southerly, over land, or move off the coast and make an over-water flight to the region. Add to this the juveniles and immatures that are making their first fall migration in the same fashion and there are more birds in fall.

Molt and plumage

Plumage is the coat of feathers that birds wear and is essential to their survival and well-being. Feathers not only provide flight and protection, but their colors and patterns play a key role in courtship and/or camouflage. Plumage also represents a bird's overall appearance, the primary factor for identification. However, feathers do not last forever and wear and tear eventually take their toll. As a result, birds undergo a process, at cyclic intervals, of losing their old feathers and growing new ones. This process, called molt, is usually prolonged and, depending upon the species, takes a few weeks to a few months or even longer to complete. Molt is also a taxing process for birds, so conditions like food, cover, etc. have to be at an optimum. All birds go through a complete molt once a year and, some species also have a partial molt by which they replace some of their feathers but not all. For example, an adult Brown Booby has one complete (all the feathers) molt a year, whereas an adult Blackpoll Warbler has one complete and one partial (head and body feathers only) molt a year. Observation of the molting process in the field is limited, but may include a soaring Red-tailed Hawk without a flight feather, a Loggerhead Kingbird with growing tail feathers of varying lengths or the transitional plumage of a Black-bellied Plover or Laughing Gull. In transitional plumage, which may be either subtle or obvious, birds show a mix of both the faded, worn feathers from the old plumage and the neater, fresher feathers of the new. Shorebirds and gulls are usually the best examples for observing a plumage in transition. For this book, the important thing is how molt changes the appearance, or plumage, of a species and whether or not it may be recognizable. In many cases, all the cyclical molts of adult and immature plumages reproduce the same color or pattern, making identification easier. There are, however, differences in plumage within some species that may be based upon a bird's age (adult or immature) or season (fall/winter or spring/summer). Being able to age and name a plumage is helpful for identification. The terms used in this book to describe the aging process or the plumage sequences of a species are named and defined as follows:

- **juvenile:** Young birds, or nestlings, after hatching, are either naked or covered with fluffy down. Usually around the time they leave the nest, they acquire their first set of real (non-downy) feathers and are then called juveniles or birds in juvenal plumage. Some larger birds, such as cormorants or herons, keep their juvenal plumage through much of their first year, while shorebirds keep theirs for only a few months and smaller land birds, such as warblers, stay as juveniles for just a few weeks.
- **immature:** At some stage, which varies among species, a bird molts and the juvenal plumage is replaced. An immature bird is defined here as one that has one or more plumages between the juvenile and the adult. The length of time a bird spends in immature plumage also depends upon the species. Larger birds, such as frigatebirds, boobies and gulls, spend several years as immatures, whereas for smaller land birds, such as vireos and warblers, the transition period may last less than a year. There are several terms to describe the various forms of immature plumages which are used to identify the age and season of individual birds. The first immature plumage after juvenile is commonly termed first-winter plumage which is acquired during the first fall and winter of its life, generally between September and March. This is followed by the first-summer plumage between April and August. By this time, the immature is one year old and, for most smaller birds, many species undergo a complete molt to adult plumage. For those species, most larger birds, that remain as immatures, the sequence continues to second winter, second summer, third winter etc. until they reach adulthood. These terms are useful for recognizing immature plumages but, for many species, the exact stage of an immature plumage is unrecognizable or unknown so that these birds are simply referred to as immatures.
- **adult breeding and adult non-breeding:** Depending upon the species, the immature plumage is eventually replaced by the adult plumage. As adults, both males and females are sexually mature and go through annual cycles of a breeding and non-breeding season. In many cases, the same appearance is kept throughout the year and is simply called the adult plumage. For example, male and female Thick-billed Vireos molt during these cycles, but their plumages look similar year round, so they would just be termed adult Thick-billed Vireos. The same is true

for Red-winged Blackbirds but a distinction would be made here between the adult male and the adult female, because males and females have different plumages. In other cases, the plumage of a breeding adult differs from that of the non-breeding adult. For example, Laughing Gulls would be known as either adult breeding or adult non-breeding and male Indigo Buntings would be an adult male breeding or an adult male non-breeding because they differ from the females.

Outline and plan of the species accounts

The species accounts represent the foundation of the book. Just over 200 species of birds are covered, of which 100 are breeding species and the rest occur as migrants. Some of those 100 breeding species have migratory populations as well. All the species are broken down into two general categories – Water Birds and Land Birds. This was done for a more convenient reference, even though it does alter some of the taxonomic order.

Each species is presented with photographs and a written description. The written description follows a consistent format with sections and information on family, status and range, description of plumage, voice, habits, similar species and additional comments. For breeding birds, the sections are in bold face followed by a paragraph, while for non-breeding birds (migrants, winter residents, etc.) the format is just a paragraph without the bold face sections. The information is the same but the format is different.

The Sections

Family: All the species are broken down into the family they represent, so the family name and a brief account are presented first. Families are a major category and, for some species, may be further classified by subfamilies. First the size of the family and its distribution in the world, or a part of it, are briefly stated. The number of species in a family ranges from small (10–50 species), medium (50–150 species) to large (150–300 species) and in some cases, very small (less than 10 species) to very large (over 300 species). Families are distributed throughout the world, in the Old World (Europe, Africa, Asia and Australia), or the New World (North, Middle and South America including the West Indies). Short descriptions follow that give general information about the shared characteristics of each family, traits that may include appearance, behavior, habitat and structural similarities and, sometimes, notes on taxonomy. Herons, ducks, shorebirds, gulls, terns and warblers are families that are more complex and challenging than the others. For this reason, there is an expanded discussion for each, which covers general topics like status and range, migration, plumage sequences and identification.

At the end of the family account, or the category marked winter residents and transients, the name, status and general range of the rarer, but usually annual transients, are mentioned but not described. There are 39 species that fall into this category. It was decided to exclude full descriptions and details of these birds because they are not among the more commonly recorded migrants and, therefore, go beyond the scope and intent of this book. They are common breeders and transients in North America and are well described and illustrated in North American field guides. They are mentioned to let the reader know that a relatively small number of these birds do move through the region on a seasonal basis. More experienced birders who are familiar with these species might also wish to know their general status.

Species name: The common name, in English, of each bird is listed first followed by the scientific name in Latin. A bold face capital Ⓔ between the common and scientific name indicates an endemic species and a bold face lower case ⓔ between the names indicates an endemic subspecies, in which case, the three-part scientific name is given. The comments section contains further information about the endemic species or subspecies. (A list of endemic species and subspecies from the region also appears on pp. 222–223.)

Photographs: Color photographs were selected to illustrate each species and to complement the written descriptions. Usually, there are two or more photographs for each species, to show not only the range of plumages within each species (such as male, female or breeding, non-breeding) but also to depict the most common way someone is probably going to observe or encounter a species, for example, by posture or habitat. In a few cases, only one photograph was necessary. Furthermore, in ten of the species' accounts, black and white line drawings were used as a visual reference, mainly because the appropriate photograph was not available. It was, however, not realistic or practical to show photographs of all the possible plumages or of all the possible positions and behaviors.

Captions are usually brief and describe the age and sex of the bird, the island in The Bahamas or Turks and Caicos Islands where the photograph was taken and the month in which it was taken. If the age or sex is not indicated, then it can be assumed that the bird is an adult or I did not know the precise age or sex and and left it out. If a photograph was taken outside The Bahamas and the Turks and Caicos Islands, then no location is given and it can be assumed that the location is the USA. The only exception is that there are nine photographs from the Cayman Islands and they have been captioned as such.

Status and range: This section gives each species a status in the region and a range of where where it may be found. Status involves two categories: the first describes an estimate of a bird's abundance or lack of abundance (presence or lack of presence) in the region and the second describes whether it is a breeder, non-breeder, migrant or visitor. If the season (winter, summer, etc.) is known, then that is also included. Status may differ from island to island or from one part of the region to another. The use of the term 'abundance' also varies for different groups of birds. Turkey Vultures are common on Andros and so are Thick-billed Vireos, but there are many more vireos than vultures. In many cases, the complete status and range of a species either within the whole region, or a part of it, is either unclear or unknown and is stated as such. Range (also referred to as distribution) is the area that a resident, migrant or visiting bird occupies in The Bahamas and the Turks and Caicos Islands. Some birds have a large range over many islands, such as the Thick-billed Vireo, while others, like the Great Lizard Cuckoo, have a limited range over only three islands. Migrant birds usually have a wide and changeable range but often a pattern emerges so that they can be assigned an overall area such as the northern or southern Bahamas.

The following terms are used to describe the overall status of each species. Numbers refer to the relative ease of searching and finding that species in the appropriate habitat and at the correct time of year or season.

- **common:** the species is present in good numbers in suitable habitat and season. It should be fairly easy to find or hear. Examples: Thick-billed Vireo and Bananaquit.
- **fairly common:** the species is present in moderate numbers in suitable habitat and season. One might expect to find the species more or less regularly, but they can be occasionally missed. Examples: Tricolored Heron and Greater Antillean Bullfinch.
- **uncommon:** the species is present in small numbers in suitable habitat and season. It is not easily or regularly found, even in

suitable habitat, and may require a special search. Examples: Bahama Swallow and Yellow-bellied Sapsucker.

- **rare:** the species is present each year, but in very small numbers – perhaps only one to five birds annually. It is difficult to find and is not expected. Examples: Red-Breasted Merganser and Summer Tanager.
- **very rare:** the species is present in very small numbers but is not annual – perhaps only one to five birds over several years. Examples: American Golden Plover and Caspian Tern.
- **accidental:** usually refers to a species that reaches the region by accident and is way out of its normal range (commonly known as a vagrant) but these accidentals are not covered in the text. For this book, the term applies only to a few cases where a breeding species occurs outside the breeding range by accident, usually singly, with no pattern of occurrence and, historically, only a few records. Examples: Turkey Vulture on Eleuthera and Red-footed Booby off East Caicos.
- **permanent resident:** a breeding species present in the region throughout the year. Examples: Common Ground-Dove and Bahama Mockingbird.

The following three terms are used to distinguish between migrants which move to, from or through the region:

- **summer resident:** a breeding species present in the region (April–October), which migrates to the region in spring (March–May), breeds during the summer season (May–August) and departs in the fall (September–October). Examples: Gray Kingbird and Black-whiskered Vireo.
- **winter resident:** a non-breeding species which is present during the winter season (November–March), for some birds (August–April), which migrates to the region in the fall (August–November), resides through the winter season and departs in the spring (March–May). Examples: Blue-winged Teal and Prairie Warbler.
- **transient:** a species that regularly, or seasonally, passes through the region between its breeding and non-breeding range, but does not reside during the winter or summer. Examples: Pectoral Sandpiper and Eastern Kingbird.
- **visitor:** a non-breeding species that does not fit into any of the above categories, but visits the region at different times of the year, usually in summer or winter. It remains for an unspecified, or variable, amount of time (from a few days to a few weeks). Examples: Forster's Tern and Black Skimmer.

- **local:** a species that occurs in localized areas – that area being determined by its habitat, such as a pond, an offshore cay or a mangrove marsh. Examples: Least Grebe and Least Bittern are found in ponds, but only in some of the ponds available, so part of their status is local. The status of breeding terns is referred to as locally uncommon, common, etc. because they breed on offshore cays and are more numerous there than in other locations.
- **introduced:** a species whose range is outside The Bahamas and the Turks and Caicos Islands, but which is deliberately, or accidentally, brought by humans and released into the region. Examples: Eurasian Collared Dove and Cuban Grassquit. The Starling and the House Sparrow, originally from Europe, were introduced into North America, but it is not known exactly how they reached the region, so they are not described as introduced.

Note: It should be mentioned that the general information about the status and range of all the birds in the region is based upon present knowledge. This information has been taken from a few published works (see Bibliography, p. 233) and from the many observations and experiences of people in the field, including my own. However, we know we don't know enough as there is still much information that is not clear or simply not known. As Clint Eastwood, playing Dirty Harry, once said: 'A man's got to know his limitations', and so it is in the region. The islands cover a huge area and are difficult to get to on a limited basis, much less a consistent one. Add to this a limited number of observers, and there are gaps in our knowledge about distribution, migratory numbers, movements, breeding, etc. While there is relatively more coverage and data from the northern Bahamas, especially New Providence and Grand Bahama, there is relatively much less news from the central and southern parts of the region. The uncertainty, or lack of information, about a more precise status is reflected in a number of species accounts where the status is simply stated as unclear or unknown. In other cases, uncertainty or unpredictability about a species (especially over a number of islands) is reflected in a status which varies from one term to another such as uncommon to fairly common or rare to uncommon.

Description: The first measurement given is for the length of a bird, from the tip of its bill to the end of its tail, and is given in both inches and centimeters. The second measurement, if given, and then only for larger birds, is for the wingspan (from the tip of one spread wing to the tip of the other). These measurements are averages and should only serve as a guideline to a bird's actual size. A general description of each species follows and includes the plumage color of both the upperparts and the underparts, usually starting with the head and ending at the tail. The eyes, bill, legs and feet are noted for their color or shape if they are good field marks. Adults in breeding plumage are presented first, followed by that of the non-breeding adult. Male and female differences are noted. If there is no mention of differences, then it can be assumed that the sexes and their plumages are similar. (Similar is a term used frequently in this section and means that differences between plumages are slight, or would involve more detailed, technical explanations.) The plumage of juveniles and immatures are described after the adults, and any observable differences are noted. If the differences are either too subtle or not mentioned, then it can be assumed the adults and immatures are of similar plumage. Any distinguishing features, or field marks, for a bird in flight, if mentioned, are given last in the description.

Voice: In many situations, it is easier to hear birds than to see them, so learning a few calls and songs can be a real asset to locating and identifying birds. However, this type of identification is usually more difficult to learn, requiring plenty of practice and persistence or birding extensively with someone who already knows. All birds have some type of vocalization which is divided into two general categories: calls and songs. Calls, or call notes, as they are often referred to, are usually simpler and shorter than songs and are used for a variety of reasons such as alarm, aggression, contact or calls around the nest. Calls may be made by any member of a species and at any time of the year. Songs may be short or long, often with variations, and are most often given by advertising adult males on their territory during the breeding season. A few species give songs at other times of the year.

The voice descriptions in the species accounts represent the most commonly heard calls, or songs, from each species but do not include all of the vocalizations that a certain species is capable of giving. Descriptions of calls are presented first, followed by descriptions of the song if the species has one. Characteristics such as loudness, length, frequency and quality are also emphasized where applicable. It should be remembered that writing and describing many of the calls and songs is largely subjective, and is not the same for everyone, since each birder usually hears or interprets the vocalizations in a different way. Some people make up phrases or sayings, not only to remember the song, but also to give it a translation when it is too difficult to describe. The song of the White-winged Dove is often described as *who cooks for you,* the Black-whiskered Vireo *cheap-John Stirrup* and the Bahama Yellowthroat *wichity wichity*. These are three renditions that are used by many but they are not absolute, and birders frequently make up their own.

Habits: This section concentrates on features of the species other than plumage or voice. These might include preferred habitats, feeding or foraging behavior, body movements, diet, nesting and any other behavior that defines the species. Brief references are made for birds that have a tendency to come to home feeders, either those filled with seeds, or, in the case of hummingbirds and Bananaquits, with sugar water. Species with a tendency to respond to pishing (see Glossary, p. 218) and squeaking are also noted, but it should be remembered that they do not always respond.

Similar species: Most species are fairly easy to identify when compared to others, but many species are more difficult because of the similarity in their size, shape and plumage as well as habitat and behavior. Any bird that is similar enough, or likely to cause confusion with the species being discussed, is listed under the heading of **Similar species** and is in bold. There are two types of presentation. One states the similar species (which has already been described or is about to be) and then discusses how it is different when compared to the species in that account. The second concerns the introduction of a new species that has not been described in any of the accounts. In this case, the common and scientific names are given along with measurements, a short sentence about status and range and one or more photographs. Comparisons with the species in that account follow the brief introduction.

Comments: This section covers any additional information that has not been covered in previous sections and may include: local names for birds, histories of introduced birds, relevant taxonomic information, information about protected species and interesting or irregular patterns of distribution in the West Indies. The scientific name of an endemic subspecies is also presented, along with any distinguishable field marks or regional differences, if they are known, or if they are observable in the field. Other subspecies are mentioned if their range relates particularly to the West Indies or to a part of it. The names and ranges for all the recognized subspecies come from the Howard and Moore text mentioned in the introductory section on subspecies.

It will come as no surprise that not all of the bird populations are doing well in the region – not only residents but also migrants. Many species are particularly vulnerable to changes in their environments and have less tolerance to human activities and abuses than others. Rather than go into the details, a sentence or two is written to underscore a problem or a potential for one. The term **Conservation** is written in bold to briefly highlight issues, or concerns, related to a species' population or any threats to that population.

Birding group from New Providence reviewing
species identification: November

Bird topography

Throughout the species accounts the descriptions, i.e. color, shape, etc. refer continually to various parts of a bird. Some are obvious like the bill or wing, but others like the supercilium or uppertail coverts are not. The figures below illustrate the main body parts and feather tracks of a bird and the terminology used in this book. Also known as bird topography.

Bahama Mockingbird

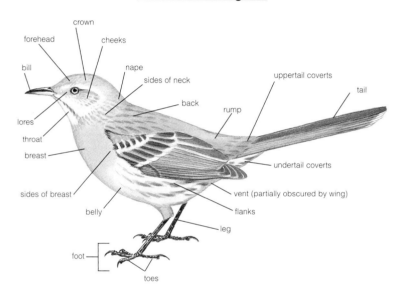

Black-whiskered Vireo

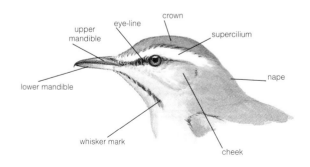

Wing of Bahama Mockingbird

folded wing

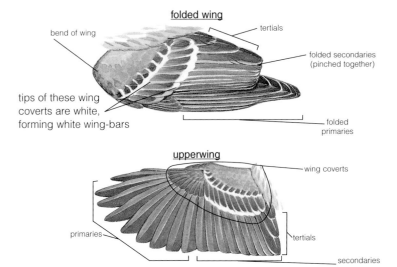

bend of wing

tertials

folded secondaries
(pinched together)

tips of these wing
coverts are white,
forming white wing-bars

folded
primaries

upperwing

wing coverts

primaries

tertials

secondaries

primaries and secondaries together form the flight feathers of the wing

underwing

leading edge of wing

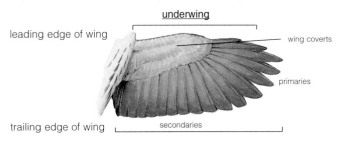

wing coverts

primaries

trailing edge of wing

secondaries

Tail of Palm Warbler

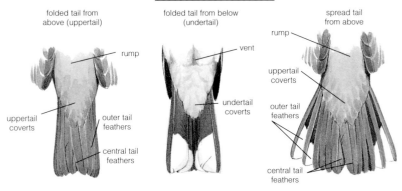

folded tail from
above (uppertail)

folded tail from below
(undertail)

spread tail
from above

rump

rump

vent

uppertail
coverts

undertail
coverts

outer tail
feathers

uppertail
coverts

outer tail
feathers

central tail
feathers

central tail
feathers

white spots on outer tail feathers can only be seen from below or on spread tail

Water Birds

◆ DUCKS AND GEESE   Family: *Anatidae*

A large well-known family found world-wide and often collectively referred to as waterfowl. Recently recognized as one of the oldest of bird families. The whistling-ducks, geese and ducks of this family are divided into separate subfamilies. Whistling-ducks have long necks and legs and are named for their high-pitched whistling calls. Both sexes are similar in plumage. West Indian Whistling-Duck is the premier resident in the region and is described in the first account. Two other species of whistling-ducks have been recorded but are not described. Fulvous Whistling-Duck is a rare (mostly winter) visitor and has been recorded on most of the islands in the region. There are only a few records for Black-bellied Whistling-Duck.

Geese are large, heavy, long-necked waterfowl that often walk and graze on land. Both sexes are similar in plumage. Two species occur in the region with Snow Goose a rare winter visitor and Canada Goose a very rare visitor, both mainly to the northern Bahamas. These two species are not described but because they are large and conspicuous, a photograph of them is included.

Canada Goose (left) with juvenal and adult Snow Goose: Grand Bahama – December

Ducks are the most numerous members of the waterfowl group and are medium to large-sized waterfowl with flattened bills, waterproof plumage and short legs with webbed feet. With few exceptions, males are more colorful than drabber females. Ducks are divided into two groups: dabblers and divers. Dabblers feed from the surface by sifting plant matter through their bills or feed by vertically tipping in shallow water with head underwater and tail above. Some also feed on land. For take off, they jump straight up in one quick movement. Divers feed underwater propelling themselves with their legs and feet. They also dive when alarmed. Take-off is accomplished by running across the water's surface using their feet and wings. Dabbling ducks have a patch of glossy color on the secondaries of the upperwing called a speculum. Divers have duller secondary feathers that lack any glossiness. The first two species and the resident population of the third species are permanent residents in the region and are described below. Migrants are described in the next section.

West Indian Whistling-Duck

Dendrocygna arborea

Caymans – October

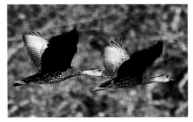

Long Island – March

Caymans – March

Status and range: Local permanent resident. Fairly common on Long Island and uncommon to fairly common on North Andros. Rare to uncommon on Abaco, Great Inagua and North and Middle Caicos in TCI. Rare visitor to other main islands. Not recorded from Grand Bahama, Bimini or Berry Islands.

Description: Length: 22 ins (56 cm); wingspan: 40 ins (101 cm). Large mostly brown duck with black eye and bill, long neck and long, thick, gray legs and feet. Dark brown stripe runs from rear of crown down along back of neck to back and contrasts with pale areas on face and neck. Distinctive black and white markings on flanks. Sexes similar. Juvenile duller brown than adult with less distinct black and white markings on flanks. In flight, head and neck are held slightly lower than back and feet project beyond tail; gray patch noticeable on upperwing.

Voice: Series of short, high, squeaky notes or harsh whistles *pisiseee*. Often calls in flight.

Habits: Spends day roosting in mangroves or other thick cover around salt or fresh-water ponds and inlets. Difficult to find. Flies out at dusk to feed during night often returning before dawn. Feeds in wetlands and also browses on land for fruit, seeds and shoots. Strong legs and feet for standing and walking.

Comments: Entire range restricted to the West Indies. **Conservation:** Population declining and considered vulnerable because of habitat destruction and illegal hunting. Protected species, it is illegal to hunt or capture.

White-cheeked Pintail   *Anas bahamensis*

New Providence – May   Female (left) and male: Abaco – May

Status and range: Locally uncommon to fairly common permanent resident on most major islands in the region including TCI. Rare visitor to Grand Bahama.

Description: Length 17 ins (43 cm). Slender and handsome dabbling duck. Head has a brown cap and nape that contrasts with white cheek, throat and sides of neck. Blue-gray bill with red patch at base. Underparts pale warm brown with black spots on the breast and flanks. Whitish tail long and pointed. In flight and certain preening positions, shows glossy green speculum with wide buff borders. Sexes similar with subtle differences (best seen on paired birds). Male a little larger with slightly brighter head, slightly brighter red patch on bill, and longer white tail; female's tail shorter and more buff-colored.

Voice: Usually silent, just low whistles or soft quacks. If seen or heard, courting male emits a high *peep peep*.

Habits: Found in both fresh and saltwater ponds, lagoons, and mangrove swamps. Feeds by tipping. Generally shy and wary throughout the region except in some developed areas where it has become habituated to people.

Comments: Commonly called 'Bahama Duck' or 'Bahama Pintail' in The Bahamas. Protected species and may not be hunted. Range outside the region includes the Greater Antilles and much of South America. White-cheeked Pintail in the region is West Indies and northern South American subspecies *A. b. bahamensis*.

Ruddy Duck   *Oxyura jamaicensis*

Resident male (left) and female: New Providence –
May

Migrant male non-
breeding: December

Status and range: Two populations in the region: one resident and one migratory. Locally common permanent resident on New Providence, rare to uncommon permanent resident on North Andros, Eleuthera, Great Exuma, and the Caicos Islands in TCI. Status of migrant birds from North America is unclear but probably rare winter resident and transient.

Description: Length: 15 ins (38 cm). Small compact diving duck. Adult male in breeding plumage has white face and bright blue bill, black crown and nape and chestnut or ruddy body. Tail feathers stiff and often cocked upwards. Resident male in region retains ruddy plumage year round but loses bill color in non-breeding season. Body of first-year male is duller and more mottled. Migrant adult male in non-breeding plumage has gray-brown body, dark cap, white face and dark bill. Adult female of both populations is brown overall with dark cap and dusky cheek crossed by single dark line.

Voice: Usually silent. During courtship display, however, resident male pumps bill against breast making low grunts and producing bubbles on the water.

Habits: Found in freshwater and brackish ponds. Feeds by diving. When alarmed, prefers to dive or swim away.

Comments: Resident birds first bred in The Bahamas in 1962 on New Providence. Has slowly increased its range since then. Protected species and may not be hunted. Resident population of Ruddy Duck in the region belongs to West Indian subspecies *O. j. jamaicensis*.

Winter Resident and Transient Ducks

A number of species of ducks migrate annually from North America to the region and either remain as winter residents or stay for a period of time and then continue their migration. Species and numbers vary from year to year. Factors affecting their presence and length of time in any one area are: amount of suitable habitat, food supply and hunting pressure. There is an annual hunting season (generally October–March) in The Bahamas and no season in TCI. Ducks generally arrive between October and November and leave the area in March or April. Depending upon the species, many of the adult males arrive in non-breeding plumage which is also referred to as an 'eclipse plumage' because it does not last that long. Generally this plumage is similar to that of the female. By early winter, most males molt to breeding plumage and are more recognizable. The eight species of ducks described below are the most commonly seen year in and year out. They are also more common in the northern Bahamas than in other parts of the region. Wood Duck and Mallard are not described and are, primarily, rare winter visitors to the northern Bahamas. It is difficult to assess whether or not mallards seen in the region are wild birds or escapees since they are commonly held in captivity.

American Wigeon   *Anas americana*

Male: Grand Bahama – March   Female: Grand Bahama – March

Length: 20 ins (51 cm). Uncommon winter resident and transient. Rare in TCI. Breeding adult male has creamy-white forehead and crown and gray face with green eye patch that extends to nape. Warm brown breast and flanks; bold white patch before black undertail. Non-breeding male in early fall with head similar to female but with rustier flanks. Female has all gray head (darkish around eye), warm-brown body and white belly. In flight, both sexes show light patch (white in male, gray in female) on the upperwing above darkish speculum. Underwing coverts are whitish. Found in fresh and brackish water. Feeds by tipping and occasionally forages on land for grasses.

Blue-winged Teal

Anas discors

Male (left) and female: New Providence – March

Non-breeding male: New Providence – October

Length: 15.5 ins (39 cm). Fairly common to common winter resident and transient. Most common duck in the region. Breeding adult male has blue-gray head with broad white crescent in front of eye. Underparts light brown, spotted with black. White patch in front of black rear end. Non-breeding male similar to female but may show hint of white crescent in front of eye. Some males may keep this plumage into early winter. Female has gray-brown head with dark eye-line, white eye-crescents and white spot at base of dark bill. Body is gray-brown with pale edges to back and wing feathers giving a scalloped appearance. In flight, upperwing of both sexes shows large, light blue patch and white bar above dark green speculum. Found in fresh and brackish water. Often in pairs by late winter. Feeds from the surface and by tipping. Fast flier with quick turns.

Green-winged Teal

Anas crecca

Male: April

Female: October

Length: 14 ins (36 cm). Rare to uncommon winter resident and transient. Rare in Caicos Islands. Small and compact duck. Breeding adult male has dark-chestnut head with green patch from eye to nape. Breast is tan with dark spots and flanks gray with white vertical bar on sides of breast. Non-breeding male similar to female. Female darkish brown and similar to female Blue-winged Teal but has thinner bill, lacks white at base of bill and has paler patch on undertail coverts. Females of both species have dark green speculum but Green-winged lacks Blue-winged's light blue patch above speculum – best seen in flight. Found in freshwater and feeds from surface and by tipping. Fast flier with quick turns.

Northern Shoveler *Anas clypeata*

Male breeding: June   Female: December

Length: 19 ins (48 cm). Uncommon winter resident and transient. Rare in TCI. Large spatulate (broad and flat) bill gives this species a unique profile. Breeding adult male has green head, dark bill and white breast with rufous flanks and belly. Non-breeding male in fall and early winter shows dull and mottled breeding plumage colors with dull whitish crescent between eye and bill. Female is brown with scalloped appearance to back and flanks and has gray-brown bill with orange lower mandible. In flight, male shows upperwing with pale blue patch and white bar above dark green speculum. Female patch is blue-gray. Found in fresh and brackish water. Feeds mainly by straining surface matter through large bill but also does some tipping.

Northern Pintail *Anas acuta*

Male: New Providence – January   Female: November

Length (male with tail): 26 ins (66 cm); female: 20 ins (51 cm). Rare to uncommon winter resident and transient. Rare in TCI. Long neck (not visible on resting birds) and tail gives both sexes streamlined profile. Breeding adult male has dark brown head with white stripe along side of neck and white breast. Flanks are gray with white patch between flank and black undertail. Long black and pointed central tail feathers. Female has warm brown head and neck with dark gray bill. Body is brown with scalloped appearance on back and flanks, white belly and pointed tail (much shorter than male's). Found in freshwater and feeds by tipping.

Ring-necked Duck   *Aythya collaris*

One male, four females: New Providence – January

Length:17 ins (43 cm). Uncommon to fairly common winter resident and transient. More common in northern Bahamas. Rare in Caicos Islands. Breeding adult male has black head with slight purple sheen and black back and breast. Gray flanks are separated from dark breast by white bar. Poorly named since male's obscure rusty ring at base of neck is almost never observed. Non-breeding male has dark head and breast, dark back and brownish flanks. Female is brown with darker crown than face, white eye-ring, thin white line extending back from eye and back is darker than flanks. Variable amount of white between eye and bill. Both sexes have blue-gray bill with white ring next to black tip and distinctive peak or bump at rear of crown. Diving duck, found in fresh, brackish and salt water. Jumps up quickly on take-off unlike other divers. In flight, has uniform gray flight feathers. See **Lesser Scaup** for similar species.

Lesser Scaup   *Aythya affinis*

Male: June   Female: March

Length: 16.5 ins (42 cm). Locally fairly common winter resident on New Providence and Eleuthera but rare to uncommon winter resident and transient on other islands in the region. Breeding adult male has light-blue bill, dark head and breast, pale gray back, white flanks and black rear end. Female is brown with dark-brown head and well-defined white patch at base of bill. Non-breeding male similar to female but lacks distinct white patch at base of bill. Both sexes have slight peak at rear of crown and, in flight, show contrasting white secondaries on upperwing. Feeds by diving in freshwater and brackish lakes. Ring-necked Duck is similar but male has black back, gray flanks and distinctive bill markings. Female Ring-necked Duck has bold, white eye-ring and less defined white patch at base of bill. In flight, Ring-necked Duck shows no white on secondaries.

Red-breasted Merganser *Mergus serrator*

Male: June

Female types: Grand Bahama –
December

Length: 23 ins (58 cm). Rare to uncommon winter resident and transient and is not recorded from TCI. Breeding adult male has dark green head with shaggy crest at rear of crown, white collar and rufous breast, black back and gray flanks. Non-breeding male similar to female. Female has rufous head with shaggy crest, pale throat and breast and gray body. Both sexes have long, thin, red bill and, in flight, show large white patch on secondaries of upperwing (male has an additional white patch above). This diving fish-eating duck is found in salt and brackish water. Frequents harbors, marinas, shallow water off coast and occasionally inland ponds and lakes.

Hooded Merganser *Lophodytes cucullatus*

Male with raised and flattened crest

Females: New Providence – January

Length:18 ins (46 cm). The only other merganser recorded in the region. Rare winter visitor to northern Bahamas and TCI. Breeding adult male has black head and neck with white patch behind eye, which becomes larger when crest is raised. Back is black and flanks rufous. Female is gray-brown overall with darker back and rusty crest on rear of crown which is most visible when crest is raised. Both sexes have thin bill (black in male, dull yellowish in female), whitish belly and long tail, sometimes cocked. Found on inland fresh and brackish water ponds and lakes.

◆ GREBES   Family: *Podicipedidae*

Small world-wide family of water birds that, from an evolutionary standpoint, is one of the oldest of bird families. They have short wings and short obscured tails. Legs of grebes are set far back on their bodies, making them excellent swimmers and divers but rather awkward out of water. Their feet have lobed or rounded projections on toes, rather than webs like ducks. Feed on small fish and invertebrates by diving or by taking aquatic insects and plant matter from the surface. Have difficulty taking off from water so often dive when alarmed. Nest on floating or anchored platforms of aquatic vegetation.

Least Grebe   *Tachybaptus dominicus*

Non-breeding: New Providence – January

Breeding: New Providence – April

Grand Bahama– September

Status and range: Local permanent resident in suitable habitat. Fairly common in northern Bahamas but uncommon to fairly common in rest of The Bahamas. Uncommon in Caicos Islands and an uncommon visitor to Turks Islands in TCI.

Description: Length: 9 ins (23 cm). Small, dark gray, diving bird with yellow eye and thin black bill with pale tip. Throat is black in breeding adult but white in non-breeding adult. Whitish belly and white patch on flight feathers visible on outstretched wing or in flight. Juvenile similar to non-breeding adult but has stripes on head.

Voice: Alarm call is single *eeek*. A high-pitched buzzy twittering or chattering frequently heard when two grebes are present.

Habits: Normally found only in fresh, or nearly fresh, water surrounded by vegetation and may be common on some golf course ponds. Usually dives when alarmed but may scamper away for a short distance across water surface using both its feet and wings. When feathers are wet and matted down from diving, looks smaller than when riding on surface with dry feathers and whitish rear end all fluffed out. Nests at any time of year and tiny chicks may be seen riding on back of adult.

Similar species: Pied-billed Grebe is larger with thicker light-colored bill and dark eyes. Overall plumage is brown rather than gray and does not have much white in flight feathers.

Comments: Fairly common in the Greater Antilles but rare to mostly unrecorded in the Lesser Antilles. Least Grebe in the region is Greater Antilles subspecies *T. d. dominicus*.

Pied-billed Grebe   *Podilymbus podiceps*

Breeding: New Providence – May

Non-breeding: New Providence – January

Status and range: Locally rare to uncommon permanent resident in northern Bahamas, Great Inagua and Caicos Islands in TCI. Uncommon to fairly common winter resident in The Bahamas and TCI. Small breeding population is supplemented in winter by more numerous migrant birds from North America.

Description: Length: 13 ins (33 cm). Compact, mostly brown, diving bird with thick stubby bill. All plumages have dark eye with narrow pale eye-ring. Breeding adult has whitish bill with black ring and black forehead and throat. Non-breeding adult has dull yellow bill without black ring and white throat. Juvenile similar to non-breeding adult but has stripes on head.

Voice: Nasal chattering similar to Least Grebe but lower pitched. Also, strange, repeated, hollow-sounding *cow cow cow cow* heard only in breeding season.

Habits: Found in both fresh and salt water. For breeding, it prefers ponds surrounded by vegetation. When threatened or approached too closely, dives or sinks slowly leaving head just above water.

Similar species: See **Least Grebe**.

◆ SHEARWATERS

Family: *Procellariidae*

Medium-sized world-wide family of pelagic (oceanic) birds with specialized tube along top of bill that covers the nostrils. Tube used for sense of smell and salt excretion and family often referred to as 'tubenoses'. They have long wings and often glide in a tilted position with one wing tip just above the water. They feed either by picking food off water's surface or by making shallow dives while swimming. Come to land only to breed and stay at sea at all other times. Audubon's Shearwater breeds in the region and is described below. Four other species, not described, are rare visitors to The Bahamas (unrecorded in TCI) and are encountered only at sea – Black-capped Petrel, Cory's Shearwater, Greater Shearwater and Sooty Shearwater. Cory's and Greater Shearwater have been reported much more often than other two species. The frequency and low numbers of this family are probably due to lack of coverage at sea but there may be natural factors involved as well.

Audubon's Shearwater

Puffinus lherminieri

August

In burrow: Cay Sal Bank – May

Status and range: Locally common spring and summer resident on Cay Sal Bank and other isolated cays in central and southern Bahamas. Uncommon summer resident on small cays in TCI. Rare to uncommon at sea in winter.

Description: Length: 12 ins (30 cm); wingspan: 27 ins (68 cm). Small shearwater with dark brown (often appearing black) upperparts and white underparts. Undertail coverts are dark but this field mark can be hard to see. Flies low over water using rapid stiff wing beats and intermittent short glides. When sitting on water, tips of folded wings do not reach end of tail.

Voice: Generally silent at sea but can be noisy and loud at night on breeding islands. Call has been described as resembling a howling cat.

Habits: Nests in cavities on uninhabited offshore cays usually from March to August. Wanders far from nest to feed and may be seen over deep water throughout the region. Feeds on surface or makes shallow dives. Occasionally found in small flocks sitting on a calm sea. Will feed in mixed flocks with terns, boobies and other shearwaters.

Comments: Audubon's Shearwater in the region is the West Indian subspecies *P. l. lherminieri*. **Conservation:** It is estimated that over 2,000 pairs of Audubon's Shearwaters nest in region approximately half of the estimated West Indies population. Breeding colonies are vulnerable to human disturbance and introduced rats and cats. On Cay Sal Bank, nesting shearwaters have been preyed upon by refugees.

◆ STORM-PETRELS   Family: *Hydrobatidae*

A small world-wide family that is among the smallest of all seabirds. They come to land only to breed and feed primarily by flying low over water and picking food off the surface of the ocean. Plumage is mostly black and white. Tiny hooked bill has single nostril tube. Three species of storm-petrels have been recorded irregularly and in small numbers from The Bahamas but not from TCI. The frequency and low numbers are probably due to lack of coverage at sea but there may be natural factors as well. Wilson's Storm-Petrel is the most likely species to be encountered and is described below. Leach's Storm-Petrel and Band-rumped Storm-Petrel are not described as there are only a few records. They also appear very similar to Wilson's Storm-Petrel and should be identified only with care and experience.

Wilson's Storm-Petrel   *Oceanites oceanicus*

Both September

Length: 7 ins (18 cm); wingspan: 16 ins (41 cm). Rare to uncommon spring transient, primarily in May, in northern Bahamas. Not recorded from TCI. Small and mostly black seabird with prominent white band on rump extending to edges of undertail coverts. Relatively long dark legs and feet. Feet have yellow webs between toes which are very difficult to see. In flight, feet extend just beyond short squared tail. Flight is direct with quick fluttery wingbeats and short glides. Strong winds can affect both flight and feeding patterns. Found at sea over deep water and flies low over ocean, searching for small food matter on the surface. Known to locate some food resources by smell. Feeds by picking at prey while hovering and pattering its feet on surface as if walking on water – behavior thought to attract or startle prey, making them easier to detect. Feeding birds attract others. Rests on water. Breeds in Antarctic regions (November to April) and migrates to the north Atlantic Ocean to spend the southern winter/northern summer (April to October).

◆ TROPICBIRDS   Family: *Phaethontidae*

A world-wide family of just three species – White-tailed, Red-tailed and Red-billed Tropicbirds – all of which are found in tropical parts of the Atlantic, Pacific and Indian Oceans. They are slim medium-sized seabirds that stay far from land except when breeding. Plumage is white, with various patterns of black on face, back and upperwings. Adult birds have long central tail feathers that trail behind in flight and sometimes appear as one streamer. Fly with stiff rapid wingbeats and feed by plunge-diving, similar to terns. Will rest on water.

White-tailed Tropicbird   *Phaethon lepturus*

Both Crooked Island – May

Status and range: Locally fairly common spring and summer resident (March–September) on or near scattered breeding islands throughout The Bahamas. Locally uncommon summer resident in TCI.

Description: Body length: 15 ins (38 cm); tail length: 12–15 ins (30–38 cm); wingspan: 37 ins (94 cm). Beautiful white sea bird with red-orange bill (a few have yellow bills) and wedge-shaped tail with two long white central tail feathers – occasionally tail feathers buff. Adult is white overall, with black eye-line, black outer primaries and black diagonal bar across inner portion of upperwing. Black areas obscured when seen from below in flight. Juvenile similar to adult but has pale yellow bill, dark bars on back and lacks long tail feathers.

Voice: Single *kip* notes given in flight near breeding areas.

Habits: Courtship flight involves two adults flying in simultaneous patterns around vicinity of breeding area. Nests in coastal limestone crannies or cliffside holes that need to be near good take-off and landing spots. Most often seen when exchanging places at nest sites as birds fly and soar just offshore before and after exchange. Forages over deep water and plunge-dives for food, preferring squid and flying fish. Frequently nocturnal.

Comments: White-tailed Tropicbird in the region belongs to West Indies and Bermuda subspecies *P. l. catesbyi*. Population in the West Indies is estimated at between 2,500 and 3,500 pairs with fewer than 500 pairs estimated in the region. **Red-billed Tropicbird** (*Phaethon aethereus*) is also found in the West Indies, mainly in Lesser Antilles, but has never been recorded in the region.

◆ BOOBIES   Family: *Sulidae*

Very small world-wide family with nine species. Large heavy sea birds with strong pointed bills and pointed wings and tail. Fly with slow wingbeats and intermittent glides. Sometimes an up and down soaring and gliding flight pattern with no wing beats when moving over open water. Feed on fish and squid by plunge-diving. Colonial nesters on uninhabited offshore cays. Development from juvenile to adult takes several years. Two species of boobies and one species of gannet are described below. Masked Booby was recorded as a breeder on one particular cay in southern Bahamas in the latter half of the 1800s but is now an accidental to very rare visitor to the region and is not described.

Brown Booby   *Sula leucogaster*

Adult: San Salvador – June

Male (left) and female: San Salvador –
June

Juvenile: San Salvador – June

Status and range: Locally common permanent resident on or near scattered breeding islands in The Bahamas. Rare to uncommon over open water elsewhere in The Bahamas. Rare to uncommon visitor over open water in TCI.

Description: Length: 30 ins (76 cm); wingspan: 57 ins (145 cm). Adult has dark brown upperparts and breast with white underparts and sharp demarcation at breast. Bill pale yellow in non-breeding adult and brighter yellow in breeding with grayish tones in male and pinkish in female. Legs and feet are yellow. Juvenile has gray bill, yellowish legs, dusky brown upperparts and mottled or smudgy brown underparts where adult is white. Demarcation at breast still visible. Juvenile retains this plumage for about a year. Subsequent immature plumages show gradual progression to white underparts.

Habits: Either flies low and plunge-dives for food at a shallow angle or flies high and plunges straight down. Nest in colonies year round on uninhabited offshore cays.

Comments: Brown Booby in the region is West Indies subspecies *S.l. leucogaster*. **Conservation:** Population of Brown Booby in West Indies, estimated at 5,000 to 7,000 pairs, has declined and is vulnerable to hurricanes, human disturbance, rats etc. In The Bahamas, population limited to only several colonies with an estimate of 500–600 pairs.

Adult – March

Immature – November

Similar species: Northern Gannet (*Morus bassanus*) Length: 37 ins (94 cm); wingspan: 72 ins (183 cm). Rare winter visitor to northern Bahamas. Stays offshore and is larger and heavier than Brown Booby. Adult gannet is all white with black wing tips; yellow wash on head and nape. Immature has variety of light and dark patterns to upperparts for several years, but head and underparts predominately white. Brown Booby in the region has no white on head or upperparts. Juvenal gannet is dark brown-gray with paler belly and white spots and specks (seen at close range) to head and upperparts. Also has distinctive, white, 'u'-shaped uppertail coverts that contrast with dark tail – a feature that Brown Booby lacks.

Red-footed Booby   *Sula sula*

January   June

Status and range: Local permanent resident off San Salvador. One to three pairs have nested on cays in Graham's Harbor, San Salvador since 1988. Accidental to very rare visitor elsewhere in the region.

Description: Length: 28 ins (71 cm); wingspan 60 ins (152 cm). Adult has two color forms in the region. One is all white with black flight feathers; other is soft brown with darker brown flight feathers and all white hindparts (rump, lower belly, upper and lower tail coverts and tail). Both forms have gray-blue bill with pink base and red legs and feet. Juveniles of both forms have darkish-gray bills, pale but dull-colored feet, brown upperparts and light brown underparts that are not demarcated on breast like Brown Booby. Some older juveniles may show an obscure breast band.

Comments: Usually fishes well out to sea for flying fish and squid during daylight or night-time hours. Feeds by diving and prey swallowed before taking flight. Harassed by frigatebirds near colonies in an attempt to make the booby disgorge its catch. Population in West Indies is estimated at 8,000 to 10,000 pairs. Red-footed Booby in the region belongs to West Indian subspecies *S. s. sula*.

Brown adults: Little Caymen

◆ **PELICANS**   Family: *Pelecanidae*

Very small world-wide family of seven species. Large water birds confined to coastal areas and inland lakes. Unique bill with large expandable pouch in which to capture fish is well known. Pelicans are fish eaters and feed by both plunge-diving and fishing from the surface. Gregarious and are often found in small flocks. Ungainly on land, they fly gracefully with deep wingbeats and soar effortlessly.

Brown Pelican   *Pelecanus occidentalis*

Adult non-breeding: Grand Bahama – March

Juvenile: New Providence – May

Status and range: Fairly common permanent resident on Great Inagua and uncommon visitor to nearby islands and TCI. Birds from North America are uncommon winter visitors to the northern Bahamas and may wander elsewhere.

Description: Length: 48 ins (122 cm); wingspan: 84 ins (213 cm). Adult is large, heavy, gray-brown bird with dark belly. Head and neck are white with face and crown washed in yellow. In breeding plumage, head turns brighter yellow and hind neck and lower neck turn chestnut. Huge bill is pale with large expandable pouch. Juvenile has gray bill and is entirely brown except for whitish belly.

Habits: Flies with slow ponderous wing beats followed by a short glide, often just above water's surface. Makes steep, twisting, head-first dives into water to catch fish. Frequents docks, fishing wharves and protected coastal waters. On Great Inagua often found over inland salt ponds.

Comments: Smaller resident Brown Pelican on Great Inagua is West Indian subspecies *P. o. occidentalis*. Larger Brown Pelican in northern Bahamas is southeastern coastal USA subspecies *P. o. carolinensis*. Subspecies are not distinguishable in the field.

◆ CORMORANTS   Family: *Phalacrocoracidae*

Small world-wide family of fairly large, dark, long-bodied water birds with long necks and slender hooked bills. They have a small featherless throat pouch called a 'gular pouch'. Swim with a low profile on the surface and dive to pursue fish and other prey. Legs set far back on body which is an adaptation for swimming and prolonged diving. Legs also used to run along water's surface to help get airborne. Feathers are not completely waterproof, so cormorants often perch with outstretched wings to allow them to dry. Nest and roost in colonies.

Neotropic Cormorant   *Phalacrocorax brasilianus*

Juvenile (left) and breeding adult (right): New Providence – December

Immature: New Providence – June

Status and range: Common permanent resident on Great Inagua and uncommon to fairly common permanent resident on New Providence. Rare to uncommon visitor to Eleuthera, Great Exuma, Cat Island, and Long Island. Unrecorded or rare elsewhere in The Bahamas. Uncommon visitor to Grand Turk in TCI.

Description: Length: 25 ins (64 cm); wingspan: 40 ins (102 cm). Adult is long-tailed, slim, all black cormorant with black feathers in area between eyes and bill (just above and including lores). Featherless throat pouch is dull yellow-orange to dirty yellow; rear portion forms a sharp point that is thinly outlined in white. In breeding plumage, fine white feathers show on sides of head and white outline of throat pouch is bolder. Juvenile is mostly black with dark brown head, neck and breast, sometimes with rusty tinge; often shows brighter yellow-orange throat pouch than adult.

Habits: Prefers freshwater or brackish ponds surrounded by trees. Gregarious and both breeds and roosts in flocks especially on Great Inagua. Flocks fly quickly in single file or 'V'-shaped formations. Usually do not rest on water so often found on perches when not feeding.

Similar species: Double-crested Cormorant is bulkier with shorter tail. Has yellow-orange bare skin in area between eyes and bill instead of dark feathers. Throat pouch yellow-orange with rear portion being rounded rather than pointed. Juvenile has pale breast and belly. Double-crested Cormorant is frequently seen along coast or in large saline ponds; occasionally freshwater ponds.

Comments: Formerly called 'Olivaceous Cormorant'. Neotropic Cormorant is slowly expanding range in the region. First documented on New Providence in 1994 and noted nesting there in 1998. May be breeding in small numbers on other islands as well as New Providence and Great Inagua.

Double-crested Cormorant   *Phalacrocorax auritus*

Juvenile: North Andros – November   Immature: Grand Bahama – January

Status and range: North American birds are rare to uncommon winter residents and visitors in northern Bahamas. Unrecorded or status unknown on other Bahama Islands. Accidental visitor to TCI. A smaller subspecies is permanent resident on San Salvador and possibly Eleuthera.

Description: Length: 32 ins (80 cm); wingspan: 52 ins (132 cm). Adult is solidly built all black cormorant with yellow-orange bare skin in area between eyes and bill (just above and including lores). Throat pouch is yellow-orange with rear portion rounded. In breeding plumage, it has two inconspicuous crests on top of head. Juvenile is dark brown with pale neck and breast. Feather wear in some birds will make pale areas almost white. Immatures darker but not all black.

Habits: Found along coast in bays or harbors or in large saltwater ponds; occasionally in freshwater ponds. Seldom mixes with Neotropic Cormorant. Rests on water or perches. San Salvador subspecies prefers brackish inland ponds and lakes often surrounded by coppice or thick vegetation.

Similar species: See **Neotropic Cormorant**.

Comments: Subspecies in San Salvador (*P. a. heuretus*) is about 20 per cent smaller than other North American Double-crested Cormorants but plumage is virtually the same. San Salvador subspecies is similar in size to Neotropic Cormorant but the same differences (shape of gular pouch and differences in lores) that apply to Neotropic and larger Double-cresteds also apply to this resident subspecies. San Salvador subspecies was formerly recognized as endemic to The Bahamas but has recently been reported nesting in Cuba.

◆ FRIGATEBIRDS

Family: *Fregatidae*

Very small world-wide family of five species. Found over tropical waters, frigatebirds are large, dark, slender sea birds that are very adept fliers but do not land on water. They have long pointed wings and deeply forked tail. Long wings and low body weight enable them to soar effortlessly. They feed by flying low over water and picking prey from the surface or by forcing other seabirds to drop their food. Known to take nestlings of other species and sometimes their own. Will also scavenge around fishing boats and coastal settlements. Adult males inflate their throat pouch of red skin like a balloon during courtship.

Magnificent Frigatebird

Fregata magnificens

| Male | Female | Juvenile |

All San Salvador – January

Status and range: Locally common permanent resident on or near breeding sites scattered throughout the region. Wanders far from nesting areas and is regular visitor in small numbers elsewhere in the region.

Description: Length: 40 ins (102 cm); wingspan: 90 ins (228 cm). A large and slender, black, fork-tailed seabird with long narrow wings. Bill is long with strong hook at tip. Adult male is glossy black with red inflatable throat pouch of bare skin. Adult female is black with white breast patch but lacks throat pouch. Juvenile has white head, breast and belly. Transition to adult plumage takes four to six years.

Habits: Nests in colonies on uninhabited offshore cays with stick nest on ground or in shrub. Steals prey from boobies and terns and is therefore often seen near their nesting colonies. Also takes flying fish and squid with low swoops over ocean's surface. Usually seen soaring over coastal waters rather than over deep offshore waters.

Comments: Also called 'Man O' War Bird'. **Conservation:** Population of Magnificent Frigatebird in West Indies has been estimated at 4,000 to 5,000 pairs and is declining. Former breeding sites have been abandoned due to human disturbance and introduced mammals such as cats and goats. Only a small portion (est. 200 pairs from four sites) of West Indies' population comes from The Bahamas.

◆ HERONS, EGRETS AND BITTERNS   Family: *Ardeidae*

Medium-sized, familiar and diverse world-wide family. Herons and egrets are often collectively referred to as 'wading birds'. Generally, herons and egrets are slender with long necks and legs while bitterns and night-herons are chunkier with shorter necks and legs. Bills vary from long to short but all are pointed and well adapted for spearing and grabbing prey. Usually feed by patiently standing, or wading slowly, in shallow fresh or salt water. Some species also hunt on land. Capture their prey with an incredibly fast thrust of the neck and bill. If prey is plentiful in one area, herons and egrets may congregate in mixed species flock. In flight, typical posture is head and neck tucked in next to body with legs protruding beyond tail. Flight is slow but steady on broad wings with deep wingbeats. They are capable of long-distance migrations and movements. During breeding season, several species develop brighter colors to lores, bill and legs and/or long feather plumes on crown, neck or body. In addition, for some species, there is a 'peak' condition in which the colors or plumes may intensify even more from the breeding plumage. This 'peak' breeding condition is held for a relatively short time at the beginning of the breeding cycle, i.e. courtship, but fades by the time the parents start caring for the young. Generally takes two years for birds to obtain their adult plumage. Plumage of both sexes similar.

This family is well represented throughout the West Indies. They are also widespread in The Bahamas and TCI but pinpointing status and range is often unclear or not known. Reasons for this are that either breeding information is lacking because areas are not covered or they are too localized or difficult to reach. Birds found in summer do not always indicate breeding as individuals may be non-breeding immatures or they may be juveniles from local or more distant colonies outside the region. Juveniles have a tendency to wander or move long distances away from their breeding locales, a behavior called 'post-breeding dispersal'. In the fall and winter, birds from North America migrate to, or through, the region but they are not distinguishable from resident birds.

Little Blue Heron with breeding feathers on
head and neck: New Providence – March

Least Bittern

Ixobrychus exilis

Female: April

Juvenile: April

Status and range: Local permanent resident. Locally common in suitable habitat on New Providence. Locally rare to uncommon on Grand Bahama, Andros and Eleuthera and rare on Abaco. Rare winter visitor to San Salvador and Pine Cay and Grand Turk in TCI. Unrecorded on other islands in the region. Some migrants from North America possibly winter in northern Bahamas.

Description: Length: 13 ins (33 cm). Smallest heron. Primarily brown and bright buff with large buff wing patches. Crown and back are black on adult male; dark brown crown and brown back on female. Juvenile similar to female but has heavy streaking below.

Voice: Common call is a series of harsh and rapid *kek* notes (about five). Call is made year round and is similar to call of Clapper Rail. A soft and low *haw haw haw haw* made during breeding season.

Habits: Found in freshwater marshes and less frequently in mangrove swamps. Very secretive and either 'freezes' when disturbed or goes into a low crouch. When feeding, stands motionless at water's edge or in tall reeds or cattails. Often seen only in flight when flushed or as it crosses an open area to another patch of vegetation.

Similar species: Green Heron is closest in size and shape to Least Bittern but is larger and darker and lacks any buff coloration on head, neck and wings. Green Heron is far less secretive and much more common.

Comments: Conservation: Least Bitterns are dependent on dense marshes for feeding and breeding. Clearance of pond-side vegetation and filling of fresh water marshes reduces what is already limited habitat. **American Bittern** (*Botaurus lentiginosus*) is the only other bittern found in the region and is twice the size of Least Bittern. It is a rare winter resident and transient on large islands of northern Bahamas.

Great Blue Heron   *Ardea herodias*

Non-breeding: New Providence –   January
December

Length: 47 ins (119 cm); wingspan: 72 ins (183 cm). Fairly common winter resident in northern Bahamas. Uncommon to fairly common winter resident in central and southern Bahamas and TCI. Some transients move through the region in spring and fall. There have been reports that Great Blue Heron breeds in the region but there are no confirmed records. Birds recorded in summer months are most likely immature non-breeders. Largest and heaviest heron in the region. Adult has white head with wide black stripe above and behind eye that extends to a few black plumes. Heavy bill is yellowish with mostly dark upper mandible. Long pale gray neck with long plumes at base; a light and dark stripe runs down front from throat to breast. Body and wings blue-gray and legs grayish. In breeding plumage, bill becomes more orange with yellow tip, plumes lengthen and legs brighter. Juvenile has dark cap, more neck and breast streaking and no plumes; dark cap lightens as bird matures. In flight, all birds show black flight feathers on upperwing contrasting with blue-gray coverts. Call a harsh deep *braak*, often given when taking off or landing. Found in both fresh and salt water and sometimes hunts on land. When foraging, stands stationary and upright or walks slowly. Feeds on a variety of prey, often quite large, including fish, reptiles and rodents. Will take birds if opportunity arises.

There is a white color form of Great Blue Heron, often referred to as 'Great White Heron' (*A. h. occidentalis*), which occurs primarily in South Florida and the Florida Keys but which has been reported, sparingly, from North Andros. Large all-white heron with heavy dull-yellow bill and dull-yellowish legs. All-white Great Egret is similar but has a bright yellow bill and black legs.

White form: Florida Everglades – February

Great Egret   *Ardea alba*

New Providence – December   Grand Bahama – January

Status and range: Uncommon to fairly common winter resident in The Bahamas and uncommon winter resident in TCI. Some transients move through the region in spring and fall. Locally common on Great Inagua but resident status there is not clear. Bred on Great Inagua in 1978 but there are no recent records. May breed on other islands in the region.

Description: Length: 39 ins (99 cm); wingspan: 51 ins (130 cm). Large all-white heron with yellow lores and heavy yellow bill. Long black legs and feet. In peak breeding, adult has green lores and long plumes from back but no head plumes. Juvenile and immature birds are similar to adult.

Voice: Similar to Great Blue Heron.

Habits: Found principally in shallow freshwater and brackish ponds, lakes and coastal lagoons. Will hunt on land and forages by stalking prey slowly or by standing motionless. Eats fish, lizards, snakes and at times birds.

Similar species: White **Reddish Egrets** are closer in size to Great Egrets than to other white herons but are still much smaller. White form of adult Reddish Egret has distinct two-toned bill and white form juvenile has all dark, or mostly dark bill, never all yellow as with Great Egret. Reddish Egret is almost exclusively a saltwater heron and is only occasionally to be found on inland freshwater ponds and lakes.

Snowy Egret   *Egretta thula*

Adult: Long Island – March   Juvenile or non-breeding adult: Grand Bahama – October

Status and range: Uncommon to fairly common winter resident in The Bahamas. Part of population on Great Inagua are permanent residents. Uncommon winter resident in TCI. Some transients move through the region in spring and fall.

Description: Length: 24 ins (61 cm); wingspan: 41 ins (104 cm). Medium-sized white heron. Adult has yellow lores, thin black bill and black legs with bright yellow feet. Some short plumes may be visible. In peak breeding, lores are reddish, feet orange and long wispy plumes on head, neck and back. Juvenile similar to adult but lacks any plumes and may have paler portions on black bill. Legs are greenish-yellow with black stripe down front; feet are yellow. Some non-breeding adults also have bi-colored legs.

Habits: Found in both shallow fresh and saltwater ponds, lakes and mangrove swamps. Feeds mainly on small fish by standing motionless, stalking slowly or actively running. Also known to wriggle or move its feet to flush prey from cover.

Similar species: White phase of juvenal **Little Blue Heron** is same size as Snowy Egret but has gray lores, thicker two-toned bill and gray green colored legs. Little Blue Heron usually feeds more slowly than Snowy Egret. White form of juvenal **Reddish Egret** is superficially similar to Snowy Egret (white with black bill and legs) but is bigger overall with larger bill, dark lores and longer all dark legs and feet.

Little Blue Heron

Egretta caerulea

Non-breeding: North Andros – April   Juvenile: Grand Bahama – December

Status and range: Uncommon to fairly common winter resident throughout the region. Has bred on Andros, New Providence and Eleuthera but breeding suspected on other islands in southern part of its range. Some transients move through the region in spring and fall.

Description: Length: 24 ins (61 cm); wingspan: 40 ins (102 cm). Medium-sized heron. Adult is entirely slate-blue with gray-green legs. Lores gray-blue and bill two-toned with gray-blue base and black tip. Breeding adult has rufous tinge to head and neck. Juvenile, for most of first year, is entirely white with gray lores, dull two-toned bill and dull yellow-green legs. For most of following year, white is intermixed with areas of slate-blue before the immature molts to adult plumage.

Habits: Found in both shallow fresh and saltwater. Slow and deliberate feeder. In typical posture, it leans forward and stares down into water.

Similar species: Snowy Egret has different bill and leg color than first year Little Blue Heron. **Reddish Egret**, of both color forms, is larger, has darker legs and is more active feeder than Little Blue Heron. Adult Reddish Egret also has brighter two-toned bill color.

Comments: Little Blue Heron is only heron in the region that is white as a juvenile/immature and dark as an adult. White plumage is only a phase until it molts to slate-blue plumage, unlike white form of Reddish Egret which remains in one color throughout its life.

Tricolored Heron   *Egretta tricolor*

Non-breeding: Long Island – March   Juvenile: Grand Bahama – September

Status and range: Fairly common permanent resident throughout the region. More common in southern Bahamas and in TCI. Also an uncommon winter resident and transient throughout the region.

Description: Length: 26 ins (66 cm); wingspan: 36 ins (91 cm). Medium-sized heron with very long bill and neck. Adult has yellow lores, dark bill with yellow lower mandible and pale yellow legs. White stripe runs from throat down front of neck. Slate-blue upperparts and breast contrast with white underparts; contrast visible both on perched birds and those in flight. During peak breeding, lores turn blue, bill blue with black tip and legs become reddish. Also white plumes on crown and reddish buff plumes on neck and back. Juvenile similar to adult but shows extensive rufous coloring on neck and wing coverts.

Habits: Found in freshwater ponds and lakes as well as brackish or saltwater. Partial to mangrove swamps and lagoons. Frequently a solitary feeder; aggressively defends feeding territory from other similar sized herons. Primarily pursues small fish by either moving quickly or slowly often in deep water.

Reddish Egret　　　　　　　　　　　*Egretta rufescens*

Adult white form and Green Heron (foreground): Great Exuma – June

Juvenal white form: Providenciales – June

Adult dark form: February

Juvenile (mix of light and dark): Grand Bahama – September

Status and range: Permanent resident in central and southern Bahamas and TCI. Common on Great Inagua and uncommon to fairly common on other central and southern islands. Uncommon in TCI. Rare to uncommon visitor to northern Bahamas.

Description: Length: 30 ins (76 cm); wingspan: 46 ins (117 cm). Larger more active heron with two color forms (sometimes referred to as a morph). Adult white form is entirely white and adult dark form has slate-blue body and dull orange-red head and neck. Both adult forms have pale yellow eyes, pink lores, pink bill with black tip and dark legs. Breeding adults have stringy plumes on rear of crown, neck and back. Juveniles have pale yellow eyes and dark legs like adults but differ with dark lores and dark bills. Juvenal dark form has mixed slate-blue and red-brown plumage without much contrast. Some juveniles show a mixture of white and dark form features but can still be identified by pale yellow eyes and dark legs. In second year (immature), base of bill starts to lighten and head and neck of dark birds become more defined red-brown.

Habits: Saltwater heron, usually found on open tidal flats or shallow saline ponds. Occasionally found in fresh water. Frequently active when feeding; prances about, changes direction, jumps and runs. Also spreads wings apparently to reduce glare on water's surface and improve sighting of prey.

Similar species: Adult Reddish Egrets, of both forms, are easily identified by bright pink and black two-tone bill. Juveniles, of either form, are more difficult to distinguish from other herons but, by concentrating on color of eyes, lores, bill and legs, identification should be possible.

Comments: Both color forms are found in the region but white form outnumbers and is seen more often than dark form. On Great Inagua, almost all the Reddish Egrets are white.

Juvenal dark form: July

Cattle Egret

Bubulcus ibis

Breeding (yellow legs obscured):
North Andros – April

Non-breeding: Grand Bahama –
October

Status and range: Locally uncommon to fairly common permanent resident in The Bahamas. Uncommon permanent resident in TCI. Birds from North America and post-breeding visitors from Bahamian and TCI colonies add to resident populations. Some transients move through the region in spring and fall.

Description: Length: 20 ins (51 cm); wingspan: 36 ins (91 cm). Short-necked and small white heron with yellow lores, short yellow bill and dark legs. In breeding season, adult has soft rusty plumes on crown, back and breast and legs are yellowish. For a short period during peak breeding, bill and legs turn reddish. Some birds retain patches of rusty wash into non-breeding season. Juvenile has dark bill for a short time before it turns yellow. In flight, Cattle Egrets flap their wings faster than other herons.

Habits: Can be seen near water or puddles but almost always feeds on land, usually in drier open grassy areas. Forages mainly for both small and large insects. Where available, it frequently accompanies livestock or other domestic animals feeding on insects they flush out. Also seen at garbage dumps. Roosts and nests in colonies over or near water in tall mangroves or other low trees.

Similar species: Other small white herons in the region have longer and darker or differently colored bills. They also forage in or near water.

Comments: Cattle Egrets are believed to have reached South America on their own from the continent of Africa. They spread northwards and were first recorded in Florida in the 1940s. First observed in The Bahamas in 1953 and are now wide-spread and common in North America and the West Indies.

Green Heron   (e) *Butorides virescens bahamensis*

Breeding: San Salvador – June   Juvenile: New Providence – May

Status and range: Common permanent resident throughout the region. Winter residents and transients from North America occur but status and extent of range is unknown.

Description: Length: 18 ins (46 cm); wingspan: 26 ins (66 cm). Most common heron in the region but not well named. Small dark heron with short yellow legs. Adult has dark crown, dark back and wings with blue-green gloss, chestnut neck and breast with some white on throat and breast. At peak breeding, adult has gray plumes on back and orange legs. Juvenile similar to adult but is brownish overall with thick brown streaks on underparts.

Voice: Very vocal. When agitated, gives a series of low *kuk kuk kuk* notes. When flushed, gives a loud skow or series of piercing *skew* notes higher than first call. Also emits a low two-note growl from cover during breeding season.

Habits: Usually solitary. Feeds in shallow fresh and saltwater often surrounded by dense vegetation but is equally at home foraging on land. Usually crouches, motionless, waiting for prey but will stalk lizards and other prey in dense vegetation. Erects crown feathers and flicks tail when alarmed. Makes nest and often perches in trees or bushes. Breeds alone or in small groups. Posture ranges from hunched or crouched position when feeding to having neck and body extended when agitated or walking.

Similar species: See **Least Bittern**.

Comments: Formerly called 'Green-backed Heron'. Locally known as 'poor-joe' in The Bahamas. Common and widespread in the West Indies. Resident Green Heron in the region is recognized as an endemic subspecies *B. v. bahamensis*. It is not known whether or not all the breeding residents in the region belong to this endemic subspecies.

Black-crowned Night-Heron

Nycticorax nycticorax

Adult plumage but still some yellow on bill (with Snowy Egret): New Providence – January

Juvenile: New Providence – October

Status and range: As permanent resident, locally uncommon on Grand Bahama and New Providence and rare on Great Inagua. Rare winter resident and transient or unrecorded on other islands in The Bahamas. Uncommon winter visitor to TCI.

Description: Length: 25 ins (63 cm); wingspan: 44 ins (112 cm). Stocky, short-necked and short-legged heron. Adult has black crown and back, gray wings and white to pale gray underparts. Black bill is stout and pointed, legs yellow. Grows two long white plumes from crown in breeding season. Juvenile is brownish with large white spots on wings and broad brown streaks on whitish underparts. Bill mostly dull yellow with some dark areas on upper mandible and tip. Immature similar to juvenile but has fewer spots and streaks and may show hint of adult facial pattern.

Voice: A loud deep *kwok* often given in flight or when flushed.

Habits: Largely nocturnal and feeds in both fresh and saltwater. During day roosts quietly in trees or shrubbery often surrounding a pond.

Similar species: See **Yellow-crowned Night-Heron**.

Yellow-crowned Night-Heron   *Nyctanassa violacea*

Adult: New Providence   May   Juvenile: San Salvador – June

Status and range: Common permanent resident throughout the region. Much less common on Grand Bahama and Abaco.

Description: Length: 24 ins (61 cm); wingspan: 42 ins (107 cm). Adult has black and white head pattern and gray body and wings. Black bill is thick and slightly rounded at tip. Legs are yellow. In breeding season, crown pale yellow with two long plumes. Juvenile is gray-brown with small white spots on wings and narrow streaks on whitish underparts. Bill is black with pale area at base. Immature is similar to juvenile but has fewer spots and streaks and may show hint of adult facial pattern. Sometimes, after Yellow-crowneds have been foraging, bill may be caked with dried mud or sand, making it appear washed out.

Voice: A loud *kwek* similar to but higher pitched than Black-crowned Night-Heron.

Habits: Forages primarily in the evening and at night but feeds during the day when necessary. Hunts mostly in salt water such as mangrove swamps and beaches but also on golf courses, hotel lawns and other open areas. Crabs are principal food. Nests in trees in small colonies.

Similar species: Adult **Black-crowned Night-Heron** has black crown and black back where adult Yellow-crowned Night Heron has black and white head and gray back. Juveniles look similar and are more difficult to distinguish. Black-crowned juvenile has larger white spots on wing and broader streaks on underparts. Bill has yellow on lower mandible and appears thinner and more pointed. Juvenal Yellow-crowned's bill is mostly black (small pale area at base) and looks relatively thicker and more rounded or stubbier.

◆ IBISES AND SPOONBILLS   Family: *Threskiornithidae*

A small world-wide family of long-legged wading birds with distinctive bills. They fly with quick wingbeats and necks extended, unlike herons. Ibises have long and strongly decurved bills which they use for probing. Spoonbills have long spoon-shaped bills used to sweep from side to side through the water. Ibises and spoon-bills belong to separate subfamilies. Roseate Spoonbill breeds in the region and both ibises are migrants. White Ibis is suspected of breeding in a number of locations but there is (as yet) only one confirmed record from The Bahamas.

Roseate Spoonbill   *Platalea ajaja*

Great Inagua – April   Immature: March

Status and range: Uncommon permanent resident on Great Inagua. Rare permanent resident on North Andros. Rare visitor elsewhere in The Bahamas. Status in TCI is unclear but recently been reported on North and Middle Caicos Islands.

Description: Length: 32 ins (81 cm); wingspan: 50 ins (122 cm). Large pink and white wading bird with a long and flat gray bill that is spoon-shaped at tip. Adult has pink back and pink wings with brighter pink patch on wing and rump. Neck and upper breast are white. Head is featherless with gray-green skin and legs mostly pink. Colors are brighter during breeding season. Juvenile is pale with pinkish cast to wings and underparts; head is feathered white and legs dark. Amount of pink increases as bird matures.

Habits: Prefers saltwater lagoons, mudflats and coastal marshes. Feeds in shallow water by walking slowly forward and sweeping spoon-shaped bill from side to side through the water. Catches prey primarily by feel rather than by sight. Often seen in small, foraging groups with other heron or egret species.

White Ibis   *Eudocimus albus*

Non-breeding: New Providence – January

Immature: New Providence – May

Length: 25 ins (63 cm); wingspan: 38 ins (96.5 cm). Uncommon to fairly common winter resident in northern and central Bahamas. Rare to uncommon winter resident in southern Bahamas. Rare visitor to TCI. There is one confirmed breeding record from Bimini in 2005. Adult is an entirely white wading bird with long strongly decurved bill. Facial skin, bill and legs are dull orange-red, becoming bright red in breeding season. Black primary wingtips most visible in flight. Juvenile has pale brown head and neck, dark brown upperparts and white underparts. Back starts a gradual molt to white plumage towards end of first year. Facial skin, bill and legs dull pinkish-orange to orange. In flight, all birds show extended neck and legs and fast wingbeats interspersed with short glides. Social and usually found in small groups. Forages in all types of wetlands including ponds, mangroves, grassy areas and coastal lagoons.

Adults in flight: Caymans – March

Glossy Ibis   *Plegadis falcinellus*

Body of Glossy Ibis shows breeding plumage (with Snowy Egret): February

Length: 23 ins (58 cm); wingspan same as White Ibis. Uncommon winter resident in northern and central Bahamas. Rare to uncommon visitor to southern Bahamas and TCI. Non-breeding adult is all-dark ibis with fine white streaking on head and neck and green gloss on back and wings. Long decurved bill is light brown and legs dark. In late winter and spring, molts to breeding plumage showing glossier wings and back plus deep chestnut to body; loses fine streaking to head and neck. Immature similar to non-breeding adult. If seen well, all Glossy Ibises show thin blue line above and below facial skin in front of eye. Flight pattern is same as White Ibis. Found alone or in small groups around freshwater and brackish marshes and ponds. Forages by walking slowly probing into shallow water or mud. If working in deeper water, may probe with entire head submerged.

Non-breeding: January

◆ FLAMINGOS   Family: *Phoenicopteridae*

Familiar and very small (five species) world-wide family of tall and long-legged wading birds with pink plumage. Thick bill with deep bend at the middle is unique to this family.

Greater Flamingo   *Phoenicopterus ruber*

Great Inagua – April

Great Inagua – April

Status and range: In The Bahamas, common permanent resident on Great Inagua. Fairly common visitor to Crooked and Acklins Island and Mayaguana and accidental to rare visitor elsewhere. A good number of birds have been seen on western side of North Andros but exact status is not known. Fairly common permanent resident on Caicos Islands but uncommon visitor to Turks Islands in TCI.

Description: Length: 46 ins (117 cm); wingspan: 60 ins (152 cm). Unmistakable. Adult is uniformly pink with long neck and long pink legs with webbed feet. Black flight feathers most visible in flight. Bill is thick, bent down at middle and mostly pale with large black tip and pink patch on lower mandible. Juvenile is gray with black-tipped gray bill. After several months, molts to pale pink immature plumage which it keeps for several years or more before acquiring adult plumage.

Voice: A goose-like *honk* in flight.

Habits: Social and usually seen in small to large flocks. Breeds in colonies where they make mud mounds for nests. Found in small to large saline ponds and lakes, tidal flats and estuaries and sometimes off beaches. Forages in deep water as well as shallow and swims readily. Feeds with head upside-down in water, filtering out small plant and animal matter using tongue to pump water in and out of bill. Pink plumage is derived from its diet of algae. Shy and does not tolerate close approach. Runs to take off and land and flies with neck and legs extended. Adults and non-breeders disperse at certain times of the year, especially adults after breeding. Movements take them to other parts of the region or, as studies have shown, to Cuba and Hispaniola.

Comments: National bird of The Bahamas. **Conservation:** Formerly common on many islands, numbers were greatly reduced by 1950s, but conservation measures on Great Inagua have increased population. Flamingos and breeding colonies are protected by law. Current population on Great Inagua and nearby islands estimated at 35,000 to 40,000. Greater Flamingo in the region is West Indies subspecies *P. r. ruber*. Also referred to as Caribbean or West Indian Flamingo. Some authorities believe this subspecies should be elevated to full species status.

Crooked Island – May

◆ RAILS, GALLINULES AND COOTS   Family: *Rallidae*

Medium-sized world-wide family of marsh and water birds with short, rounded wings and long legs and feet. Bills vary from short to long and tails are small. Rails are secretive, frequently nocturnal and very good at skulking through thick marsh vegetation. They will also swim if necessary. Gallinules and Coots appear more like ducks and are much less secretive than rails. They inhabit fresh and brackish water ponds and swim regularly. Will also feed on land.

Clapper Rail   ⓔ *Rallus longirostris coryi*

USA (east coast) – August

North Andros – October

Status and range: Locally fairly common to common permanent resident in The Bahamas. Uncommon permanent resident in TCI.

Description: Length: 14 ins (36 cm). Large gray-brown rail with long and thick, slightly decurved bill. Back is gray with dark brown markings. Whitish throat and neck and breast buff to buffy-gray. Flanks, belly and undertail are gray with white barring. Short tail often cocked.

Voice: A series of *kek-kek-kek-kek* notes that speeds up then slows down. Usually noisiest at dawn and dusk. Calling by one bird usually draws responses from others in the area. Heard much more often than seen.

Habits: Almost exclusively a bird of mangrove swamps. Forages as tide goes out. Mostly nocturnal in some areas. Walks, runs or swims, but seldom flies. Flicks tail when walking. Has uncanny ability to slip between tangled mangrove roots. Feeds mostly on fiddler crabs.

Comments: Clapper Rail in the region is recognized as an endemic subspecies *R. l. coryi*. Outside region, common in Greater Antilles but as a different subspecies.

Besides the resident Clapper Rail, three other species of rails have been recorded in the region and they are all thought to be transients. Sora is the most frequently encountered and is described below. Virginia Rail (*Rallus limicola*) has only been recorded relatively recently and locally on Grand Bahama. Status there is not clear. Black Rail (*Laterallus jamaicensis*) has only a few records from North Andros and Eleuthera.

Sora   *Porzana carolina*

April

Length: 8.5 ins (21 cm). Uncommon winter resident and transient throughout the region. Small rail with short, stubby, yellow bill and dull greenish-yellow legs. Adult has gray head with black patch in front of eye and black throat. Back is brown with thin black and white streaks. Flanks barred black and white and undertail coverts dull white. Fall juvenile is similar to adult but lacks black in face and is buffier on head, neck and breast. Alarm call a sharp *keeek*. Sometimes gives long high descending 'whinny' with a whistled two-note ending. Heard more often than seen. Primarily frequents freshwater and brackish marshes and ponds edged with thick vegetation. Also found in mangrove swamps. Feeds on aquatic insects and marsh seeds. Secretive and rarely flies. Winter resident throughout the West Indies. Soras regularly migrate considerable distances between breeding and non-breeding ranges. They migrate at night and routes include over-water flights.

Common Moorhen

Gallinula chloropus

Non-breeding: New Providence – March

Breeding: New Providence – May

Juvenile: New Providence – October

Status and range: Fairly common permanent resident in northern and central Bahamas. Uncommon permanent resident in southern Bahamas and in TCI.

Description: Length: 14 ins (35 cm). Head and body slate-gray; wings and back dark brown. White line runs along flanks and undertail coverts have dark center with extensive white outer feathers. Legs and feet yellow-green with extremely long toes. Breeding adult has red bill with yellow tip and red shield on forehead. Bill and shield duller in non-breeding adult. Juvenile overall looks paler, has duller bill and legs, whitish throat and pale gray underparts.

Voice: Alarm call a series of *kiks*. Common call is hoarse and cackling series of quick *keh* notes which then slows down to more nasal whining at the end. Pitch varies from low to high.

Habits: Found in freshwater and brackish ponds. Long toes enable it to walk across thick vegetation on water's surface or around edges. Moves head and flicks tail as it walks and swims. Will also forage on land, including golf courses and often in company with American Coot. When alarmed, it beats a hasty clumsy retreat back into water or into vegetation.

Similar species: American Coot in all plumages, has more uniform slate-gray coloring, thicker white bill and lacks white flank line. Undertail coverts show slightly less white than Common Moorhen.

American Coot   *Fulica americana*

New Providence – January   New Providence – December

Status and range: Common winter resident and uncommon permanent resident in The Bahamas. Migrants from North America add to resident population during winter season. In TCI, common winter resident on Caicos Islands but uncommon on Grand Turk. Breeding in TCI is not confirmed for year round residents.

Description: Length: 15.5 ins (40 cm). Overall, slate-gray duck-like bird with black head and neck. Undertail coverts dark with white outer feathers. White bill has partial black ring near tip. Forehead shield is white with red-brown spot on top. Legs and feet pale olive. Toes have lobes or rounded projections which help bird to swim. Juvenile similar to adult but with duller bill and paler head, neck and body.

Voice: Wide mixture of toots, chicken-like clucks and guttural churring noises.

Habits: In winter, often found in large flocks on both fresh and brackish water. Feeds on vegetation by short dives or by tipping, like dabbling duck. Moves head as it swims. Also feeds on land especially golf courses. May aggressively defend breeding or feeding territory. Requires a long run and patters with its feet across land or water to take off.

Similar species: See **Common Moorhen**.

Purple Gallinule

Porphyrio martinica

Adult: New Providence – May

First-winter: Grand Bahama – February

Length: 13 ins (33 cm). Rare to uncommon winter resident and transient in northern and central Bahamas. Rare winter resident and transient in southern Bahamas and in TCI. Adult is a striking purple-blue bird with glossy green back and wings and all-white undertail coverts. Red bill with yellow tip and light blue shield on forehead. Legs and feet bright yellow with extremely long toes. Fall juvenile is buffy brown with dark greenish back and wings. Bill darker than adult. Starts to show some blue on underparts by mid-winter. Alarm call similar to Common Moorhen. Almost always found in freshwater ponds surrounded by thick vegetation. Long toes enable it to walk across thick vegetation on water's surface or in low bushes and trees that over-hang water or that grow around edge. Does not forage on open golf courses unlike moorhen and coot. Flicks tail while walking. Looks cumbersome and awkward but is capable of migrating long distances including over-water flights.

LIMPKIN   **Family:** *Aramidae*

A New World family with a single species. Limpkin is a long-billed and long-legged wading bird of swamps and wetlands that feeds primarily on snails and mollusks. Utilizes several types of habitat in The Bahamas. Taxonomists classify Limpkins as not being related to herons or ibises despite appearances.

Limpkin   *Aramus guarauna*

North Andros – April

New Providence – May

Status and range: Locally uncommon permanent resident on Abaco and New Providence. Fairly common on North Andros and Eleuthera. Accidental visitor to other large islands in the region.

Description: Length: 26 ins (66 cm); wingspan: 40 ins (102 cm). Large, dark-brown, long-legged bird. Bill thick and long, partially pale orange and slightly decurved. Head and neck show dense white streaks. Dark brown back and wing coverts with bold, triangular, white spots. In flight, long neck is extended, body slightly hunched and legs extended well beyond tail.

Voice: Call a loud, piercing, drawn-out scream *krr-eeoooo*, usually made at dawn, dusk or during night. Also a fast series of *kip* notes.

Habits: Forages day or night in wet or dry, grassy and brushy areas and around margins of ponds. Diet probably includes aquatic and land snails, reptiles and insects. Also seen in fairly dense coppice or edges of pinewoods that are near wetlands or open areas. Slow strolling walk with jerky motion and tail flicking. Roosts in trees; sometimes calls from treetops.

SHOREBIRDS

The next four families of plovers, oystercatchers, stilts and sandpipers are collectively referred to as shorebirds in North America and the West Indies. In Europe and Asia, they are known as waders. Found world-wide, shorebirds range in size with varying bill and leg lengths which determine their foraging behavior. They are usually found in or near all types of fresh and saltwater habitats, some preferring drier areas. Identification of many shorebirds may be made on the basis of bill size, leg length, body shape and feeding behavior. Identification based on plumage is more subtle and difficult because a shorebird's plumage changes, depending upon the age of the bird and the season. With some species, changes are dramatic, with others, less so. Some knowledge of the variation between the different plumages and when they occur is helpful. There are three principal types of plumage: adult breeding (April–August/September), adult non-breeding (August/September–March/April) and juvenile (August–October/ November). These months apply to migrant shorebirds and not to the few resident species as their breeding cycle starts earlier in the year. Shorebirds do not molt or change their plumage all at once, so there is a transition period from one plumage to the next. The months indicated above are a general time period when certain plumages or those in transition occur. In transitional plumage, which may be either subtle or obvious, birds show a mix of both faded and worn feathers from the old plumage and the neater fresher feathers of the new. Both males and females are generally similar in appearance but there are a few distinctions which are noted in the species accounts.

During fall migration, any or all of the three main types of plumage and a variety of some in transition may be encountered in the more common species. It is also a time when, generally, more color is observed in shorebirds, especially in the early stage of fall migration. When adults reach the region in the fall, they will more than likely be in some type of faded and worn breeding plumage, or be in some form of transitional plumage which would be a patchy appearance of faded feathers from the breeding plumage and fresher but duller-colored feathers of the non-breeding plumage. Usually, by October, they will be seen in complete non-breeding plumage and, while the feathers are new and look more uniform, the overall appearance is generally some form of dull gray and/or brown. Juveniles differ from adults (especially earlier in fall) mainly because their plumage is fresher and brighter than the worn feathers of the breeding adult or an adult that is in transition. Many juveniles of several species will also have a crisp scaly appearance or pattern to the back and wings, which is created by pale or buff-colored edges to dark feathers. Later in fall, juvenal feathers fade and, generally, by November (sooner in some species) they will have lost, or almost lost, their juvenal plumage and will be molting to their first winter plumage which is similar to that of the adult non-breeding. By the following spring, a few of these immatures may remain in the region for the summer as non-breeders, most in a partial breeding plumage. They do not go north with the adults. The adults, in spring, whether they are migrating from the region or from areas outside the region, will likely be in some state of transition to breeding plumage. Full breeding plumage is not encountered that often.

PLOVERS   Family: *Charadriidae*

A medium-sized family of shorebirds found throughout the world. Compactly built, they range in size from small to medium with short necks and short thick bills. They have relatively large heads and eyes, long pointed wings and many have white stripe on upperwing. Inhabit open beaches, tidal flats and areas of short grass. Nest on the ground in the open. Have habit of running quickly and then stopping abruptly. Feed by picking off ground or making shallow probes. The region is well represented by six plover species described below – first three are breeders and last three are transients.

Snowy Plover   *Charadrius alexandrinus*

Cat Island – May   Breeding male: Florida – late March

Status and range: Uncommon permanent resident and fairly common summer resident in central and southern Bahamas and TCI. Some birds appear to withdraw from these areas in winter but their status is not well known as movements of these populations have not been studied, making it difficult to distinguish between residents and non-residents. Accidental visitor to Abaco, Andros, Great Exuma and Cat Island. Not reported from other northern and central Bahamian islands.

Description: Length: 6.25 ins (16 cm). Small pale plover with thin black bill, white forehead and gray legs. Upperparts are pale brown-gray and underparts white. Breeding adult male has black mark on forecrown and small black patch behind eye and on side of breast. These areas duller on adult female and absent on non-breeding adult and juvenile. In flight, shows white stripe on upperwing; rump and upper-tail coverts same color as back with dark patch on end of tail.

Voice: Calls include low *purrt* and softly whistled *tu-wheet*.

Habits: Prefers drier rather than wetter areas. Often seen on shores of interior saline ponds, dry mudflats and sandy beaches. Runs more often than flies. Long breeding season. Nests in the open in small depression on ground.

Similar species: See **Piping Plover**.

Comments: Known as 'Snowy Plover' in the New World and 'Kentish Plover' in the Old World. Subspecies in region *C.a. nivosus* is same as that in USA and rest of West Indies. **Conservation:** Threatened species in USA due to human disturbance, habitat loss and increased predation. Population in The Bahamas and TCI also vulnerable, for the same reasons but conservation status not well known.

Wilson's Plover   *Charadrius wilsonia*

Male showing some breeding feathers on head: Grand Bahama – December

Male: Ragged Islands – May

First-winter birds (similar to non-breeding adult): Grand Bahama – December

Status and range: Common summer resident in central and southern Bahamas and TCI. Uncommon to fairly common summer resident in northern Bahamas. Status of birds seen during winter is not clear because it is not known whether they are permanent or winter residents.

Description: Length: 8 ins (20 cm). Brown-backed plover with distinct, thick, all-black bill, white forehead and underparts and pale-colored legs. Breeding adult male has black forecrown, black lores and wide black breast band; black areas replaced by brown in breeding adult female and non-breeding adults. Some breeding males show hint of rust coloring behind eye. Juvenile similar to non-breeding adult but brown breast band sometimes incomplete and upperpart feathers thinly edged in buff, creating slightly scaly appearance. In flight, shows white stripe on upperwing and dark patch on end of tail.

Voice: Call notes include quick whistled *whit* and louder *wheet*.

Habits: Frequents beaches, low rocky areas, tidal flats and usually drier parts of lagoons and saline ponds. Forages by day and night. Nest is shallow scrape on open ground.

Similar species: See **Semipalmated Plover**.

Killdeer   *Charadrius vociferus*

Both New Providence – May

Status and range: Fairly common to common permanent resident in central and southern Bahamas and TCI. Uncommon in northern Bahamas. In winter, migrants from North America supplement local populations.

Description: Length: 10.5 ins (27 cm). All ages and seasonal plumages similar. Fairly large brown-backed plover with red eye-ring, fairly thin black bill and dull pale-colored legs. Dark band on forecrown divides white forehead from white supercilium. Underparts white with two distinctive black bands – one on breast and other as collar around neck. Bands look wider or narrower, depending upon bird's posture. Long tail projects beyond tips of folded wings; visible on standing bird. In flight, especially when landing or in display, shows brownish-orange rump and uppertail coverts, black band near tip of tail and prominent white stripe on upperwing.

Voice: Calls a loud *kill-deer kill-deer* and a repeated *k'dee-dee-dee*. Noisy and easily agitated. Often first bird to sound alarm, causing other shorebirds in area to take flight.

Habits: Very adaptable. Found along coast, near ponds and mudflats, and inland on lawns, short grassy fields and golf courses. Feeds day or night. Nests on ground and, if disturbed at nest, will sometimes do pretend 'broken-wing' display to draw intruder away.

Similar species: Two bands on breast area and brown-orange color of rump and uppertail coverts distinguish Killdeer from all other plovers and shorebirds in the region.

Black-bellied Plover   *Pluvialis squatarola*

Adult male breeding: May

Non-breeding (with turnstone):
Eleuthera – March

Juvenile: October

Non-breeding showing black armpits:
Caymans – March

Length: 11.5 ins (29 cm); wingspan: 29 ins (74 cm). Common winter resident and transient throughout the region. A few non-breeders remain through summer. Known as Black-bellied Plover in New World and Grey Plover in Old World. Largest plover in region with conspicuous black eye (except in breeding plumage), thick black bill and long dark gray legs. Breeding adult male is boldly checkered black and white above and solid black below with white vent and undertail coverts. Breeding adult female duller with more black and white mottling to underparts. This striking plumage or (more likely) one that is in transition between this plumage and non-breeding plumage is likely to be encountered either before birds leave the region in spring (April–May) or when they arrive back in early fall (August–September). In fall and winter, non-breeding adult has light brown-gray upperparts with weak patterns and white underparts with dusky wash on breast mixed with a few light streaks. Juvenile similar to non-breeding adult but upperparts and wing are more evenly and boldly patterned with mottled white or pale yellow-buff; makes some juveniles look gray and others warm brown. In flight, all plumages show white stripe on upperwing, white uppertail coverts and white underwing with prominent black patch at base next to body, often referred to as black 'armpits'. Common call a mournful three-note whistle *plee-oo-wee*; also a single *plee*. Found on rocky coastlines, beaches, estuaries, tidal flats and at edges of salt ponds. Feeds day or night. Shy and does not usually allow a close approach. Long-distance migrant that nests on tundra areas of northern North America. **American Golden-Plover** (*Pluvialis dominica*) is only other large plover in the region and is quite similar to Black-bellied (especially non-breeders and juveniles) but is very rare transient throughout the region and unrecorded from several islands.

Semipalmated Plover

Charadrius semipalmatus

Breeding: April

Non-breeding: New Providence – October

Length: 7.25 ins (18 cm). Uncommon winter resident and common transient (mainly in fall) in The Bahamas. Common winter resident and transient in TCI. A few non-breeders remain through summer. Small plover with short bill, dark brown upperparts, white underparts and yellow-orange legs. Adult breeding plumage, seen in spring, has orange bill with black tip, white forehead with black forecrown that extends to black face and a complete black breast band. Breast band may be thin or wider depending on bird's posture. Non-breeding adult has whitish supercilium, darker bill and duller legs. Also black areas of breeding plumage turn dark brown. Juvenile in early fall similar to non-breeding adult but has thin buff edges to back feathers and duller legs. In flight, all plumages show long wings with white stripe on upperwing and dark patch near tip of tail. Call a clear rising two-note whistle *chu-weee*. Found on wide open beaches, tidal flats, low rocky areas and margins of inland lakes, ponds or pools, often seen with other shorebirds. Long-distance migrant. Nests on ground in dry arctic tundra areas of northern North America. **Wilson's Plover**, also a small brown-backed plover, has noticeably thicker and longer, all-black bill and duller colored legs.

Piping Plover

Charadrius melodus

Breeding: April

Non-breeding: New Providence – October

Length: 7.25 ins (18 cm). Uncommon winter resident in northern Bahamas. Unrecorded on some of the large islands in central Bahamas and all of southern Bahamas. Status on Caicos Islands in TCI is unclear. Small plover with short stubby bill, pale sandy upperparts, white underparts and yellow-orange legs. Adult breeding plumage, seen in early spring, has yellow-orange bill with black tip, black bar on forecrown and black breast band (sometimes broken in centre of breast). Non-breeding adult and juvenile have black bill and pale sandy patch on sides of breast – black bar on forecrown is absent. In flight, shows white stripe on upperwing, sandy back, whitish uppertail coverts and black patch near tip of tail. Call a soft whistled or piping *peep* or *peep-lo*. Strictly coastal. Usually seen on sandy beaches, mudflats and low rocky areas. **Snowy Plover** is also a small pale-backed plover but has thinner all-black bill and gray legs. In flight, less contrast between back and uppertail coverts. **Conservation:** Occurs primarily in USA and Canada, where it is considered an endangered species due to loss of habitat, increased human activity and predation on beaches where it breeds. Same problems affect Piping Plovers wintering in the region.

◆ OYSTERCATCHERS   Family: *Haematopodidae*

Small world-wide family (eleven species) of large entirely black or black and white shorebirds. Strong, red, dagger-shaped bill and long, heavy, pink legs. Bill is used to pry open shellfish or mollusks and to probe mud flats, beaches and, in some cases, inland pastures.

American Oystercatcher   *Haematopus palliatus*

Adult: New Providence – April

Status and range: Permanent resident. Locally uncommon in central and southern Bahamas and TCI. Uncommon on New Providence, rare to uncommon on Abaco, Bimini and Andros but not recorded from Grand Bahama.

Description: Length: 18 ins (46 cm); wingspan: 32 ins (81 cm). Large black and white shorebird. Both adults have thick bright orange-red bill, red eye-ring around yellow eye and sturdy, pale, pink legs. Head and neck solid black and back dark brown with white underparts. Bold, white, wing stripe and white area at base of tail; both conspicuous in flight. Juvenile similar to adult but has dusky bill with orange base and duller eye color.

Voice: Common call a loud whistled *wheep*. Mated pairs noisy when greeting each other.

Habits: Frequents rocky shorelines looking for mollusks and shellfish but will also probe for food on beaches and tidal flats. Nests on ground on offshore cays. Low reproductive rate and only averages one chick per year. Wary and does not usually allow close approach.

◆ STILTS AND AVOCETS

Family: *Recurvirostridae*

Very small world-wide family with seven species. Tall, slim, black and white shore-birds with small heads, elongated necks, thin bills (curved upwards on Avocets) and very long legs. Black-necked Stilt is the sole representative of stilts in the region and is described below. American Avocet, not described, is an accidental to very rare visitor.

Black-necked Stilt

Himantopus mexicanus

Long Island – March

Crooked Island – May

Status and range: Uncommon to fairly common summer resident in northern Bahamas but rare summer visitor to Bimini and Grand Bahama. Common permanent resident in central and southern Bahamas and TCI.

Description: Length: 14 ins (36 cm). Tall, slender, black and white shorebird with long, black, needle-like bill and long, bright, pink-red legs. Back of adult male glossy black; female brown-black. Juvenile similar to female but back feathers have thin buff edges and legs are duller. In flight, white lower back and rump form a wedge into black back and legs extend well beyond tail.

Voice: Common call notes *yip* or *kek*. Alarm call a loud incessant *kek-kek-kek-kek*.

Habits: Frequents shallow freshwater, brackish and saline ponds in open areas or those surrounded by thick vegetation such as mangroves. Often in loose flocks with other stilts and shorebirds. Feeds by walking with long strides and picking prey from surface. Vigilant and noisy, quickly sounds alarm when approached.

◆ SANDPIPERS   Family: *Scolopacidae*

Large and diverse world-wide family which is also the largest of the shorebird families. Small to large shorebirds with tapered bodies and slender bills and legs. Necks vary from long and slender to short and thick. Wings relatively long and pointed, making for fast and strong flight. Most nest on ground in arctic tundra areas of North America, making them long distance migrants. Outside breeding grounds, sandpipers often found in mixed species flocks. Willet is the only member of the sandpiper family that breeds in the region.

Willet   *Catoptrophorus semipalmatus*

Great Exuma – June

Breeding 'Eastern Willet':
Providenciales – June

Non-breeding 'Western Willet': Florida – March

Status and range: Locally fairly common summer resident in central and southern Bahamas and in TCI. Uncommon summer resident or visitor in northern Bahamas. Transients and a relatively few wintering birds occur but their status is unclear or unknown.

Description: Length: 15 ins (38 cm); wingspan: 26 ins (66 cm). Large sandpiper with straight heavy bill and long, stout, gray legs. Breeding adult has gray-brown mottled back and wings and dense but fine streaking on head, neck and breast. Rest of underparts white with barring along sides of breast and flanks. Non-breeding adult is plain gray overall with white from belly to undertail coverts. Juvenile similar to non-breeding adult but has brownish tinge overall with buff edges to feathers on back and wings. In flight, all plumages show conspicuous black and white wing pattern on both upper and underwing.

Voice: Alarm call a loud repeated *kip kip kip*. Song, often given in flight, a loud *pee wee willet*. Very vocal in breeding areas but fairly quiet in non-breeding season.

Habits: Found on tidal flats, beaches, brackish inland ponds and in mangrove swamps. Forages by shallow probes and picking from water's surface. Nest is shallow scrape on ground, often well away from water and usually in short vegetation.

Comments: There are two separate breeding populations of Willet and they are represented by two subspecies. Breeding Willet in the region and eastern North America is subspecies *C. s. semipalmatus*, known as 'Eastern Willet'. It is believed that Eastern Willets migrate to the region to breed and leave after they have finished in late summer. It is also thought that some Eastern Willets migrate through the region in spring and fall and that a few may overwinter, especially in the more south-ern areas. However, their status and range are not well known, if at all. *C. s. inorna-tus*, known as 'Western Willet', breeds inland in Western North America and part of population spends winter in coastal regions of eastern USA and Florida. Some birds reach the region but how many and how far south they go is unknown. Western Willet has been recorded during winter and early spring from a few locations in the northern Bahamas especially Abaco. It is very similar in non-breeding plumage to Eastern Willet but Western Willet is slightly larger with a relatively longer thinner bill and longer legs. These traits, however, are difficult to discern without practice, experience or a side-by-side comparison.

Winter Resident and Transient Sandpipers

Most sandpipers are long-distance migrants and many species pass through the region during migration. There are more birds in fall than in spring due to their more easterly migration route and the influx of juveniles. In fall, adults tend to migrate southwards early, before the juveniles, leaving the breeding grounds in July and August. The result is that adult sandpipers start to appear first in the region between mid-July and September and, usually the first species to appear, are Lesser Yellowlegs, Short-billed Dowitchers and Least Sandpipers. Juveniles start arriving between September and October but there is a considerable overlap when both adults and juveniles may be present at the same time. The majority of sandpipers either stop briefly and then continue their southbound route, or they simply overfly the region altogether. A few remain throughout the winter season. Even then, there may be considerable movement within the region to locate adequate food resources.

The sandpipers described below are the most likely species to occur in the region, either as winter residents or transients. A description of the traits common to each sandpiper is presented first, followed by a brief description of the three main plumages (adult breeding, adult non-breeding and juvenile). It is not practical to have a photograph for all the possible plumages, so a few of the more typical examples are presented. Although the plumage of first-winter immatures and non-breeding adults are generally similar, there are some cases where they may be distinguishable and those photographs are noted (see Stilt Sandpiper or Lesser Yellowlegs). First-winter shorebirds retain their old juvenal wing coverts, which contrast with the new (but duller) feathers on the back. Sometimes this is obvious while other times it is not. Because of plumage variation, season, feather wear, etc. it can be quite difficult to age every individual sandpiper either in photos or the field, so it is often enough just to identify the species. Eighteen species of sandpipers are covered in the species accounts with the last five species treated as a group – the smallest sandpipers.

Ruddy Turnstones in flight: Long Island – March

Greater Yellowlegs   *Tringa melanoleuca*

New Providence – November

Non-breeding Greater with Lessers:
Grand Bahama – December

Lesser Yellowlegs   *Tringa flavipes*

Grand Bahama – October

First-winter: New Providence –
October

Greater Yellowlegs Length: 14 ins (36 cm) and **Lesser Yellowlegs** Length: 10.5 ins (27 cm). Uncommon to fairly common winter residents and fairly common to common spring and fall transients throughout the region. A few non-breeders remain in summer. Lesser Yellowlegs is the more common of the two. Size difference obvious when two species are seen together but size difficult to estimate when one bird is by itself.

Traits common to both species: Long thin bills, slender bodies and long yellow legs. Mottled gray, black and white upperparts and white underparts. Backs and wings mottled darker on adult breeding and juvenile but are plainer gray on non-breeding birds. In flight, both show white uppertail coverts and thinly barred white tail with legs extending beyond tail. Habit of bobbing heads and tails when alarmed. Found in a number of shallow fresh and saltwater habitats.

Differences: Bill of Greater Yellowlegs is longer and appears slightly upturned; bill of Lesser Yellowlegs is shorter and straighter. One way to gauge this difference is to compare bill length of each with width of head (back of head to base of bill). Greater's bill is distinctly longer than width of head; Lesser's bill is same length or only slightly longer. In breeding plumage, both species have darker backs but Greater's throat and neck have bold dark streaks, dark spots on sides of breast and bars on flanks. Lesser has fine streaking on neck and on sides of breast but not as strongly streaked or barred below as Greater. Plumage of non-breeding adult is similar for both; best distinguished by bill length and voice. Juvenal Greater has white throat with distinct dark streaks on neck and breast; juvenal Lesser has fine streaks with smudgy-gray wash across breast. Common call of Greater Yellowlegs is loud whistled *tew tew tew*, given in series of three or four notes. Lesser's call a softer *tu* or *tu-tu*. Both have similar single note alarm calls which are often repeated.

Solitary Sandpiper — *Tringa solitaria*

Breeding: late April

Non-breeding: New Providence – October

Length: 8.5 ins (22 cm). Rare to uncommon winter resident and uncommon to fairly common transient in The Bahamas. Uncommon transient through TCI. Slender sandpiper with bold white eye-ring, thin straight bill and long, dull, yellow-green legs. Back and wings are dark brown with white spots and underparts whitish. In flight, shows dark underwing, dark rump and central tail feathers with outer tail feathers white with black bars. Breeding adult has dense streaks on head and breast, non-breeding adult and juvenile have browner wash to head and breast and duller spots on back and wings. Call note, mostly in flight, is high pitched *teet-wheet* (similar to Spotted Sandpiper). Feeds along margins of any small fresh or brackish water ponds or pools, usually alone.

Spotted Sandpiper   *Actitus macularius*

Breeding: May

Non-breeding: Grand Bahama – March

Juvenile: Grand Bahama – October

New Providence – January

Length: 7.5 ins (19 cm). Uncommon winter resident and uncommon to fairly common transient throughout the region. Small short-necked sandpiper with gray-brown upperparts, white underparts and long tail that extends well beyond wing tips on standing bird. Has habit of frequently moving rear end up and down. Short flights with rapid stiff wingbeats interspersed with short glides, usually low over water. (This is not the flight pattern during migration, however.) Breeding adult has dark eye-line with thin white supercilium and pale orange bill with small dark tip. Black spots on underparts and pale pink to yellow legs. Non-breeding adult has prominent white crescent below eye, dull bill color and no dark spots on underparts. Also shows small white wedge between bend of wing and pale brown area on sides of breast. Juvenile very similar to non-breeding adult but has light buff and black bars on wing coverts. Call a high whistled *peep-peep*, often extended. Similar to Solitary Sandpiper but lower pitched and without same quality. Feeds along edges of both fresh and saltwater habitats, including rocky coastlines. Usually alone.

Ruddy Turnstone   *Arenaria interpes*

Breeding: New Providence – May   Non-breeding: Grand Bahama –
                                   December

Length: 9.5 ins (24 cm). Common winter resident and transient throughout the region. A few non-breeders remain through summer. Chunky shorebird with slightly upturned, short and pointed, dark bill. Bold, dark, breast pattern and short orange legs. In flight, shows striking black and white pattern on back, wings, and tail. Breeding adult has distinct black and white facial pattern and rich chestnut on back and wings. In non-breeding plumage, facial pattern is browner and duller and chestnut replaced by dark brown. Juvenile similar to non-breeding adult but has rusty edges to back and wing feathers. Calls include a series of low-pitched rattles and various twittering notes; also a sharp *kew*. Feeds along rocky coastlines, beaches and edges of inland ponds. Uses bill to turn over stones and debris searching for food. Also scavenges around man-made sources such as garbage dumps, picnic spots, outside hotel restaurants and fish or conch-cleaning areas, becoming quite tame in some cases.

Whimbrel   *Numenius phaeopus*

April

Length: 17.5 ins (45 cm). Rare winter visitor and transient in The Bahamas. Uncommon winter visitor and transient in TCI. A few are probably winter residents. Large brownish shorebird (largest in region) with long decurved bill. Dark bold stripes on head, fine streaks on paler neck and breast, barred flanks and pale belly. Bill color is dark or dark with pinkish-red base on lower mandible. Legs long and gray. All plumages similar but juvenile has brighter pattern of pale dots or spots on back and wings. In flight, the back, rump and tail are also brownish. Call, mostly in flight, a loud, rapidly repeated whistle *whi whi whi whi whi*. Found in a number of habitats including beaches, mudflats or rocky shorelines.

Red Knot   *Calidris canutus*

Molting to breeding plumage: late April   Non-breeding: March

Length: 10.5 ins (27 cm). Locally uncommon to fairly common winter resident on Abaco. Rare to uncommon winter visitor and transient in rest of region. Some populations have shown a serious decline in recent years. Fairly large chunky sandpiper with dull olive legs and dark bill that appears short for size of bird. Breeding adult has mottled gray and black back with distinctive rufous face, breast and belly. Transition to or from breeding plumage often shows pale rufous blotches to underparts. This plumage more likely to be seen than full breeding adult. Non-breeding adult has uniform gray upperparts, whitish supercilium and whitish underparts; some streaks on breast and bars on flanks. Juvenile similar to non-breeding adult but has pale and dark edges to back and wing feathers, giving a slightly scaly appearance. In flight, all plumages show pale gray uppertail coverts and tail with fine barring on coverts. Forages primarily on open tidal mudflats.

Dunlin   *Calidris alpina*

First-winter. February   October

Length: 8.5 ins (22 cm). Locally uncommon to fairly common winter resident on Abaco. Rare winter visitor and transient in rest of region. Unrecorded from several islands. Small and compact sandpiper with longish black bill (noticeable droop at tip) and short black legs. Often has a short-necked hunched appearance. Generally by time adult or juvenal Dunlin reach the region in late fall, they are in non-breeding or first-winter plumage: gray-brown upperparts and whitish underparts, gray wash to neck and breast and diffuse streaks to flanks. It is possible that a few Dunlins seen in early stages of fall migration or later stages of spring migration may show black blotching on belly (note photo above) and some red-brown feathers on upperparts as they start transition from or to breeding plumage. Flight call a raspy *kreee*. Forages primarily on mudflats but may also be found on inland ponds. Has similarities to non-breeding **Western Sandpiper** but Western is smaller with shorter bill and whiter neck and breast.

Short-billed Dowitcher   *Limnodromus griseus*

In transition to breeding: April

Non-breeding: February

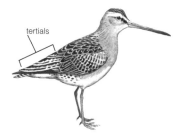

Fresh juvenile

First-winter (still showing some pale internal markings on tertials): October

Length: 11 ins (28 cm). Uncommon winter resident and fairly common transient in The Bahamas. Fairly common winter resident and transient in TCI. Stout sandpiper with extremely long, straight, dark bill and long, dull, yellow-green legs. Darker cap contrasts with prominent whitish supercilium. White wedge from uppertail coverts to middle of back, visible in flight. Breeding adult has dark back and wings, rusty wash on neck and breast spotting, white belly and undertail coverts with barred flanks. Non-breeding plumage is gray to brown-gray above, white below with gray wash of streaks on breast and light barring along flanks. Fresh juvenile has buffy breast and cleaner underparts without heavy spotting and barring. Back and wing feathers dark with broad rusty edges; tertial feathers also with rusty internal markings. Flight call usually given just as it takes off, especially when startled, is rapid and soft *tu-tu-tu*. Similar to call of Lesser Yellowlegs but faster and longer. Prefers shallow brackish or saltwater areas as well as tidal flats where it probes the mud with rapid up-and-down movements. In the region, it is most likely to see adult dowitchers in non-breeding plumage or some type of transitional plumage closer to non-breeding than breeding. This is especially true for birds in fall migration. Juveniles, in early fall migration, are likely to show bright feathers which fade by late October and then molt to first-winter plumage which is similar to non-breeding adult. **Long-billed Dowitcher** (*Limnodromus scolopaceus*) has only been recorded twice in the northern Bahamas. Very similar to Short-billed Dowitcher and is best distinguished by familiarity with the two species and by call, a sharp high *keek*.

Stilt Sandpiper

Calidris himantopus

Breeding: June

Starting transition to breeding plumage on head: April

First-winter: New Providence – October

Non-breeding: Long Island – March

Length: 8.5 ins (22 cm). Rare to uncommon winter resident and uncommon to fairly common transient in The Bahamas. More common in central and southern Bahamas. Fairly common transient and winter resident in TCI. Slim sandpiper with fairly wide whitish supercilium, long dark bill with very slight droop at tip and long yellow-green legs. In flight, shows whitish uppertail coverts and grayish tail. Breeding adult has rufous cheek, dark blotchy back and heavily-barred underparts. Non-breeding adult plain gray above and white below with some streaks on neck and breast. Juveniles, in early fall, are dark above with conspicuous pale edges to feathers, creating scaly appearance; back turns gray later in fall for first-winter plumage. Feeds by probing, sometimes with quick up-and-down motion (like dowitcher but not as extensive), in both fresh and saltwater ponds and pools. Often wades up to belly and immerses head.

Pectoral Sandpiper
Calidris melanotos

Breeding adult: April

Juvenile (bill muddy from probing): New Providence – early November

Length: 8.5 ins (22 cm). Uncommon fall transient and rare spring transient in The Bahamas and TCI. Absent in winter. Medium-sized sandpiper with fairly short, slightly decurved, mostly dark bill and dull yellow legs. In all plumages, good field mark is dense thin streaking on breast sharply contrasting with unmarked white underparts. Males noticeably larger than females when seen together. Breeding adult has dark back and wing with buff to rufous edges to feathers. Juvenile similar to adult but has buffy wash to breast streaking and brighter colored edges to back and wing, creating a striking scaly pattern. Flight call a low harsh *chrrk*. Favors short grassy areas along edges of fresh or brackish water ponds and puddles; sometimes open mudflats. Often has an upright posture with neck extended, especially when alarmed.

Wilson's Snipe
Gallinago delicata

New Providence – October

October

Length: 10.5 ins (27 cm). Uncommon winter resident throughout the region but unrecorded from several major islands in central Bahamas. All seasonal plumages similar. Compact brownish shorebird with short neck, short legs, very long sturdy bill, striped head and bold stripes down back. Belly is white and sides of breast and flanks strongly barred. Call note on take-off is scratchy *sckait sckait*. Forages in shallow water, wet grassy areas, thick reeds or vegetation surrounding ponds. Secretive and prefers cover, often crouching when alarmed. Usually flushes before being seen with fast twisting flight. Superficially resembles dowitcher but plumage and behavior are different. Formerly called 'Common Snipe'.

Smallest Sandpipers

Commonly referred to as 'peeps' in North America and the West Indies. They are referred to as 'stints' in Europe and Asia. The five species described here can be a difficult group to identify since they are small, hard to observe well, move around a lot and seasonal plumage differences are often subtle. Size is helpful but usually only when there are other peeps nearby for comparison. Bill length and shape are important but a sense of these field marks usually occurs only after practice and experience.

Sanderling   *Calidris alba*

Non-breeding: Grand Bahama – December

Non-breeding (worn): Long Island – March

Juvenile: early September

In transition to breeding (rufous feathers on wing): April

Length: 8 ins (20 cm). Uncommon to fairly common winter resident and transient in The Bahamas. Fairly common in TCI. Largest member of the 'peeps'. Small sandpiper with relatively heavy, straight, black bill and short black legs with hind toe absent. In flight, shows bold white wing stripe on upperwing; underwing is white. Non-breeding adult pale gray above and white below with small black area at bend of folded wing, sometimes obscured. This plumage is paler than any of the other peeps in non-breeding plumage. Juvenile in early fall migration is similar to non-breeding adult but has black and white checkered pattern on upperparts and more prominent black area at bend of wing. Breeding adult has rufous head, breast and upperparts but this plumage is not likely to be seen in region. Birds in transition may show some rufous feathers on back, wing, head or breast in spring (April–May) or late summer (August). Call note a simple *kip*. Feeds on sandy beaches, often running in and out with waves, or on tidal flats and inland salt ponds.

Semipalmated Sandpiper   *Calidris pusilla*

In transition to breeding: late April

April

Juvenile: September

Length: 6.25 ins (16 cm). Uncommon to fairly common transient through the region. Status of winter residents unclear because they are difficult to identify in this plumage and even more difficult to distinguish from Western Sandpiper. Probably a very rare winter resident in northern part of region and relatively more common (but still rare) in southern part including TCI. Small sandpiper with black legs and short, straight, black bill. Bill shape varies from being short and blunt at tip (sometimes appearing tubular) to longer and more tapered with thinner tip. Tendency is for males to have shorter bills and females longer bills. Non-breeding plumage uniformly brown-gray above and white below. Breeding adult in spring migration has mottled, mostly gray and black back and wings, white underparts with light streaks on sides of breast. Some birds have rufous tinge to crown and cheeks. Juvenile, in fall migration, similar to breeding adult but has cleaner pattern to back and wings; dark feathers neatly edged white and/or buff giving scaly appearance. Main flight call note a low short *churk*. Does, however, make other calls, especially when in group. Found on tidal flats and along edges of ponds and lagoons. Feeds on dry mud as well as shallow water.

Western Sandpiper   *Calidris mauri*

In transition to breeding: late April

Mostly in non-breeding: September

Juvenile: September

First-winter but still an area of rufous in scapulars: September

Length: 6.5 ins (16.5 cm). Uncommon fall and rare spring transient through the region. Rare winter resident throughout the region but complete status unclear, due in part, to difficulty in distinguishing from Semipalmated Sandpiper. Small sandpiper with short black legs and relatively long, slightly decurved, black bill. Females have longer bills than males and show more of a slight droop at tip. Non-breeding plumage is uniformly brown-gray above and white below. Adult breeding plumage unlikely to be seen in the region but late spring and early fall migrants may show transitional plumage with varying amounts of rufous on crown, cheeks and back plus streaking on breast. Juvenile, during fall migration, differs from breeding adult by lack of rufous on head and reduced streaking on breast. Also, just above wing, they show distinctive row of dark feathers edged bright rufous (called scapulars) which contrast with duller back and wing feathers. Main flight call a thin and high *cheet*. Does, however, make other calls especially when in groups. Forages around most shoreline habitats especially mudflats.

Even on close examination, non-breeding plumage of both Western and Semipalmated Sandpiper is virtually the same and identification may only be made carefully by bill size and shape and call note. The bill of Western is, on average, longer with slight droop at tip than shorter, straighter and blunter bill of Semipalmated. However, because there is considerable overlap in bill size when comparing male Westerns and female Semipalmateds, many birds go unidentified as to which species they belong to.

Least Sandpiper   *Calidris minutilla*

Worn non-breeding: Long Island – March

Molting to breeding: – April

Juvenile: September

First-winter: Grand Bahama – late October

Length: 6 ins (15 cm). Uncommon winter resident and fairly common transient in northern and central Bahamas. Common in southern Bahamas and in TCI. Smallest and most numerous peep in the region. Has short, slightly decurved, dark bill which is relatively thick at base and which tapers to a fine point. Short yellow-green legs but light conditions or mud stains may obscure leg color. All plumages have brown to brown-gray upperparts, white underparts and some form of light streaking and/or brown wash on neck and upper breast. Non-breeding plumage has brown-gray back, wings and breast. Breeding adult and juvenile have darker backs and wings with rufous and buff edges to feathers but juvenile has brighter colors and broader edges. Distinguished from Semipalmated, Western and White-rumped Sandpiper by bill size and shape, breast pattern, browner tones to back and wings and leg color. Common flight call a high *kreeet*. Found on mudflats and inland ponds where it sometimes feeds just a short distance away from water in low grasses or vegetation around edges. Wades in shallow water but generally not as often as either Semipalmated or Western.

White-rumped Sandpiper   *Calidris fuscicollis*

Breeding: May

Non-breeding: Grand Bahama – late October

Juvenile (with Least Sandpipers): Grand Bahama – late October

Juvenile: Grand Bahama – late October

Length 7.5 ins (19 cm). Rare to uncommon transient throughout the region. Tendency to be later migrant in spring (late April – late May) and in fall (late October – early November) and possibly overlooked. Larger than other three peeps but not Sanderling which it usually is not seen with. Long-winged sandpiper; folded wings extend beyond tip of tail on standing bird. Short black legs and black bill with a slight droop at tip. Base of lower mandible dull red and only visible at close range. Whitish uppertail coverts (rump area) most visible in flight or certain preening positions. Non-breeding plumage has brown-gray upperparts, brown-gray wash and light streaks to upper breast and white underparts with obscure streaks along flanks. Breeding adult has dark back and wing feathers with rufous and pale buff edges. White underparts have dark streaks on neck, sides of breast and on flanks. Fall juvenile similar to breeding adult but brighter above and lighter streaking below. Flight call note a high squeaky *jeet*, unlike other peeps. Forages around borders of fresh and saltwater ponds and lagoons. Often feeds with other peeps which helps with size comparisons.

GULLS, TERNS AND SKIMMERS   Family: *Laridae*

Medium-sized world-wide family of pelagic and coastal birds which has four different subfamilies: jaegers/skuas, gulls, terns and skimmers. Only gulls and terns and one skimmer are covered here.

Gulls

Gulls are a subfamily (*Larinae*) of the family *Laridae*. They are fairly small to large-sized web-footed birds with stout bills and bodies. They regularly swim and are found along coasts and on large inland lakes and ponds. They eat just about anything and are also excellent scavengers, often congregating in the region at public beaches, garbage dumps and fish-cleaning areas where they scrounge for food. Gulls nest in colonies.

The identification of adult gulls is relatively straightforward but recognizing immatures, especially in their first year, can be more of a challenge, since they vary in appearance. Immatures are also known for some individual variation in plumage, even within the same species and the same age. A basic understanding of the different forms of plumage and the time at which they occur is often the key to correct identification. All gulls have one juvenal plumage and then a succession of immature plumages before they reach adult plumage. This process takes between two and four years to complete, depending upon the species. The smallest gulls take two years, medium-sized three and the largest four years to obtain adult plumage. All forms of immature plumage are named by the age of the bird (first-year, second-year, third-year, etc.) and by the season (winter or summer). A typical sequence of development would be juvenile (August–September) to first-winter (September–April) to first-summer (April–August) followed by second-winter (September–April) to second-summer, etc. until they become adults. At certain times of these months, birds may show a transitional plumage where the birds have a mixture of worn feathers from the old plumage and neater feathers of the new plumage. Adult gulls have an annual breeding and non-breeding plumage. Generally, gulls are darkest overall in juvenile and first-winter plumage and they become progressively lighter as they mature to adulthood. Having some knowledge of the juvenile and first-winter plumage is usually more important than knowing the later immature plumages. Despite the details, often the most useful identification features for gulls are their size and shape and color of bill, back and legs. Gulls are often found in mixed flocks with other gulls, so comparisons are often possible.

First-winter Lesser Black-backed Gull: New Providence – January

First-winter Herring Gull (with Laughing Gulls): Grand Bahama – December

Laughing Gull   *Larus atricilla*

Breeding: Eleuthera – March

Non-breeding: New Providence – January

Faded juvenile: New Providence – early October

First-winter: New Providence – December

Status and range: Locally fairly common to common summer and winter resident in The Bahamas. Common summer resident in TCI. In summer, disperses throughout central and southern parts of the region to breed. In winter, concentrates in coastal towns and settlements, mainly in northern Bahamas, especially Nassau. Winter population increases as winter residents and transients arrive from North America.

Description: Length: 16.5 ins (43 cm); wingspan: 40 ins (102 cm). Long-billed and long-winged medium-sized gull that takes three years to reach adult plumage. (Months given below in parentheses are approximate months during which plumage described, or transitional phase to that plumage, occurs in the region.) Breeding adult (February–September) has black head with distinctive white crescents above and below eye, dark red bill and dark legs tinged with red. Back and wings dark gray with black outer primaries. Underparts and tail are white. Non-breeding adult (August–March) acquires white head with gray smudge behind eye and back of head. Red bill becomes blacker and white eye-crescents still visible. Juvenile (July–September) mostly brown (dark brown at first fading to lighter brown) with scaly appearance to back and wings. Develops dark gray back and whiter head with dark patch behind eye when in its first-winter plumage (September–April). First-winter birds also have dark gray sides to breast and flanks and white tail with wide dark band at tip. Brown wing coverts from juvenal plumage are retained and contrast with dark gray back. For next two years, Laughing Gull gradually loses brown wing coverts, gray sides of breast and flanks and tail band so that, by third winter, it is in non-breeding adult plumage. By following spring, it is in adult breeding plumage and ready for courtship and family.

Voice: Short call *kee-aw*. Long call loud and repeated laugh-like *ah-ah-ah-ah* that starts rapidly and then slows down. Noisy, even in non-breeding season, especially in groups.

Habits: Breeds in thick ground cover on offshore cays. Frequents harbors, beaches and inland ponds; also found offshore. Forages for fish and crustaceans but will scavenge in garbage dumps and seek handouts from people. Will also take other birds' eggs and sometimes nestlings, especially terns. Increasing population poses threat to tern colonies.

Breeding: Great Exuma – June

Non-breeding: Grand Bahama – January

In flight, all Laughing Gulls show some dark outer primaries; more extensive in first year birds. In fresh non-breeding plumage, may also show a few white tips to primaries.

Winter Resident and Transient Gulls

The following four species of gulls are winter residents, arriving mostly in November and departing in March, although some may be present as early as October or as late as May. The majority appear to be winter residents but a few may be transients wintering further south. These species have been reported the most frequently but populations vary from year to year. However, all these gulls are more common and regular around Nassau Harbor. They are usually found in adult non-breeding or first-winter plumage so these plumages are emphasized. However, usually by February or March, the white unstreaked head of breeding plumage will show in many of the adults. Ring-billed Gull takes three years to develop adult plumage while the other large gulls take four years. Two other species are not described: Bonaparte's Gull and Black-headed Gull are both rare winter visitors to the region.

Ring-billed Gull   *Larus delawarensis*

Adult non-breeding: Grand Bahama – January

First-winter: New Providence – November

Length: 18 ins (46 cm); wingspan: 48 ins (123 cm). Uncommon to fairly common winter resident and transient in northern and central Bahamas. Much less common further south. Rare to uncommon in TCI. Larger than Laughing Gull and more common than the other three wintering species. Non-breeding adult has lightly streaked white head and neck, pale gray back and wings and white underparts. Bill is yellow with black ring near tip, tail white and legs and feet dull yellow. First-winter Ring billed Gull has white head and nape with some streaks and flecks; white underparts with light brown flecking and spotting. Back is pale gray and wing coverts brown and white. Bill is pink with black tip. White rump and mottled brown tail with dark band at tip. Legs and feet pink. In second-winter, Ring-billed Gull looks similar to adult.

First-winter: April

Herring Gull

Larus argentatus

Adult non-breeding: New Providence – December

First-winter: New Providence – December

Juvenile: Grand Bahama – early November

Non-breeding adult sitting with first-winter and second-winter standing: New Providence – January

Length: 25 ins (64 cm); wingspan: 58 ins (147 cm). Uncommon winter resident and transient in northern Bahamas. Rare to uncommon further south and in TCI. Noticeably larger than Ring-billed Gull. Non-breeding adult has streaked to lightly streaked white head and neck, pale gray back and wings and white underparts. Bill is yellow with red spot near tip. Rump and tail white and legs and feet pink. Well known for some variation in immature plumages, especially first year. General characteristics of first-winter Herring Gull are all brown plumage with mottled back and wings. Bill is black with a variable amount of pink at base; some bills mostly pink with black tip. Rump light brown and tail dark brown. Legs and feet pink. Juveniles sometimes appear in fall and are similar to first-winter but have all dark bills and darker brown heads and bodies. The Herring Gull does not acquire pale gray back feathers usually until its second winter. Subspecies in region is *L. a. smithsonianus* often referred to as American Herring Gull.

Lesser Black-backed Gull

Larus fuscus

Adult non-breeding: Eleuthera – March

Possible third-winter (with Laughing Gulls): New Providence – December

Second-winter: New Providence – January

First-winter: Eleuthera – March

Length: 21 ins (53 cm); wingspan: 54 ins (137 cm). Rare to uncommon winter resident and transient in northern Bahamas. Locally, sometimes fairly common. Not reported from other Bahamian islands or TCI. Originally a European gull, now found regularly in North America. Slightly smaller than Herring Gull. Non-breeding adult has streaked white head and neck (streaking heaviest around eye), dark gray back and wings (darker than Laughing Gull) and white underparts. Bill is yellow with red spot near tip, rump and tail white, legs and feet yellow. First-winter Lesser Black-backed Gull very similar to first-winter Herring Gull but bill is all black, head and underparts paler, back and wings darker and slightly more contrast between rump and tail. Also, overall appearance of first-winter Lesser Black-backed is slightly darker and grayer than brownish first-winter Herring. Lesser Black-backed Gull does not acquire dark gray back feathers until second winter. Subspecies in region is *L. f. graellsii*.

Great Black-backed Gull

Larus marinus

Adult: February

Second-winter: New Providence – December

Both first-winter: New Providence – December

Length: 30 ins (76 cm); wingspan: 65 ins (165 cm). Rare to uncommon winter resident and transient on Grand Bahama, Abaco and New Providence. Rare in the Exumas and San Salvador; not reported from other islands or TCI. Big and bulky gull, larger than Herring Gull. Non-breeding adult has faintly streaked white head, black back and wings and white underparts. Large and heavy bill is yellow with red spot near tip. Rump and tail white and legs and feet pink. First-winter Great Black-backed Gull has mostly white head, mottled back, checkered black and white wings and white underparts with some streaks and flecks. Bill is black, rump and tail white with dark band at tip and legs and feet pink. Great Black-backed Gull does not acquire black back feathers until second winter.

Terns

Terns are a subfamily (*Sterninae*) of the family *Laridae*. They are small to medium-sized web-footed birds that superficially resemble gulls but have more slender bills and bodies, narrower pointed wings and shorter legs. Terns forage while flying and catch their prey by plunge-diving or picking from the water's surface. They rarely swim and do not scavenge like gulls. They breed in colonies and many defend nest site with persistent alarm calls and dive-bombing. Eight species of terns breed in the region in scattered colonies and are described below. They also occur, in fewer numbers, as transients in spring and fall but these would not be distinguishable from the breeding terns. Royal Tern and Sandwich Tern are also winter residents. Breeders arrive from mid-April to early May and, usually, depart the breeding site by the end of August. A few may linger in the area into September. Adult breeding and juvenal plumages are described because they are the most likely plumage to be encountered, although the period during which juveniles may be seen is brief and is usually limited to breeding areas. Identification of juveniles is made easier because they usually travel with the adults and leave the region together. Adult non-breeding plumage is also briefly described because it is occasionally encountered in fall. It takes several years or more for terns to reach adulthood but terns born in the region are not usually seen during these years as they remain closer to their wintering grounds and do not return to the breeding areas until they are sexually mature. In any case, the plumage of immature terns is generally similar to that of non-breeding adults. Nesting terns are particularly vulnerable to human disturbance and predation from cats, dogs and Laughing Gulls, so there is always a vital and legitimate concern for their protection.

Sandwich and Roseate Tern colony: Exumas – June

Gull-billed Tern   *Sterna nilotica*

Adult breeding: Great Exuma – June   Non-breeding: winter

Status and range: Locally fairly common summer resident in central and southern Bahamas and in TCI. Rare to uncommon summer visitor in northern Bahamas.

Description: Length: 14 ins (35 cm); wingspan: 34 ins (86 cm). Breeding adult has black cap and nape, thick black bill (more gull-like) and relatively long black legs. Pale gray upperparts, including rump and tail and white underparts. Tail is short and moderately forked. In flight, primary tips medium gray, when seen from above but appear darker from below. Non-breeding adult has white head with small dusky patch behind eye but bill remains black. Juvenile similar to non-breeding adult but has brown tinge to crown and back.

Voice: A harsh *key-wick*. Not as noisy as other terns.

Habits: Nests in small colonies along coast. Does not plunge-dive but makes graceful downward swoops to snatch prey from water or land. Only tern in region that regularly feeds for insects over fields and other open areas. Also takes small lizards off higher branches of coppice areas.

Similar species: Combination of thick black bill, pale appearance to body and wings and feeding behavior distinguish Gull-billed Tern from all other terns in the region.

Comments: Not a prolific species and most likely overlooked. It is estimated that only 100–150 pairs breed in the region but that number could be higher.

Royal Tern   *Sterna maxima*

Non-breeding adults: Grand Bahama – February

Breeding caps: Cay Sal Bank – May

Juvenile: August

Status and range:: Locally uncommon summer resident in The Bahamas and in TCI. In northern Bahamas, locally uncommon to fairly common winter resident. More common in winter in northern Bahamas than in southern parts of region as population increases with arrival of winter residents and transients from North America.

Description: Length: 20 ins (51 cm); wingspan: 41 ins (104 cm). Large crested tern with long orange bill and black legs. Plumage most often seen is non-breeding which has mostly white head with black shaggy crest at rear of crown, light gray upperparts, white underparts and relatively short white tail with moderate fork. Breeding adult (April – June) has full black cap and reddish-orange bill. Head molts back to mostly white before breeding season ends. In flight, outer primaries are dark when seen from above but paler from below. Juvenile has head much like non-breeding adult but has pale orange-yellow bill and dark or light legs. Also dark gray primaries and gray bars on secondaries. Juvenal plumage may be kept well into fall – even November.

Voice: Loud and hoarse *kre-errk*, mostly given in flight.

Habits: Breeds in small colonies on uninhabited offshore cays. Feeds by plunge-diving usually within sight of land but occasionally well offshore. Mostly coastal, it prefers pilings, docks and buoys for resting. Tern most likely to be seen in winter.

Comments: Not a large population of Royal Terns breed in the region; estimates are between 100–150 pairs but that number could be higher.

Similar species: Royal Tern is largest and most regularly seen tern in the region and only tern with orange bill. **Caspian Tern** (*Sterna caspia*) length: 21 ins (53 cm); wingspan: 50 ins (127 cm) is a very rare non-breeding visitor to northern Bahamas, Great Inagua and TCI. Unreported from other islands. Although significantly rare, it is mentioned here because of its close resemblance to Royal Tern. Caspian Tern is larger and bulkier than Royal Tern with thicker darker red bill not thinner orange bill of Royal. Cap of non-breeding Caspian Tern dusky and streaked throughout, without white forehead and crown of Royal. Caspian also has less of a crest. In flight, Caspian shows dark primaries on underside of wing, whereas Royal shows darker primaries on upperwing.

Non-breeding Caspian Tern: January

Non-breeding Royal Tern: Grand Bahama
– February

Sandwich Tern   *Sterna sandvicensis*

Breeding adults: Great Exuma – June

Non-breeding (with Laughing Gull): September

Status and range: Locally uncommon to fairly common summer resident through-out The Bahamas and TCI. Rare to uncommon winter resident in southern Bahamas and TCI.

Description: Length: 15 ins (38 cm); wingspan: 34 ins (86 cm). Medium-sized crested tern. Adult has long narrow black bill with yellow tip and black legs. Pale gray upper-parts and white underparts. White tail moderately forked and tail feathers do not extend past tip of folded wing. Breeding adult has full black cap early in breeding sea-son (April and May) but cap starts to molt to white soon afterwards. By the time birds leave breeding area, they have white heads with just rear portion and crest remaining black. Non-breeding plumage held for most of year. In flight, dark outer primaries when seen from above but paler from below. Juvenile has shorter bill than adult with-out yellow tip; crown is dusky and there are dark markings to back and wings.

Voice: A sharp and rasping two-note *skree-ick* similar to Roseate and Royal Terns.

Habits: Breeds on uninhabited offshore cays often in company with other tern species such as Royal or Roseate Terns. Forages over shallow inshore water as well as over deeper open water. Feeds by hovering and then plunge-diving for small fish. Regularly joins feeding flocks of mixed species.

Similar species: Breeding **Roseate Tern** is similar to Sandwich Tern but does not have a crest, has different bill and leg color combination and longer outer tail feath-ers. Both species can be difficult to identify at a distance, especially in flight.

Comments: Breeding population of Sandwich Tern in the West Indies estimated to be 2,000 to 3,000 pairs with an estimate of 300 pairs nesting in the region. **Conservation:** Nesting birds are vulnerable to human disturbance and eggs and chicks are susceptible to various predators – from crabs to Laughing Gulls.

Roseate Tern   *Sterna dougallii*

Breeding adults: Great Exuma – June

Status and range: Locally rare to uncommon summer resident throughout the region.

Description: Length: 15 ins (38 cm); wingspan: 29 ins (74 cm). Breeding adult has black cap and nape, long and slender bill and red legs. Bill is black most of year but, during breeding season, its color ranges from black with orange-red base to mostly orange-red with black tip. Most colorful when adults start feeding chicks. Upperparts pale gray and underparts white. Tail white and deeply forked with long outer tail feathers that extend well beyond tip of folded wing. In flight, outer three primaries dark when seen from above but almost white from below. Adult gradually develops white forehead and dark bill as it molts to non-breeding plumage after leaving breeding site. Some birds also lose long tail feathers at this time. Juvenile has dark to dusky head, black bill, black legs and scaly dark marks on back and short tail.

Voice: A sharp grating *chi-vick* given mostly in flight. Similar to Sandwich and Royal Terns.

Habits: Nests on ground or rock ledges in the open on uninhabited offshore cays, often in company of Sandwich or Royal Terns. Feeds over shallow inshore water or deeper open water. A forceful plunge-diver, it appears to fly into the water, sometimes submerging itself completely. Regularly joins feeding flocks of mixed species. May change breeding site from year to year. When adults and juveniles leave breeding areas, it is not known whether they leave the region altogether or move well offshore to feed and then leave, or both.

Similar species: See **Sandwich Tern** and **Common Tern**.

Comments: Roseate Tern gets name because, at beginning of breeding season, breast and belly sometimes have faint rose blush, visible only in good light. **Conservation:** Breeding population in the West Indies is considered to be threatened and estimated at 4,000 to 6,000 pairs, a reduction of over 40 per cent from past numbers. In the region, it is estimated that there are between 800 and 900 breeding pairs. Roseate Tern colonies are very sensitive to human disturbance and excessive predation from Laughing Gulls and/or introduced pests such as rats. Traditional breeding sites may be abandoned sometimes in the middle of the season.

Least Tern

Sterna antillarum

San Salvador – June

Adult breeding: April

First-winter: August

Status and range: Locally fairly common to common summer resident throughout the region.

Description: Length: 9 ins (23 cm); wingspan: 20 ins (51 cm). Smallest tern in the region. Breeding adult has black cap, black nape and black lores with white forehead. Thin yellow bill has small black tip and legs are yellow-orange. Pale gray upperparts, including rump and tail, and white underparts. Tail short and moderately forked. In flight, two black outer primaries when seen from above, but pale gray from below. In non-breeding adult, bill is black and white forehead extends into crown. Juvenile has dusky crown, blackish bill, dark shoulder bar (or carpal bar) and dull markings on back and wings.

Voice: Call note a *kip kip*. Alarm call is a harsh *zweep*. Common call around colonies a shrill *chitit-whitit chitit-whitit*.

Habits: Nests in colonies on sandy beaches, flat rocky shores or on rocky islands of inland salt ponds. Aggressive and noisy when defending nest. Flies with rapid wingbeats (more so than other terns) and usually hovers before plunge-diving. Forages mainly over shallow inshore coastal waters and inland ponds, sometimes over deeper ocean water.

Comments: Conservation: Preference for open coastal breeding sites, especially beaches, leads to conflict with recreational development and human disturbance. An estimated population of between 600 and 650 pairs breed in the region but that number could be higher.

Bridled Tern   *Sterna anaethetus*

Adult breeding: Great Exuma – June

Juvenile (left) and adult at sea: late   San Salvador – June
August

Status and range: Locally fairly common to common summer resident throughout the region.

Description: Length: 15 ins (38 cm); wingspan: 30 ins (76 cm). Breeding adult has black crown, nape and eyeline, black bill and black legs. White forehead extends as line above and behind eye. Upperparts dark gray with brown tinge and underparts white. Pale collar difficult to see. Deeply forked tail is dark gray with white on several outer tail feathers. Non-breeding adult similar but has paler crown and nape. In flight, underwings white with dark gray flight feathers but base of primaries also white. Juvenile similar to adult but has smudgy-to-white head and shorter tail; also thin white irregular lines on back and wings.

Voice: Relatively quiet. Mellow *kahrr* sound on breeding grounds. Alarm call a *wrep wrep* resembling a puppy's bark.

Habits: Strictly pelagic except during breeding season. Nests under ledges or crevices in loose colonies on rocky uninhabited offshore cays, often on outer fringes of Sooty Tern and Brown Noddy colonies. Forages over deep water well offshore and feeds by picking from water's surface; shallow plunge-dives are infrequent. Concentrates where predatory fish chase smaller fish to surface. Regularly joins feeding flocks of mixed species. Occasionally seen at sea standing on floating debris.

Comments: Estimates of Bridled Tern pairs total 4,000–6,000 in the West Indies and 2,000–2,500 in the region. Could be even more but some productive areas have not been surveyed recently.

Similar species: Sooty Tern looks quite similar but, when seen standing at close range, the two species can be distinguished fairly easily by viewing extent and shape of white over eye and back color. However, from further away, white over eye is difficult to see and bright sunlight can lighten or darken back color, especially on birds in flight. At a distance, Sooty Tern uniformly black from crown to tail, whereas Bridled Tern shows more contrast between black crown, paler collar and dark gray back. When tail is spread, Sooty shows narrow white outer tail feathers and Bridled shows more extensive white. In flight, base of primaries on underwing is darker on Sooty, lighter on Bridled.

Underwing of Sooty Tern (left) and Bridled Tern (right)

Sooty Tern   *Sterna fuscata*

Adult breeding: Great Exuma – June

Status and range: Locally common summer resident throughout the region.

Description: Length: 16 ins (41 cm); wingspan: 32 ins (81 cm). Breeding adult has black crown, nape and thin line in front of eye. Also black bill and legs. White forehead patch extends just over eye. Uniform black upperparts and white underparts. Deeply forked tail black with white on just outermost tail feathers appearing as mostly black tail with thin white edges. Non-breeding adult similar but some birds may have paler crown and nape. In flight, underwings white with dark gray flight feathers. Distinctive juvenile is all dark gray with lightly-spotted upperparts, white vent and undertail coverts.

Voice: Noisy. Call described as a raspy *wide-a-wake*. Also a single nasal *wack*.

Habits: Strictly pelagic except during breeding season. Forms large breeding colonies on uninhabited offshore cays, often with Brown Noddies and Bridled Terns. Nests in open or under vegetation. Feeds over deep open water by picking and occasionally makes shallow plunge-dives. Concentrates where predatory fish chase smaller fish to water's surface. Regularly joins feeding flocks of other mixed species. Sometimes nocturnal. Does not sit on water and rarely stands on floating debris.

Similar species: See **Bridled Tern**.

Comments: Champion flyers – adults stay aloft until they return each year to breeding areas. Thought to sleep while flying. Juvenal Sooty Terns, after leaving breeding sites, cross Atlantic Ocean to west coast of Africa and remain there as immatures for several years before returning to breed for first time. Incredibly, they are thought to stay on the wing the entire time. By far the most numerous breeding tern in the West Indies (estimates at 250,000 pairs) and in the region (estimates at 8,000 pairs).

Brown Noddy

Anous stolidus

Adult breeding: Grand Turk – June   New Providence– June

Status and range: Locally fairly common to common summer resident throughout the region.

Description: Length: 15 ins (39 cm); wingspan: 32 ins (81 cm). Slick and subtly good looking tern. Adult is all dark brown with white forehead that blends to pale gray crown and part of nape. White crescent below eye and bill is long and black. Legs also black. Long wedge-shaped tail only visible when spread; when folded, looks rounded rather than pointed like other terns. Appears black against bright sea or sky. Juvenile similar to adult but has browner head.

Voice: A low-pitched growl around breeding areas.

Habits: Strictly pelagic except during breeding season. Nests on ground in open or in low bushes on uninhabited offshore cays. Often seen in company with Sooty and Bridled Terns. Forages over deep water and concentrates where predatory fish chase smaller fish to surface. Feeds by flying low and picking food from surface and occasionally makes shallow plunge-dives. Regularly joins feeding flocks of mixed species. Will rest on water unlike Sooty and Bridled Terns.

Comments: After Sooty Tern, Brown Noddy is the most numerous breeder in the region. An estimated 4,500 pairs nest in The Bahamas and TCI and an estimated 15,000 pairs breed in the West Indies.

Transient Terns

In addition to the breeding terns, there are three tern species that occur in the region as transients or visitors and are described below. Common Tern and Black Tern pass through the region in spring and fall. The bulk of the two populations probably move well offshore but some birds come to the coast or further inland to feed or roost. Common Tern is seen significantly more often than Black Tern. Forster's Tern is a rare fall and winter visitor to the northern Bahamas.

Common Tern   *Sterna hirundo*

Adult breeding: early June

Transition to non-breeding: September

Non-breeding: Mayaguana – early October

Length: 15 ins (38 cm); wingspan: 30 ins (76 cm). Rare to uncommon spring and fall transient throughout the region. Pobably more common than records indicate. Breeding adult, seen during spring migration, has black crown and nape, orange-red bill with black tip and orange-red legs. Medium gray upperparts, grayish under-parts and white rump and tail which contrast with gray back. These tones of gray will look darker under an overcast sky and lighter in sunlight. Tail feathers do not reach tip of folded wing. In flight, primaries have thin dark tips when seen from above but are darker from below. Roseate Tern is sometimes mistaken for Common Tern in spring and summer when Roseate's bill is partially, to mostly, orange-red with black tip but largest amount of bill color occurs in mid-summer when Common Tern is not usually in the region. Also Roseate's plumage is paler, has little contrast between back and rump and has longer tail streamers. For adult non-breeding Common Tern, seen during fall migration, forehead becomes white, bill and legs turn black, and primaries darker from above and below. Also develop dark shoulder bar (or carpal bar) on leading edge of wing. First-year immature is similar to non-breeding adult.

Black Tern   *Chlidonias niger*

Breeding

Transition

Non-breeding

Non-breeding: Grand Bahama –
September

Length: 9.75 ins (25 cm); wingspan: 24 ins (61 cm). Rare spring and fall transient throughout the region and may be overlooked. Most fall records occur between July 15 and September 15. Recorded sparingly which may be due to time of year and limited coverage. If inland, usually seen over fresh and brackish water ponds and wetlands. Low, buoyant and erratic flight with downward swoops to pick food off water's surface. Small tern with short dark bill, mostly dark legs and short squared tail. In spring, adult has unmistakable black head, breast and belly with white vent and white undertail coverts. Black and white areas contrast with gray back, wings and tail. In late summer and early fall, non-breeding adult has rear of crown and part of cheek smudgy black, gray upperparts and mostly white underparts. In flight, good field mark is vertical dark bar on sides of breast. Some birds may have patchy black and white plumage as they molt from breeding to non-breeding plumage. Subspecies in region is *C. n. surinamensis*.

Forster's Tern   *Sterna forsteri*

Non-breeding: February   Non-breeding: August

Length: 14.5 ins (37 cm); wingspan: 31 ins (79 cm). Rare fall and winter visitor to Grand Bahama and Abaco with few records elsewhere in The Bahamas. Not reported from TCI. Plumage seen in region is non-breeding which is similar for adult and first-winter immature. Pale gray upperparts and white underparts. Primaries dusky-to-pale gray and bill dark and legs dull orange. Most distinctive field mark is white head with black oval-shaped mask around eye. Rear part of mask not connected to white or dusky nape. In fall, non-breeding Common Tern looks similar to Forster's Tern but black around eye is connected to black nape and not isolated as in Forster's. Common Tern also has darker primaries and a dark shoulder or carpal bar.

Skimmers

Skimmers are a subfamily (*Rynchopinae*) of the family *Laridae*. Found worldwide with just three species – Indian Skimmer, African Skimmer and Black Skimmer from the Americas. Skimmers are all about their bills and feeding behavior. Bill is thick and tapered towards tip with upper mandible considerably shorter than lower mandible. Feed by flying low over water with lower mandible skimming or ploughing just below surface and when they contact fish, upper mandible slams shut.

Black Skimmer   *Rynchops niger*

Non-breeding (with Royal Tern and Laughing Gull): Grand Bahama – December

Length: 18 ins (46 cm); wingspan: 44 ins (112 cm). Winter visitor; rare in northern Bahamas and much rarer and irregular on Great Inagua and in TCI. Distinct bill is orange-red at base and black towards tip. Slim body (black above and white below), long black and white wings and short orange-red legs. Non-breeding adult has white collar; breeding adult all black. Juvenile has duller bill color, brown mottling on crown and nape and dark brown upperparts and wing with scaly appearance. Often found with resting terns and/or gulls. Coastal species around harbors, bays and inlets.

Land Birds

◆ NEW WORLD QUAIL   Family: *Odontophoridae*

Small, New World family, quails are generally small ground-dwelling birds with short bills and necks. Wings short and rounded. Legs short but sturdy and used for running and scratching ground for food. There are no native quail in the region or in the West Indies.

Northern Bobwhite   *Colinus virginianus*

Male: New Providence – May   Female: New Providence – May

Status and range: Introduced species. Locally uncommon permanent resident on Abaco, Andros and New Providence. Not found on other islands or TCI.

Description: Length: 9.75 ins (25 cm). Small and round-bodied, reddish-brown bird with dark barring on pale breast and belly. Short rounded wings and short gray tail. Adult has distinctive facial pattern with dark crown and stripe through eye which contrasts with prominent supercilium and throat. Throat white on male, buff on female. Male sometimes raises crest.

Voice: Call note is a soft whistled *hoy*. Song a whistled *bob-WHITE*. Heard more often than seen.

Habits: Prefers brushy fields and open woodlands. Feeds on ground for seeds, berries, plant buds and insects. Usually found in pairs or in groups of several birds, called coveys. Prefers to run rather than fly. When flushed, covey will burst out in all directions with rapid wingbeats.

Comments: Native to eastern North America where historically they have been valued by hunters. Probably introduced to The Bahamas in colonial times as game bird. In season, it is legal to hunt Northern Bobwhite in northern Bahamas.

◆ NEW WORLD VULTURES   Family: *Cathartidae*

Very small family of birds (seven species) found only in the New World. Large and dark with long broad wings that are built for soaring. Head and nape are feather-less, bill long and sharply hooked at tip. They feed on carrion and have sharp vision to detect carcasses on the ground, often cueing in on other soaring vultures. Recent research indicates that New World Vultures are not related either to vultures in the Old World or other birds of prey but rather to storks. However, because they super-ficially appear like birds of prey i.e. in their soaring ability and hooked bills, they are described in this section with hawks and falcons rather than with the water birds.

Turkey Vulture   *Cathartes aura*

Abaco – February   North Andros – May

Status and range: Common permanent resident on Grand Bahama, Abaco and Andros. Accidental to very rare visitors elsewhere in The Bahamas. Not found in TCI. Status of transients or visitors not known because they are not distinguishable from residents.

Description: Length: 26 ins (66 cm); wingspan: 67 ins (170 cm). Large all-black bird, most often seen soaring. On underside of wing, paler flight feathers sometimes look silvery in the right light. Tail is long and slightly rounded. Head and nape are hairless with red skin in adult, black skin in juvenile. Bill white in adult, dark in juvenile.

Habits: Feeds on carrion. Soars overhead searching for potential food using its eyesight and sense of smell (unique for a bird). Frequently scavenges at garbage dumps and road kills. When soaring, wings are held in shallow 'V' and, at times, bird rocks from side to side. Cumbersome flapping on take off from perch or ground. Often feeds and roosts in groups. Spreads wings to the sun presumably to warm body, dry off any moisture, or realign feathers.

Comments: There are a few 'relatively recent' records of **Black Vulture** (*Coragyps atratus*) from northern Bahamas but it is still considered very rare.

HAWKS   **Family:** *Accipitridae*

This family and the next, falcons, are often referred to as birds of prey or raptors. Hawks form a large world-wide family noted for their powerful sharply-hooked bills, strong legs and sharp talons. They have exceptional eyesight and hearing and hunt by soaring or from a perch. Osprey and Red-tailed Hawk each belong to a separate subfamily: *Pandioninae* for Osprey and *Accipitrinae* for Red-tailed. There is some debate among taxonomists as to whether or not Osprey should be classified as a family by itself. Osprey and Red-tailed Hawk are the two resident hawks in the region and are described below. Three other raptors are not described. Swallow-tailed Kite is rare spring transient in northern Bahamas, Sharp-shinned Hawk is very rare transient through the region and Northern Harrier is rare transient and winter visitor throughout the region.

Osprey   *Pandion haliaetus*

Resident subspecies: Providenciales – June

Resident subspecies: Crooked Island – May

North American subspecies: February

Status and range: Resident subspecies is common permanent resident in central and southern Bahamas. Slowly extending range northwards. Fairly common permanent resident in TCI. North American birds are uncommon to fairly common winter residents and transients in northern Bahamas, although some have been recorded in central and southern Bahamas. Status in that area not known.

Description: Length: 23 ins (58 cm); wingspan: 63 ins (160 cm). Large fish hawk. Dark brown above and white below. Underwing coverts white with dark patch at bend of wing. Flight feathers barred; tail has medium barring. Resident birds have white head with thin dark line behind eye making head look whiter. Winter residents and transients from North America have slightly streaked cap and thick dark line through eye making head look darker. When soaring, wings are slightly bent along leading edge, rather than straight like vultures or red-tails which gives Osprey distinctive profile.

Voice: A series of short high-pitched whistles.

Habits: Mainly fish-eating. Frequently soars over inland lakes, estuaries or along coastlines. Usually hovers just before diving. Catches fish by plunging head and feet first into water or, if fish is close to surface, simply snatches it with feet and talons. Barbs on soles of feet help hold wriggling fish. Builds large nest of sticks, often on offshore cays, which it usually uses year after year.

Comments: Resident Osprey in the region is West Indian subspecies *P. h. ridgwayi*.

Red-tailed Hawk *Buteo jamaicensis*

Adult: May   Adult (captive and permanently injured): Grand Bahama – February

Status and range: Uncommon to fairly common permanent resident on Grand Bahama, Abaco and Andros. Unrecorded or accidental visitor elsewhere in The Bahamas and TCI.

Description: Length: 19 ins (48 cm); wingspan: 49 ins (124 cm). Large hawk with broad rounded wings and short wide tail which is rufous in adult. Adult dark brown above and white below sometimes with band of dark streaks across belly. Seen in flight from below, flight feathers lightly barred with dark tips and dark bar along leading edge of inner wing. Juvenile similar to adult but tail is brown with thin black bands.

Voice: A harsh, thin, downward scream *keeeeeerrr*.

Habits: Often seen soaring over open fields and pinewoods or perched at edges of these habitats. Occasionally stands on telephone pole. At times, soars with Turkey Vultures. Feeds on rodents, reptiles and birds.

Comments: Red-tailed Hawk is widespread in North America and the Greater Antilles. In The Bahamas it belongs to the same subspecies as is found in South Florida *B. j. umbrinus*.

◆ FALCONS   Family: *Falconida*

Medium-sized world-wide family and noted for their long pointed wings and long tails. They hunt by fast pursuit or by diving. American Kestrel is described below followed by briefer descriptions of Merlin and Peregrine Falcon. These falcons belong to the subfamily *Falconinae*.

American Kestrel   *Falco sparverius*

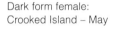

Light form female: San Salvador – January

Dark form female: Crooked Island – May

North American male: February

Status and range: Resident subspecies with two color forms: one with light (white) underparts and one with dark (rufous) underparts. Light form has significantly larger range and is much more common than dark form. Light form is common permanent resident in central and southern Bahamas and in TCI. Less common in northern Bahamas. Dark form is uncommon permanent resident on San Salvador, Rum Cay and Crooked and Acklins Islands but status unclear on other southern islands. Migrant kestrels from North America are uncommon winter residents and transients in northern Bahamas and rare or unrecorded elsewhere in the region.

Description: Length: 10 ins (25 cm); wingspan: 22 ins (56 cm). Small well-marked falcon. Both sexes have rufous back and tail and white face with two black vertical lines, one behind and another below eye. Male has blue-gray wings and unbarred tail with black band near tip. Female has rufous wing coverts and barred tail. Resident light form has white underparts with little streaking on breast and variable streaking or spots on flanks. Dark form has rufous chest, flanks and most of belly, giving female mostly rufous overall appearance. Juvenile similar to each respective adult. Male kestrel from North America has buffy underparts with bold spots, while underparts of female have large brown streaks.

Voice: Common call is a rapid or slower series of sharp high-pitched notes *klee-klee-klee*, etc. Noisy during breeding season.

Habits: Preys primarily on large insects and lizards and, to lesser extent, on small birds and rodents, by diving from exposed perch. Occasionally North American birds may hover over potential prey and then dive. At times hunts by pursuit. Fond of perching on telephone poles and lines. Nests in cavities or tops of dead palms.

Similar species: Merlin (present only in winter) is stockier and darker overall with heavy streaking on underparts. Hunts by pursuit, rather than hovering or pouncing from perch. Almost never found on telephone poles and lines.

Comments: Resident subspecies of American Kestrel in The Bahamas and TCI is recognized as same as Cuban subspecies *F. s. sparverioides*. However, plumage color and patterns in populations of American Kestrels in the West Indies are variable and some authorities believe that some resident kestrels in the region show a mix of plumage characteristics from both Cuban subspecies and Hispaniolan subspecies *F. s. dominicensis*.

The next two falcon species are both uncommon winter residents and transients. They occur throughout the region and are usually solitary in nature.

Merlin   *Falco columbarius*

Immature or female: Grand
Bahama – February

In flight from below

Length: 10 ins (25 cm); wingspan: 24 ins (61 cm). Small dark falcon with dark streaks on pale underparts and dark tail with thin light bars. Male has blue-gray upperparts, while female and juvenile have dark brown upperparts. Facial markings are inconspicuous. Hunts from all types of habitats and pursues small birds with fast and direct flight. Seldom soars and does not hover like some migrant American Kestrels. Sightings of females and juveniles seem more frequent than males.

Peregrine Falcon

Falco peregrinus

Adult with prey: March

Juvenile from below

Length: 18 ins (46 cm); wingspan: 41 ins (104 cm). Large stocky falcon, spectacular flier. Adult has black crown and facial patch that extends through and below eye and contrasts with white throat and breast; gives bird a hooded appearance. Back and wings blue-gray and underparts white with fine bars on belly, vent and undertail coverts. In flight, underwing has fine dark barring throughout. Juvenile similar to adult but is dark brown above and heavily streaked below. Some juveniles have paler crown and less of a hooded appearance. Peregrine Falcon hunts birds by pursuit or by long fast dives called a stoop. Will also soar while looking for prey. Frequently found near or along coastline. Peregrine, including streaked juvenile, is larger than Merlin with longer and wider wings, more rounded tail tip and more conspicuous facial pattern.

◆ PIGEONS AND DOVES   Family: *Columbidae*

A very large and familiar world-wide family (over 300 species) of fruit and seed-eating birds. Most feed on ground but a few forage in trees. They have small rounded heads with short bills and compact bodies with short wings and legs. When walking on ground, head moves back and forth. Songs contain low cooing notes. They drink water by sucking, unlike most other birds who must scoop up water and throw head back to swallow. Several species are hunted as game birds. Nine species from this family breed in the region and are described below. Three of the species are introductions.

Rock Pigeon   *Columba livia*

Natural plumage: New Providence – May

Mixed plumages: Grand Bahama – December

Status and range: Introduced species. Fairly common permanent resident in populated areas of Grand Bahama, Abaco, New Providence and Eleuthera. Uncommon on other islands as far south as Crooked Island. Some populations may be free-flying but are domestic birds. Not found in TCI.

Description: Length: 12.5 ins (32 cm). This is the common street pigeon of towns and settlements and plumage varies. Natural plumage (most like wild birds) is gray with dark head and neck, sides of neck iridescent green-purple and two black stripes on upperwing. Squared gray tail with black band on tip. In flight, shows white rump and white underwings. Rock Pigeons are often raised in captivity and selectively bred to develop a wide variety of colors. Color variations are common including mostly dark, white and brown birds with variety of intermediate plumages.

Voice: Typical call a low gurgle ending in a soft *cooo*.

Habits: Forages on ground around settlements looking for seeds and fruit. In some towns, very tame and approaches closely for hand-outs. When flushed, takes off with loud wing-claps.

Similar species: An entirely dark Rock Pigeon may resemble **White-crowned Pigeon** but White-crowned inhabits more natural areas such as tall trees and coppice and is much wilder and more skittish. It also has white crown and is usually not found on ground.

Comments: Native to Europe, Asia and North Africa, Rock Pigeons have been widely introduced but mainly as domesticated birds (many of which became feral) and not as wild birds. They were introduced as domestic birds into North America, probably in colonial times, and have spread throughout the region. Formerly called Rock Dove.

White-crowned Pigeon

Patagioenas leucocephala

Grand Bahama – February

Grand Bahama – October

Status and range: Fairly common to common throughout The Bahamas. Uncommon in TCI. Studies have shown that status includes permanent residents, summer residents, winter residents and transients. Inter-island movements are common and other movements are influenced by food supply and hunting pressure.

Description: Length: 13.5 ins (34 cm). Large but slender entirely dark gray pigeon with white forehead and crown and green iridescent lines along sides of neck. Bill is red with pale tip. Female similar to male but crown duller. Juvenile is brown-gray with gray crown and lacks neck iridescence. In flight, which is fast and direct, white crown of adults is difficult to see.

Voice: Main song a deep *coo*, followed by a repeated *coo-ca-coo* with last note dropping in pitch. Song has slightly hoarse quality. Also a *whoo-ca-coo* sound.

Habits: Favors trees, seldom found on ground. Primarily feeds on berries and fruit. Long breeding season lasting from April to September. Nests mainly on offshore cays in small to large colonies and commutes daily to main islands to feed. At certain times, berries of poisonwood tree are a critical food source for nesting success. Sits tight when approached, then flushes with loud wing-claps. Very skittish especially during hunting season. More often seen flying rather than perched.

Similar species: See **Rock Pigeon** and, for its call, **Caribbean Dove**.

Comments: This is the premier game bird of The Bahamas and there is a long-standing tradition of hunting White-crowned Pigeon. Hunting season starts in fall and ends in early spring. There is no hunting season in TCI. Primary range is from southern tip of Florida, The Bahamas and the Greater Antilles. **Conservation:** Should include the protection of both breeding and non-breeding habitats and proper enforcement of hunting regulations.

Eurasian Collared-Dove   *Streptopelia decaocto*

New Providence – December

Coffee brown plumage: Great Exuma – June

New Providence – May

Tattered bird: New Providence – October

Status and range: Introduced species. Permanent resident around towns and settlements. Common on Grand Bahama and New Providence, fairly common on Abaco and Bimini and uncommon to fairly common on Andros, Berry Islands, Eleuthera and Great Exuma. Not found in TCI.

Description: Length: 13 ins (33 cm). Adult is large dove that has incomplete black collar with white border. Pale gray plumage with slightly darker brown-gray back and contrasting dark primaries. (Some birds, found mainly on New Providence, have coffee-brown plumage rather than pale gray.) Long squared tail with brown-gray central tail feathers and broad white tips to outer tail feathers, base of tail dark. Seen from below, underside of folded tail mostly white with dark base, although base obscured by long gray undertail coverts. Juvenal plumage, held only for short time, is similar to adult but lacks black collar and is paler overall.

Voice: At times, may call incessantly, giving quick three-note *ka-KOO-koo* with emphasis on longer second note. Third note lower-pitched. Also a nasal growl-like *hreeegh*, often given in flight just before landing.

Habits: Prefers developed areas and farms and is not above scrounging through garbage or rubbish areas. Not found in extensive pinewoods or coppice. Almost always forages on ground. Perches in open often on power lines and poles. In courtship flight, climbs upwards then soars on steeply-raised wings, its tail spread, and returns to perch, usually giving growl-like call just before landing. When flushed or alarmed, takes off with loud wing-claps. Frequently feeds on seeds spilled from bird feeders.

Comments: Native to Asia, it has spread throughout Europe. Introduced in Nassau in 1974, it has expanded rapidly throughout northern Bahamas and Florida. Now spreading across North America. Spreading slowly to less-developed islands in central Bahamas but not yet reported from southern Bahamas. Reason for coffee-brown plumage of some collared-doves is not known. Furthermore, other collared-doves, mostly on New Providence, have tendency to get into some pretty dirty areas and soiled colors may stain feathers, mainly head and breast, making them look quite dark or filthy.

White-winged Dove

Zenaida asiatica

Cayman Islands – March

Cayman Islands – October

Status and range: Uncommon to fairly common permanent resident in central and southern Bahamas and in TCI. Rare visitor to or unrecorded in northern Bahamas. Found on small cays as well as on large islands. Dispersal patterns or movements of this species in the region are not well known.

Description: Length: 12 ins (30 cm). Stout light gray-brown dove with pale gray belly, vent and undertail coverts. Red eye surrounded by blue skin with small lateral black mark below eye. White patch or bar on upperwing conspicuous in flight and appears as white line along lower edge of folded wing. Squared tail with outer tail feathers tipped in white with black border. Seen from below, folded tail has broad white tip with dark base.

Voice: Common song a slightly hoarse *woo-koo woo woo* sometimes described as 'who cooks for you'. Also a series of *woo* notes and other variations of main song.

Habits: Usually a ground feeder. Found in dry scrubland, mangrove swamps, woodlands and gardens. Comes to feeders.

Similar species: Only dove in region with distinctive white wing patches on upperwing.

Zenaida Dove

Zenaida aurita

Caymans – March

Cat Island – May

Status and range: Permanent resident throughout the region. Rare to uncommon in northern Bahamas, fairly common to common in central and southern Bahamas and fairly common in TCI. Found on small cays as well as on large islands.

Description: Length: 11 ins (28 cm). Stocky brown dove with warmer or cinnamon tones on face and breast. Black line behind eye and black mark below eye. Dark spots on wing coverts and tertials. Adult has small iridescent violet patch on sides of neck. Secondary feathers on wings are tipped in white showing in flight as thin white trailing edge and on folded wing as small white patch. Tail is rounded with brown central tail feathers and outer tail feathers tipped in gray with thin black border. Juvenile similar to adult but paler and lacks iridescence on neck.

Voice: Song a mournful *whoo-oo hoo hoo hoo*. Last three notes are on an even pitch. Song is similar to Mourning Dove but slightly faster with less inflection on first two notes. Takes practice to distinguish.

Habits: Ground feeder that prefers undeveloped areas. Usually found in or near pinewoods in northern Bahamas and in coppice or thick scrub on other islands. Mostly found alone or in pairs. Shy and retiring and does not usually allow close approach. Often seen only in flight. Little or no wing whistle on take-off.

Similar species: Mourning Dove is slightly paler and more slender (less stocky) with longer pointed tail that flashes more extensive white when spread. Also lacks white tips to secondaries. Mourning Dove however prefers more developed areas and has habit of sitting on telephone wires.

Comments: Range outside the region restricted to the Greater and Lesser Antilles and Yucatan Penninsula of Mexico. Formerly Florida Keys but now only accidental visitor there and South Florida. Zenaida Dove in the region is Greater Antillean subspecies *Z. a. zenaida*.

Mourning Dove

Zenaida macroura

Grand Bahama – November   April

Status and range: Fairly common permanent resident throughout the region. Common and widespread in North America, migrants most likely occur as well but they are not distinguishable from resident birds.

Description: Length: 12 ins (30 cm). Slim dove with gray-brown upperparts and paler head and underparts. Black line behind eye and black mark below eye. Dark spots on wing coverts and tertials. Adult male has pink tones on breast and small patch of iridescent feathers on sides of neck. Adult female has smaller iridescent patch. Both have long pointed tail with brown central tail feathers and shorter graduated outer tail feathers tipped in white. When spread, tapered tail with white spots distinctive. Juvenile lacks iridescence on neck and is duller than adult with scaly appearance to back and wings.

Voice: Song a mournful *whoo-oo hoo hoo hoo*. Last three notes being on an even pitch. Very similar to Zenaida Dove but slightly slower and with more inflection on first two notes.

Habits: Feeds on ground and prefers developed areas, farmlands, roadsides and open country. Not found on smaller cays. Fast and straight flight. Wings make whistling sound on take-off; slightly less audible in flight.

Similar species: See **Zenaida Dove**.

Common Ground-Dove

Columbina passerina

Male: New Providence – May   Female (front) and male (behind): South Andros – May

Status and range: Common permanent resident throughout the region.

Description: Length: 6.5 ins (16.5 cm). Very small gray-brown dove with black spots and lines on wings. Feathers of crown, nape and breast have dark edges, creating scaly appearance. Short tail has dark outer tail feathers with tiny white tips. Adult male has small dark pink-red bill with black tip, blue-gray crown and nape and pink cast to head and breast. Adult female has darker bill and more uniform color around head and breast. Juvenile similar to female but with some back and wing feathers edged whitish. All plumages have rufous coloring in primaries and rufous on under-wing, most conspicuous in flight.

Voice: Long series of repeated notes *woop woop woop*.

Habits: Feeds on ground and when flushed flies to spot further along ground or flies to low perch. Usually in pairs or in small flocks. Walks slowly or quickly and moves head back and forth. Shuns deep coppice, preferring open areas, scrublands, roadsides and gardens. Comes to seed feeders.

Comments: One of the most common birds in the region and locally called 'Tobacco Dove'. Common Ground-Dove has two subspecies in the region. *C. p. bahamensis* is found only in The Bahamas, TCI and Bermuda (perhaps an introduction there) and *C. p. exigua* found only on Great Inagua in southern Bahamas and Mona Island between Hispaniola and Puerto Rico. Inaguan birds described as paler and smaller than other subspecies but that is difficult to distinguish in the field.

Caribbean Dove

Leptotila jamaicensis

Caymans – October

Status and range: Introduced species. Uncommon to fairly common permanent resident on New Providence. Not found on other islands or in TCI.

Description: Length: 12 ins (30 cm). Large, stocky, ground-dwelling dove with gray crown and white forehead, face and underparts. Nape and sides of neck are reddish-brown with some iridescence below nape. Plain gray-brown back and tail, outer tail feathers dark with white tips. Reddish-brown underwings visible in flight.

Voice: Song a high-pitched three note *coo ca cooo* with last note dropping in pitch. Voice is similar to White-crowned Pigeon but higher pitched and with greater drop in last note.

Habits: Forages on ground in thick coppice or secondary growth, often in same habitat as Key West Quail-Dove. Usually walks away when disturbed or flies a short distance and lands again. Can be difficult to find. Sings from medium-high perch.

Comments: Formerly called 'White-bellied Dove'. Range is limited to Jamaica and Cayman Islands in the West Indies and Yucatan Peninsula of Mexico. Jamaican birds were introduced onto New Providence presumably to stock island with birds after hurricanes in late 1920s.

Key West Quail-Dove   *Geotrygon chrysia*

Both Grand Bahama – late October

Status and range: Permanent resident in the region. Uncommon to fairly common in northern Bahamas but not found on Bimini or Berry Islands. Rare in central Bahamas and not found in southern Bahamas. Rare to uncommon on North Caicos and Pine Cay on Caicos Islands in TCI.

Description: Length: 12 ins (30 cm). Large and bulky ground-dwelling dove with small head and short tail. Rich red-brown back, wings and tail (with no white tips). Underparts pale gray. Crown and nape iridescent green with broad white facial stripe below eye. Both female and juvenile duller and browner but still show white facial stripe. Underwings are also red-brown so any Key West Quail-Dove in flight should be distinguishable by size and coloration.

Voice: Song a slow, drawn-out, mournful monotone rather like sound of someone blowing across mouth of a bottle.

Habits: Forages on ground among dead leaves in thick coppice, secondary growth and scrub. Usually seen alone on ground or flying low across an open area or road. Will scurry away when approached. Sings from medium-high perch. Difficult to see and may be more numerous in some areas than realised.

Comments: Range restricted to The Bahamas, TCI and Greater Antillean islands of Cuba, Hispaniola and Puerto Rico. Formerly found in Florida Keys but now only accidental both there and South Florida.

Grand Bahama

◆ PARROTS   Family: *Psittacidae*

Very large (over 300 species), well-known, colorful family of birds with distinctly wide and strongly decurved bills used for cracking nuts and seeds, grabbing fruit and climbing on trees. Use feet like hands when feeding. Most common in tropics. Many parrot species are endangered through habitat destruction and illegal pet trade.

Cuban Parrot   (e) *Amazona leucocephala bahamensis*

Abaco – April

Great Inagua – March

Status and range: Locally fairly common permanent resident on southern Abaco and Great Inagua. Not found on other islands or in TCI.

Description: Length: 12 ins (30 cm). Large and short-tailed green parrot with mostly white head, green nape and rose-colored (pink-red) throat. On Great Inagua, rose coloring extends farther up cheek than on Abaco birds. Blue primaries most conspicuous in flight. Blunt head and short rapid wingbeats identify birds in flight.

Voice: Noisy. Typical parrot squawks, shrieks and screeches. Loud and can be heard from long distances. Often calls while flying.

Habits: Eats fruit, nuts and seeds. On Abaco, usually found in pinewoods but will fly to coppice areas and settlements to search for additional food. On Great Inagua, it is found throughout the island and sometimes in Matthew Town. Abaco parrots nest in natural limestone cavities in the ground and Great Inagua parrots nest in tree cavities. Usually travel and feed in small groups, dispersing only during breeding season in late spring and early summer.

Comments: Cuban Parrot in The Bahamas is recognized as an endemic subspecies *A. l. bahamensis* and locally referred to as 'Bahama Parrot'. In addition to The Bahamas, this species is found only on Cuba and the Cayman Islands.

Conservation: Cuban Parrot is flagship species for conservation in The Bahamas and habitat on both islands is protected by national parks. Protected by Bahamian law and taking it for a pet is illegal. Approximately 1,000 to 1,500 parrots remain on Abaco and it is thought that there may be twice as many or more on Great Inagua. Population is relatively stable but these birds are still vulnerable, especially on Abaco. Increases in the number of feral cats and introduced raccoons pose a serious threat to these ground-nesting parrots.

◆ CUCKOOS AND ANIS

Family: *Cuculidae*

Medium-sized family of fairly large, slender, long-tailed birds found world-wide. Their tails make up about half the birds' total length. Eat insects, larvae and small reptiles. Some are tree-dwellers, while others often feed on the ground. All are proficient at clambering through thick brush. Each outer tail feather of cuckoos in the region is shorter than previous feather i.e. graduated lengths. This shows as distinctive pattern of white spots on folded tail when seen from underneath or when tail is spread. Cuckoos in the region are brown and white with strong bills. Anis are black and have high-ridged bills.

Mangrove Cuckoo

Coccyzus minor

Both Great Exuma – June

Status and range: Permanent resident throughout The Bahamas. Generally less common in northern Bahamas (only a few reported from Grand Bahama) and more common in central and southern Bahamas. Uncommon permanent resident in TCI.

Description: Length: 12 ins (30 cm). Slim long-tailed bird with black mask and gray crown. Gray-brown upperparts and white underparts with buffy wash which is slightly stronger on belly, vent and undertail coverts. (Some birds more strongly washed with buff throughout.) Upperwing brown with no rufous in primaries. Bill is decurved with upper mandible dark and lower mandible yellow with dark tip. Central tail feathers gray-brown while shorter and graduated outer tail feathers are black tipped in white, presenting conspicuous white spots on underside of folded tail.

Voice: Call a series of low and throaty *gaw gaw gaw kow kow kow* notes sometimes ending with a hollow *koowp*. Also a few *kow* notes.

Habits: Usually found in dense scrub and coppice. Less numerous in tall mangrove stands despite name. Heard more often than seen. Secretive and forages slowly often with long pauses looking for prey.

Similar species: Yellow-billed Cuckoo (*Coccyzus americanus*) Length: 12 ins (30 cm). Regular spring (April–May) and fall (October–November) transient through the region. More common in southern Bahamas and TCI in fall. Spends winter in South America. Small dark area around eye (not mask), totally white underparts (not buff) and rufous in primaries (not brown) which are visible on folded wing and conspicuous in flight. Lower mandible and base of upper mandible are yellow – more yellow than Mangrove's. Undertail pattern similar.

April

Great Lizard-Cuckoo   (e) *Saurothera merlini bahamensis*

Adult: North Andros – May   Juvenile: North Andros – October

Status and range: Permanent resident on only three islands in northern Bahamas. Fairly common on North and South Andros, uncommon on Eleuthera and very rare on New Providence. Not found on other islands or in TCI.

Description: Length: 21 ins (53 cm). Impressive large cuckoo with gray-brown upperparts and pale gray underparts blending to rufous flanks, belly, vent and undertail coverts. Primaries tinged rufous. Long and pointed darkish bill, slightly decurved at tip. Adult has red skin around eye, dull yellow in juvenile. Extremely long gray-brown central tail feathers; shorter and graduated outer tail feathers are black tipped in white presenting conspicuous white spots on underside of folded tail.

Voice: Call is a very loud, long and rapid series *kek-kek-kek-kek-kek-kek*, etc. sometimes with a scratchy *kawick* at the beginning or end. Also a short growled *ta-coo*. Louder, longer and faster than Mangrove Cuckoo.

Habits: Found in pinewoods with brushy understorey or edges. Also dense coppice and shrubs. Despite size, agile in thick vegetation. Prey includes small lizards, large insects, birds' eggs and sometimes nestlings. When flushed, usually flies or glides only short distance. Adept at running on ground. Generally secretive and difficult to locate, especially during non-breeding season. However, when agitated or curious, may permit close approach.

Comments: Great Lizard-Cuckoo is found only in the West Indies and range restricted to The Bahamas and Cuba. In The Bahamas, recognized as an endemic subspecies *S. m. bahamensis*. Locally called the 'rain crow' on Andros. **Conservation:** Small population on New Providence severely threatened and vulnerable due to habitat destruction from development. Its future there is doubtful if not already over.

Smooth-billed Ani   *Crotophaga ani*

New Providence – January   New Providence – March

Status and range: Common permanent resident throughout the region.

Description: Length: 14 ins (35 cm). Unmistakable. Entirely black long-tailed bird with distinctively wide decurved bill that has high ridge on upper mandible (almost parrot-like). Tail appears loosely connected to body and is about one half of bird's length. In proper light, shows faint purple gloss on wings and tail. Juvenile is duller black, has lower ridge on bill and brown tinge on wings. Anis fly weakly with several flaps and glides; landings are often awkward.

Voice: Vocal and noisy. No song but common call note a scratchy, whining and rising *whee-ink*. Also gives variety of short grunts and whistles.

Habits: Prefers open areas with thick grasses and bushes, sometimes lawns and golf courses. Feeds on ground or in low shrubs looking primarily for insects but also small lizards and sometimes fruit. Highly social and usually seen in groups. Nests in pairs or more often in groups where all members may participate in nest building, laying eggs and raising young. If cold or wet, will perch with wings and tail outspread towards sun. Roosting birds, if cold, sit closely side by side.

Comments: Because anis have such an unusual appearance, they are subject to many local names: 'long-tailed crow' and 'cemetery bird' to name but two.

◆ BARN OWLS AND TYPICAL OWLS   Families: *Tytonidae and Strigidae*

Two well-known world-wide families, the first one small and the second large. Owls from both families are mostly nocturnal birds of prey with large heads, short necks and eyes that face forward. Can turn their heads more than 180° to either side. They have excellent hearing and silent flight which enables them to track down prey in darkness. Kill and hold their prey with strong sharp bills and talons. Prey often swallowed whole. Owls are divided into two families which are separated by structural features such as shape of face, tail and feet. One representative of each family occurs in the region.

Barn Owl   *Tyto alba*

In threat display: New Providence – winter

Status and range: Uncommon permanent resident throughout The Bahamas and Caicos Islands in TCI.

Description: Length: 16 ins (41 cm). Large light-colored owl with heart-shaped white face and dark eyes. Upperparts light orange-brown with fine gray and white markings. Underparts and underwing mostly white. Males paler than females. In poor light or at night, appears ghostly white, especially in flight.

Voice: Not vocal but calls include either hisses, shrieks or clicks heard mainly around roost site or nest. Does not hoot.

Habits: Roosts and nests in abandoned buildings, caves, ledges in blue holes and other dark inaccessible spots. Hunts at night from perch or flies low over open areas or near settlements and pounces on prey (rats, insects, reptiles and birds). Seen in daylight when flushed from roost.

Burrowing Owl   *Athene cunicularia*

Cat Island – May

Florida – May

Status and range: Permanent resident. Locally uncommon to fairly common on Cat Island and Great Inagua. Rare to uncommon on South Andros, very rare on Grand Bahama and rare on New Providence. Status on other islands unclear. Not found in TCI.

Description: Length: 9.5 ins (24 cm). Small, ground-dwelling, brown owl with yellow eyes, white throat and long legs. Heavy white spotting on dark-brown upper-parts and brown and white barred underparts. Short tail also barred. Juvenile has buffy underparts with little or no barring.

Voice: Male breeding call a high *ka-coo*. Also gives a raspy alarm note.

Habits: Most active at dusk and at night but more active during day when feeding chicks. Feeds mainly on insects and small lizards. Sometimes seen standing near nest hole in broad daylight and will bob up and down if agitated. Prefers open areas with short grass or bare ground. Nest is burrow in ground that it excavates with bill and legs. Thin soil and limestone base of islands limit natural nesting sites so often nests in man-made embankments.

Comments: Subspecies in The Bahamas, *A. c. floridana* is same subspecies as found in Florida. **Conservation:** Population of Burrowing Owl in The Bahamas has declined over past 25 years. There is now an urgent need for a survey of this species and appropriate conservation action.

◆ NIGHTHAWKS AND NIGHTJARS   Family: *Caprimulgidae*

Medium-sized world-wide family of well-camouflaged birds that feed at dusk and at night. They have large eyes and small bills with huge mouths. Feed on insects caught in flight. Relatively long wings and tails. Nest and rest on ground or on low branches. Sit on branch lengthwise rather than across it. Nighthawks have long pointed wings and pursue insects in open air. Nightjars have rounded wings and feed in coppice and dense habitats.

Antillean Nighthawk   *Chordeiles gundlachii*

Female on nest: Great Exuma – June

Male: Great Exuma – June

Male: Providenciales – June

Status and range: Common summer resident and transient throughout the region. Arrives in late April and departs by mid-September. A few birds remain into October.

Description: Length: 8.5 ins (22 cm); wingspan: 21 ins (53 cm). Slender bird with small head and tiny dark bill. Upperparts dark and densely mottled with white, gray and warm brown; underparts light buff with black bars. Male has white bar across throat, female's bar off-white. Long pointed wings have bold white band across primaries, conspicuous in flight and also visible on folded wing of perched bird. Male's band slightly larger and more distinct than female's. Folded wings do not extend past tip of tail. Long tail slightly forked at tip. Male tail has indistinct white bar across dark outer tail feathers, visible from below or if tail is spread; female lacks this bar. Both sexes have small white feather near bend of wing, unique to nighthawks and visible on folded wing but sometimes obscured. Juvenile lacks both throat bar and bold white band on wing.

Voice: A buzzy *pitty-pit-pit* given in flight. Males call frequently at dusk in spring and early summer. In display flight, male dives and pulls up abruptly, primary feathers bent down to make barely audible woosh at bottom of dive. For nighthawks, known as 'booming display'.

Habits: Feeds by catching flying insects high or low over open areas or above tree-tops. Bouyant flight with glides but appears erratic when quick moves or steep dives are made for prey. Usually seen feeding at dusk or on cloudy days. After heavy day-time rain sometimes feeds in loose flock low over golf courses or open fields. Nests on open ground, often under an isolated bush, on gravel or sand.

Comments: Breeds only in the West Indies and South Florida. Antillean Nighthawk in the region and in South Florida is subspecies *C. g. vicinus*. Formerly considered West Indian subspecies of Common Nighthawk. Locally called 'mosquito hawk' or 'pidda-ma-dick'. Winter range is un-known but thought to be South America.

Similar species: Common Nighthawk (*Chordeiles minor*) Length 9.5 ins (24 cm); wingspan: 24 ins (61 cm). Rare to uncommon transient through the region but un-recorded from several islands in central and southern Bahamas. Closely resembles Antillean Nighthawk and only reliably distinguished in the field by voice. Gives nasal *peent*, very different from call of Antillean. Unfortunately, Common Nighthawk does not call much during spring migration and both nighthawks are usually silent in fall.

Male: May

Probable female: May

Chuck-will's-widow

Caprimulgus carolinensis

In migration: Florida – April

Status and range: Uncommon winter resident in northern and central Bahamas as far south as Great Exuma. Status on other islands unknown. Rare winter resident on Great Inagua and TCI. Recently confirmed as breeder on Grand Bahama and Abaco but status and numbers unclear.

Description: Length: 12 ins (30 cm). Large, densely mottled, warm to gray-brown bird with broad rounded wings and long rounded tail. Breast darker than brownish buff throat. Male has white outer tail feathers which are buff on female and most visible in flight.

Voice: Nocturnal song a loud whistled and distinct *chup-whill-wheeeow* often repeated. First note softer and may not be heard at a distance. Starts calling in early spring, silent at other times.

Habits: Active at dawn, dusk and moonlit nights. Almost always heard rather than seen. Bird of thick coppice and pinewoods. Rests and nests on ground. Catches large insects while flying low. Also known on occasion to consume small birds. Secretive and well camouflaged and population probably fairly small, so rarely seen.

Similar species: Could be confused with **Antillean Nighthawk** if seen perched or flushed during day. Nighthawk would be smaller, more slender and grayer than larger, bulkier and browner Chuck-will's-widow. Nighthawk would also have white patches on wing.

Comments: Its secretive habits and camouflaged plumage make it very difficult to find and study. It is unclear if calling chucks in early spring are residents or birds calling before migrating north or both.

 **HUMMINGBIRDS** **Family:** *Trochilidae*

Smallest of birds, hummingbirds comprise a very large and distinct New World family of more than 300 species. They have long slender bills and tongues which are well-adapted for probing flowers for nectar. Insects and spiders are also an important part of their diet. In many species, males have brilliant iridescent feathers especially on the throat (called a 'gorget' in hummingbirds) while females and immatures are less colorful, making them more difficult to identify. A unique wing movement allows hummingbirds not only to hover over flowers, but also to fly backwards, sideways, and up and down. Wings move so quickly that they appear as a blur.

Cuban Emerald   *Chlorostilbon ricordii*

Female: Grand Bahama – February

Male: Grand Bahama – February

Possible immature: Grand Bahama – March

Status and range: Fairly common permanent resident on Grand Bahama, Abaco and Andros. Not found on other islands or TCI.

Description: Length: 3.7–4.2 ins (9.5–10.5 cm). Adult male is iridescent metallic green all over. Appears dark in poor light. Prominent white spot behind eye, white vent and undertail coverts and long, dark, deeply forked tail. Adult female has metallic green upperparts and light gray underparts. Sides of neck, breast and flanks mottled metallic green. White area behind eye extends over dark cheek. Tail not as deeply forked as male's. Dark bill of both sexes straight to slightly decurved. Lower mandible of male (best seen from below) dull red with dark tip; only red at base on female. On perched birds, tail extends well past wing tips. Immature plumages poorly known and very difficult to identify in the field, but similar to adult female.

Voice: Song a high and thin *see see see see*. Call note metallic and 'buzzy' given singly or repeated (similar to a chatter). Might hear whirring or hum of male's wings in flight.

Habits: Found in pinewoods, brushy undergrowth, coppice edges and residential gardens. Male often perches on exposed twig. Feeds on nectar from flowering shrubs and trees and small insects. Comes to hummingbird feeders. Aggressive in breeding and feeding areas, will chase away much larger birds. Aggressive nature of Cuban Emerald may account for low population of Bahama Woodstar on islands inhabited by both species.

Similar species: Compared to female Cuban Emerald, female **Bahama Woodstar** has rufous on underparts and rufous tips on shorter more rounded tail. Female and immature **Ruby-throated Hummingbird** has less white behind eye (just a spot), less metallic green flanks and white tips to shorter tail feathers.

Comments: Found only in the West Indies and range restricted to Cuba and three northern Bahama islands listed above. Reported from South Florida but not officially documented.

Bahama Woodstar
(E) *Calliphlox evelynae*

Adult male: New Providence – December

Adult female: Grand Bahama – February

Immature male: New Providence – October

Adult male: Great Inagua – winter

Status and range: Permanent resident. Fairly common to common throughout the region, including TCI. Rare to uncommon on Grand Bahama, Abaco and Andros where Cuban Emerald also occurs.

Description: Length: 3.5–3.75 ins (9–9.5 cm). Native hummingbird of the region. **Adult male** has dusky metallic green upperparts with iridescent purple-red throat that will look black depending upon angle of light. Broad white band separates dark throat from dusky green lower breast, flanks and belly which are suffused with light to strong rufous. Long, deeply-forked tail and narrow, black, outer tail feathers with bold rufous edges to inner portion. Folded tail from below appears black with rufous centre. **Adult female** has dusky metallic green upperparts and white to dull-white throat and breast with pale rufous flanks and belly. Long tail not as deeply forked and more rounded than male's. Outer tail feathers rufous at base, black in middle and rufous at tip. Folded tail from below appears black with large rufous tips. Both sexes have dark straight to very slightly decurved bill, small white dot behind eye and small bright rufous patch on sides of breast that extends into underwing. At rest, tail extends well past wing tips. **Immature** of both sexes similar to adult female but immature male shows some iridescent spots on whitish throat and has duskier flanks and belly. Female immature has paler rufous on flanks and has buff tail tips which can appear whitish when backlit. May be too difficult to identify sex of some immatures. In Great and Little Inagua subspecies, purple-red throat iridescence on adult male extends to forehead. Adult female and immature plumages poorly known.

Voice: Call notes include single and double chip notes: *chit* or *chitit*. *Chit* note can be in rapid series. Song has *chitit* notes and rising *teeee* at the end.

Habits: Found in all island habitats such as coppice edges, woodland clearings, dry scrub, coastal scrub forest and residential gardens. Feeds by hovering over flowers and taking nectar with long bill and tongue. Will also take small insects. Comes to hummingbird feeders. Breeds year round. Female builds nest and raises young.

Comments: Bahama Woodstar in the region is an endemic species with two recognized subspecies: *C. e. lyrura* on Great and Little Inagua and *C. e. evelynae* on all other islands including TCI. There are several records from southeast corner of Florida.

Similar species: Ruby-throated Hummingbird (*Archilochus colubris*) Length 3.75 ins (9.5 cm). Rare transient and possible winter resident in northern Bahamas. Metallic green above, dingy white below and small white spot behind eye. Adult male has ruby-red throat, dingy green flanks and dark tail with no rufous. Female and immature have dusky to pale buff flanks and white tips on outer tail feathers; tail length of Ruby-throateds is shorter than Bahama Woodstar. Bahama Woodstar has more rufous on sides of breast, flanks and tail.

Immature male: September   Adult female: April

KINGFISHERS   **Family:** *Alcedinidae*

Medium-sized world-wide family with most species occurring in warmer climates of the Old World. They have large heads and bills and proportionally smaller bodies. Typically forage over water for fish although some species forage over land for insects and small lizards. The most common and widespread kingfisher in North America occurs in the region.

Belted Kingfisher   *Ceryle alcyon*

Both Grand Bahama – October

Status and range: Uncommon to fairly common winter resident and transient throughout the region.

Description: Length: 13 ins (33 cm). Large-headed bird with long, heavy, dark bill and short tail. Shaggy crest often raised. Both sexes have slate-blue upperparts, broad white collar, white underparts and blue breast band. In addition, female has rust-colored breast band and rusty flanks.

Voice: Call is a loud, harsh, dry rattle. Often given in flight as an alarm or territorial dispute.

Habits: Mostly solitary and often perches on tree limbs, power lines or other conspicuous perches over or near shallow water. Vigorously defends perch from other kingfishers. Catches fish by plunge-diving after hovering over prey or by diving directly from perch. Fishes in both fresh and salt water. Skittish bird and usually does not tolerate close approach.

◆ WOODPECKERS

Family: *Picidae*

Large and well-known family found throughout the world. Birds with strong bills which they use to drill holes in trees and then use their extraordinarily long tongues to reach grubs and other insects. They nest in cavities they have carved into trees. In addition, they have strong feet and toes (usually two forward and two backward) to facilitate climbing up tree trunks and stiff tails to brace themselves. Woodpeckers have an undulating flight. Breeding woodpeckers in northern Bahamas are an important part of the ecosystem as other species, such as Bahama Swallow and La Sagra's Flycatcher, use their abandoned nest holes.

West Indian Woodpecker

ⓔ *Melanerpes superciliaris*

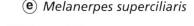

Female: Abaco – October

Male: Abaco – October

Male: San Salvador – June

Status and range: Uncommon to fairly common permanent resident on Abaco, including larger offshore cays. Rare to uncommon and vulnerable (a low population) permanent resident on San Salvador. Formerly found on Grand Bahama. Not found on other islands or TCI.

Description: Length: 10 ins (25 cm). Largest woodpecker in the region. Bold black and white barring on back, rump and wings. Underparts creamy-gray with some red wash on belly. Barred flanks and undertail coverts. Male has red crown and nape; only nape is red on female. Abaco male has bold black mark above and behind eye. Female's black mark similar but extends as spots onto crown. San Salvador birds are slightly lighter and smaller and appear to have smaller black mark above eye. In breeding plumage, males from both islands have more white in face and yellow tinge to breast and belly.

Voice: Common call a loud and rolling *churrr churrr* given as contact call between paired adults. *Chur* call is a series of notes run quickly together. Also a sharp *chiv chiv chiv.*

Habits: Frequents pinewoods, coppice, orchards and settled areas (especially those with coconut palms) on Abaco. On San Salvador, frequents coppice areas and appears to prefer to nest in dead Sabal Palms. Feeds on insects, larvae, fruit and small lizards. Can be difficult to find.

Comments: West Indian Woodpecker in The Bahamas has two recognized endemic subspecies: *M. s. blakei* on Abaco and *M. s. nyeanus* on San Salvador and formerly Grand Bahama. Found only in the West Indies and range restricted to Cuba, Grand Cayman in the Cayman Islands and the two islands in The Bahamas. Formerly called 'West Indian Red-bellied Woodpecker' or 'Cuban Red-bellied Woodpecker'. Impact of extensive logging on Grand Bahama during 1950s and 1960s is believed to have caused, or at least had something to do with, the loss of West Indian Woodpecker on that island. Recently West Indian Woodpecker was discovered nesting (2002) around McLeans Town at eastern end of Grand Bahama. Status and subspecies yet to be determined but origin most likely Abaco.

Yellow-bellied Sapsucker   *Sphyrapicus varius*

Female: New Providence – November   Juvenile (losing brown tinge on face): January

Length: 8.5 ins (22 cm). Uncommon winter resident and transient throughout the region. Even on islands where it has never been reported, there are trees bearing its distinctive drilling pattern of holes. Black and white woodpecker with irregular barring on back and white patch on dark wing. Striped black and white face pattern. Adult male has red forehead and throat; female has red forehead and white throat. Face and underparts of fall juvenile tinged brown; lacks solid forehead color of adult. In flight, all birds show white patches on wings and whitish rump. Mostly silent but call note a whiny *keeah*. Drills on live trees in distinctive pattern – series of shallow holes in horizontal line. Drinks flowing sap and eats insects attracted to it. Also feeds on berries and fruit. Prefers semi-open habitats including gardens and ornamental trees, usually not seen in deep coppice. Rather solitary and inconspicuous. Breeds throughout parts of northern North America and is highly migratory, wintering far south of its breeding range. In the West Indies, winters mainly in The Bahamas and the Greater Antilles. **Hairy Woodpecker** lacks white-wing patch, barring on back and red forehead of adult. Also has very different call note.

Hairy Woodpecker   (e) *Picoides villosus*

Male: Abaco – February   Female: Grand Bahama – October

Status and range: Fairly common permanent resident on those northern Bahama islands with pinewoods: Grand Bahama, Abaco, North Andros and New Providence. Not found on other islands or TCI.

Description: Length: 8 ins (20 cm). Black and white woodpecker with white central panel on black back, white spots on black wing and dingy white underparts. Black tail has white outer tail feathers. Male has red mark on nape.

Voice: Common call note a loud and high *keek*. Also a sharp and loud rattle or chatter call (quickly repeated series of *keek* notes).

Habits: Primarily a bird of the pinewoods but also found in other wooded habitats.

Similar species: See **Yellow-bellied Sapsucker**.

Comments: Widespread in North America and parts of Middle America. Range in West Indies restricted to northern Bahama islands. Hairy Woodpecker in The Bahamas has two recognized endemic subspecies: *P. v. piger* on Grand Bahama and Abaco and *P. v. maynardi* on North Andros and New Providence. Differences between two subspecies include duskier underparts, fine streaks on pale area of back and some black bars on white outer tail feathers on *P. v. piger* compared to *P. v. maynardi* but these features are difficult to discern in the field. Bahama subspecies of Hairy Woodpecker is smaller than North American subspecies.

◆ TYRANT FLYCATCHERS   Family: *Tyrannidae*

Largest New World family of birds with over 400 species that feed primarily on insects but take berries and fruit when opportunity arises. Most flycatchers are dull-colored with non-musical songs. They have keen eyesight, broad flat bills and tactile bristles at base of bill which make them well adapted for capturing insects. Feed by flying from perch and snatching insects in mid-air, often returning to same perch. May also hover and snatch insects from foliage or take insects from ground.

   Eight species of flycatchers from the region are described below. Three are permanent residents, one is summer resident and four are transients. Two other species, Acadian and Scissor-tailed Flycatcher, are not described and both are considered rare transients mainly in the northern Bahamas.

Cuban Pewee   ⓔ *Contopus caribaeus bahamensis*

Grand Bahama – February   Abaco – January

Status and range: Permanent resident. Fairly common to common on Grand Bahama, Abaco, Andros, New Providence and Cat Island. Uncommon on Eleuthera. Not found on other islands or TCI.

Description: Length: 6 ins (15 cm). Smallest Bahama flycatcher. Dark head with distinct white crescent behind eye and slight crest or peak to rear of head. Bill is broad and flat with pale orange base on lower mandible. Dark gray-brown upperparts tinged olive and dull white underparts have gray-brown wash on sides of breast and flanks. Darker wings have faint wing-bars. Some birds have pale yellow tinge to underparts.

Voice: Call note a quick and soft *tit-tit-tit*. Song most often heard is high whistled *DEE dee-dee* with emphasis on first note and then descending. Also a faster and longer song *DEE-dee dee-dee-dee-dee* heard at dawn.

Habits: Found in both pinewoods and broad-leaved coppice. Flycatches from conspicuous, sometimes very low, perch. Flicks tail upon returning to perch. Usually approachable.

Comments: Found only in the West Indies and range restricted to northern Bahamas and Cuba. Also accidental to South Florida. Formerly treated as sub-species of Greater Antillean Pewee and formerly called by that name. Cuban Pewee in The Bahamas is recognized as an endemic subspecies *C. c. bahamensis*. Also referred to as 'Crescent-eyed Pewee'.

Similar species: The following two species of transient flycatchers are similar in size, coloration and habits as Cuban Pewee.

Eastern Wood-Pewee   *Contopus virens*

May   April

Length: 6.25 ins (15.9 cm). Rare fall transient mainly in northern Bahamas. Similar to Cuban Pewee but overall slightly darker, has longer wings and slightly stronger wing-bars. Face is darker with thin indistinct eye-ring instead of bold crescent behind eye. Has tendency to sit exposed on dead twig or limb next to an open area. Call is a thin and high plaintive *tweee* or a dry *wit*.

Eastern Phoebe   *Sayornis phoebe*

June   October

Length: 7 ins (18 cm). Rare transient and winter resident mainly in northern Bahamas. Gray-brown upperparts with darker head, long dark tail and faint wing-bars. Whitish underparts (especially throat) with smudgy wash on sides of breast and many birds show yellow wash on belly. Dark head contrasts with white throat. Dark bill and no marks around eye, unlike orange lower mandible and bold crescent behind eye of Cuban Pewee. Has habit of frequently pumping tail down then up. Seems to prefer brushy or wooded habitats around small freshwater ponds. Call note a sharp *chip*.

La Sagra's Flycatcher   (e) *Myiarchus sagrae lucaysiensis*

Grand Bahama – March   Grand Bahama – December   Abaco – February

Status and range: Permanent resident. Fairly common to common on Grand Bahama, Abaco, Andros, New Providence and Eleuthera. Uncommon on Great Inagua. Reported sparingly from central and southern Bahamas but status unclear. Not found in TCI.

Description: Length: 7.5 ins (19 cm). Medium-sized flycatcher with gray-brown upperparts, soft gray throat and breast with pale yellow wash on belly, vent and under-tail coverts. Darker brown cap blends gradually into grayer cheeks. Wing coverts and tertial feathers edged white with rufous edges along primaries. Brown outer tail feathers have rufous edges on inner part of each feather, only seen from below on folded tail. When plumage is worn and dull, yellow wash and rufous coloring reduced. Juvenile similar to adult but has slightly brighter rufous on wings and tail.

Voice: Call note a loud and rising whistled *wheet*, sometimes doubled. Song, often at dawn, a series of intense or less intense *wheet* notes combined with notes that have a buzzy or raspy quality.

Habits: Found in pinewoods, coppice, mixed woodlands and tall brushy growth mostly in understorey. Sits motionless, sometimes leaning forward rather than sitting erect. Will also hover to catch prey or pick berries from foliage. Has ability to raise crest feathers or flatten them changing appearance of crown. At times, during non-breeding season, can be secretive and hard to find.

Similar species: Loggerhead Kingbird is larger with heavier bill. Head is darker with sharper demarcation between color of head, cheek and throat. Has no rufous in wings or tail.

Comments: Found only in the West Indies and range restricted to The Bahamas, Cuba and Grand Cayman in the Cayman Islands. Also rare visitor to South Florida. Formerly treated as subspecies of Stolid Flycatcher and formerly called by that name. La Sagra's Flycatcher in The Bahamas is recognized as an endemic subspecies *M. s. lucaysiensis*.

Gray Kingbird *Tyrannus dominicensis*

Cay Sal Bank – May

New Providence – May

Juvenile: Grand Bahama – September

Status and range: Common summer resident and transient throughout the region. Arrives in April and leaves in October but migrating birds may appear in March or linger into November.

Description: Length: 9 ins (23 cm). Conspicuous kingbird with gray upperparts and white underparts. Dark mask around eye and large broad black bill. Darker wing patterned with pale edges to feathers. Tail is forked or notched at tip. Juvenile similar to adult but wing pattern shows buff edges to feathers.

Voice: Fairly quiet in migration but noisy during breeding season. Pairs especially noisy when greeting each other in early part of breeding season. Call note a loud sharp *pi-cheeer*, last note with more chatter. Song a longer variation of call note and often given at dawn.

Habits: Seems comfortable around both inhabited and uninhabited areas. Nests in urban settings, gardens, coppice and mangroves. Not found in interior of extensive pinewoods but sometimes found along edges. Very aggressive when defending territory. Often seen perched and flycatching from power lines and poles. Will take large insects which they beat against perch before swallowing. In some places, feeds at night on insects attracted to streetlights. At times, seen in large numbers migrating south in fall.

Similar species: Loggerhead Kingbird darker above; squared tail with thin dull white tip. The two species are not usually found together.

Comments: Common summer breeder throughout the West Indies, Florida Keys and coastal areas of Florida. Gray Kingbirds in The Bahamas and TCI are migratory and leave the region after breeding. In other areas of the West Indies, they are found year-round. Migratory birds are thought to spend winter season in northern South America.

Loggerhead Kingbird (e) *Tyrannus caudifasciatus bahamensis*

Grand Bahama – April

Grand Bahama – February

New Providence – May

Status and range: Permanent resident. Common on Grand Bahama, Abaco and Andros and fairly common on New Providence. Not found on other islands or in TCI.

Description: Length: 9 ins (23 cm). Adult has dark upperparts and white underparts with large black bill. Dark head contrasts with paler gray-brown back and sharply contrasts just below eye with white cheek and throat. Black mask around eye, visible only in good light. Feathers on dark wing are edged in white. Underparts white; lower belly, vent and undertail coverts lightly washed in yellow, especially during breeding season. Yellow wash on underwing coverts visible only when wing is raised. Squared tail dark with dull white tip. Juvenile similar to adult but wing pattern shows buff edges to feathers.

Voice: Call note a loud, sharp, slightly buzzy *tireet* often repeated. Song a loud rolling *pirri-pirri-pirri*.

Habits: Primarily a pinewoods species but also found in habitat near pinewoods such as coppice and secondary growth – sometimes gardens. Insects main diet but takes berries and small lizards. Hunts from interior of habitat as well as from exposed perches. Appears to retreat deeper into pinewoods when Gray Kingbirds are present.

Similar species: See **La Sagra's Flycatcher** and **Gray Kingbird**.

Comments: Found only in the West Indies and range restricted to The Bahamas and the Greater Antilles. Loggerhead Kingbird in The Bahamas is recognized as an endemic subspecies *T. c. bahamensis*.

Two other species of kingbird are rare but regular transients in the northern Bahamas and are described below. In the rest of the region, they are mainly unrecorded but there are records of Eastern Kingbird from the Exumas, Cat Island and Providenciales in the Caicos Islands. Eastern Kingbird may also be uncommon in late summer/early fall (mid-August–September) when their fall migration is at its peak. Western Kingbird is found almost exclusively in fall but there are spring records and it is a probable winter resident or visitors.

Eastern Kingbird   *Tyrannus tyrannus*

May   August

Length: 8.5 ins (21.6 cm). Relatively smallish kingbird with dark upperparts and contrasting white underparts. Black head and smallish-looking bill, dark gray back and black tail with white tip. Black head contrasts sharply with white throat and sides of neck. Underparts white with some smudginess on breast. At times, appears like smaller version of Loggerhead Kingbird. Usually found on an exposed perch. Often found with Gray Kingbirds in migration and not vocal.

Western Kingbird   *Tyrannus verticalis*

May   June

Length: 8.75 ins (22.2 cm). Pale gray crown and back with darker wing and black tail; thin white edges to black outer tail feathers. Underparts have whitish throat blending to grayish breast with bright lemon yellow belly and undertail coverts. Yellow extends to underwing coverts. Prefers exposed perches but will glean insects or berries from foliage. Call a sharp *kip*.

◆ VIREOS

Family: *Vireonidae*

Small New World family which superficially resemble warblers. Vireos are small birds with large-looking heads and stout bills, which have tiny hook at end of upper mandible. Feed on insects and their larvae and also take berries and fruit more so than warblers. Foraging behavior is slow and deliberate, less active than warblers. Typically persistent singers during breeding season and call notes typically involve scold or alarm notes.

Thick-billed Vireo

(e) *Vireo crassirostris*

Cat Island – October

Worn plumage: Great Exuma – June

Status and range: Common permanent resident throughout most of The Bahamas. Common permanent resident on Caicos Islands but not found on Turks Islands in TCI.

Description: Length: 5.25 ins (13.3 cm). Common vireo in the region with relatively thick light gray bill and dark brown eye. Thin dark line in lores with broad yellow stripe above. Incomplete and thin pale yellow eye-ring with gap (sometimes colored black) above eye. Upperparts mostly uniformly brown-olive and wings dark with two white wing-bars. Underparts pale yellow with throat and undertail coverts slightly paler. Underpart color ranges from lightest yellow in northern Bahamas to brightest yellow in southern Bahamas and Caicos Islands. Yellower birds also have relatively more yellow-green on upperparts. Occasionally yellower birds are found in northern Bahamas.

Voice: Scold note a harsh and nasal *anh anh*, often steady and repeated. Song is loud usually five-note phrase *chip chip CHUWEE chip*. Frequently repeated and with several variations. Also gives rambling song which is continuous jumble of brief, squeaky, buzzy and nasal notes. Sings while foraging. Birds in Caicos Islands have more chatter in song.

Habits: Found in thick coppice, brushy margins of pinewoods and low, dense, dry scrub. Secretive and prefers to stay inside cover but is responsive to pishing.

Similar species: See **White-eyed Vireo**.

Comments: Thick-billed Vireo in the region has two recognized endemic subspecies: one in The Bahamas, *V. c. crassirostris*, and one in the Caicos Islands of TCI, *V. c. sta-lagmium*. Caicos birds average slightly smaller than Bahama birds but this is not noticeable in the field. Found only in the West Indies with an interesting distribution pattern. Range restricted to The Bahamas, Caicos Islands, Cayman Islands and only one island each off Cuba and Haiti but not main islands. Also rare visitor to South Florida.

Black-whiskered Vireo
Vireo altiloquus

Adult: New Providence – May

Immature: Grand Bahama – early October

Status and range: Common summer resident (April–September) on all major islands in The Bahamas except San Salvador and Rum Cay where it is not found. Common summer resident in TCI.

Description: Length: 6.25 ins (16 cm). Large vireo with relatively thick long bill. Gray crown with white supercilium and dark line running through red-brown eye. Thin dark 'whisker' mark on throat can be difficult to detect. Upperparts olive-green, including wing, with no wing-bars. Underparts mainly dull-white with pale yellow wash on vent and undertail coverts. Immature in fall similar to adult but slightly duller with browner eye.

Voice: Call or alarm note a nasal whine-like *yaah.* Song is an often repeated two to three-note warbled phrase with a slight burry quality. Full song described locally as 'cheap-John Stirrup, sweet-Joe Clare.' May be persistent singer in spring and early summer.

Habits: Primarily found in tall broadleaf trees in coppice and secondary growth, sometimes in ornamental trees around gardens. Dry scrub and mangroves in southern areas of region. Moves slowly through upper branches or remains still for long periods, so may be hard to find at times. Usually responds to pishing.

Comments: Widespread breeder in the West Indies. Population in The Bahamas and TCI migrates to northern South America. Also breeds in parts of the Florida Keys and coastal areas of South Florida.

Similar species: Red-eyed Vireo (*Vireo olivaceus*) Length: 6 ins (15 cm). Rare to uncommon fall transient and very rare spring transient through the region. Very similar to Black-whiskered but lacks 'whisker' mark and has relatively smaller bill. In fall, most Black-whiskered Vireos have left region before most migrant Red-eyed Vireos have arrived but there is some overlap. Call or alarm note similar.

Immature: October

Grand Bahama – October

Winter Resident and Transient Vireos

There are five species of vireo that are either annual winter residents or transients in the region. White-eyed Vireo and Yellow-throated Vireo are described below. Red-eyed Vireo has been described as similar species to Black-whiskered Vireo. Blue-headed Vireo, rare winter visitor to northern Bahamas and Philadelphia Vireo, rare fall transient, are not described.

White-eyed Vireo   *Vireo griseus*

Both immatures: Grand Bahama – October

Adult: Grand Bahama – October

Length: 5 ins (12.7 cm). Uncommon winter resident and transient throughout the region. More common in fall in northern Bahamas. Adult has white eye and yellow 'spectacles'. Crown gray-green and back olive-green with contrasting gray coloring on nape and along sides of neck. Wings are dark with two white wing-bars. Throat and underparts white to pale gray which contrast with pale yellow sides of breast and flanks. Fall immature similar to adult but has brownish eye. Immature retains dark eye through fall and sometimes into winter. Habitats include coppice, thick scrub and secondary growth. Likes to stay hidden in cover. Scold notes harsh and raspy sometimes like a 'chatter'. Some birds sing during winter season and song similar to Thick-billed Vireo. **Similar species:** Adult **Thick-billed Vireo** has dark eye. However, Thick-billed Vireo is easily confused with immature White-eyed Vireo in fall which has dark eye. Thick-billed lacks gray contrast on sides of neck and lacks contrast between pale yellow flanks and whitish underparts. Also, eye-ring of Thick-billed is less complete and duller. Scold notes of both are similar but Thick-billed's scold is slower with little or no chatter.

Yellow-throated Vireo   *Vireo flavifrons*

Length: 5.5 ins (14 cm). Rare to uncommon winter resident and transient throughout

April

the region. More brightly colored than the other vireos. Bold yellow eye-ring connected to yellow lores making it look like spectacles. Bright yellow throat and breast with rest of underparts white. Upperparts yellow-olive with gray rump and gray uppertail coverts. Wings dark with two white wing-bars. Found in a variety of wooded habitats, usually in upper portions. Recognizable scold notes a harsh *chi-chi-chi-chur-chur-chur*, rapid at first, then trailing off.

CROWS   **Family:** *Corvidae*

Well-known, medium-sized, world-wide family of birds. Crows are noisy large black birds often found in flocks. They are also generalists surviving in a wide variety of habitats and feeding on a wide variety of food.

Cuban Crow   *Corvus nasicus*

North Caicos – June   Providencialis – June

Status and range: In TCI, locally common permanent resident on North and Middle Caicos. Uncommon on Providenciales. Not found on Turks Islands or The Bahamas.

Description: Length: 18 ins (46 cm). Large all-black crow with slightly glossy sheen. Flat head and heavy pointed bill with conspicuous nostril opening on upper mandible. Short tail and thick powerful legs. Build appears like small raven.

Voice: Loud and noisy especially in a group. Frequent call resembles gobbling of a turkey but can also sound like squeaky brakes on car.

Habits: Gregarious outside breeding season. Frequents open areas near vegetation and coppice, also human settlements and agricultural areas. Eats insects, fruit, seeds, eggs and reptiles – just about anything.

Comments: Found only in the West Indies and range restricted to Caicos Islands and Cuba.

SWALLOWS AND MARTINS   Family: *Hirundinidae*

Medium-sized world-wide family of streamlined and graceful birds. Swallows are aerial specialists that catch insects in mid-air. Characteristic flight includes gliding and soaring with intermittent rapid flapping. They have small bills with large mouths and long pointed wings. Tails slightly to deeply forked. Gregarious, many species breed in colonies. Some species make cup-shaped nests from mud while others nest in cavities. They do not sing but make short chirping sounds and twittering notes. Bahama Swallow and Cave Swallow breed in the northern Bahamas and six species are transients.

Bahama Swallow   Ⓔ *Tachycineta cyaneoviridis*

Abaco – February

Adult in flight from below

Status and range: Uncommon to fairly common permanent resident on Grand Bahama, Abaco and Andros. Rare to uncommon spring transient on New Providence where it formerly bred. Accidental to very rare visitor on other islands in The Bahamas or unrecorded. Not recorded from TCI.

Description: Length 5.75 ins (14.6 cm). Sleek and elegant swallow. Adult male has dark green crown, nape and back with dark green-blue wings, rump and tail. Upperparts appear black in poor light but glisten in good light. Bright white cheek and white underparts. Tail deeply forked and, on perched birds, tail feathers extend well past folded wing. Adult female similar but slightly duller. Underwing of both adults shows sharp contrast between dark flight feathers and white wing coverts, visible in flight from below. Juvenile similar to adult but has gray-brown upperparts, white underparts and less deeply forked tail; underwing coverts are duller white but still shows some contrast with dark flight feathers.

Voice: Call note a quiet cheeping *chi-cheep*.

Habits: Breeding habitat limited to pinewoods. Nests in natural cavities such as old woodpecker holes and crevices or crannies of old buildings. Forages (often quite high) over pinewoods and open areas such as fields, clearings and mangroves, sometimes garbage dumps. Often perches on dead snags and telephone wires.

Comments: Bahama Swallow in The Bahamas is an endemic species breeding only in the pinewoods of Grand Bahama, Abaco and Andros. Cuba and South Florida are the only other locations where they have been recorded. Movements and winter range of this species are not well understood. It is much harder to locate during fall and winter months than during spring and summer. Some birds appear to migrate outside the region as Bahama Swallow is a rare winter resident in eastern Cuba from January to March. Adult (mostly in spring) and juvenal (summer) birds are rare and irregular visitors to South Florida and Florida Keys.
Conservation: Population is not large overall and is considered vulnerable due to its restricted pinewoods habitat and limited nesting sites.

Similar species: See **Tree Swallow**.

Tree Swallow   *Tachycineta bicolor*

Adult (note underwing): July   Adult in flight from below

Length: 5.75 ins (14.6 cm). Uncommon transient mainly through northern Bahamas. Occurs in winter but status unclear. Rare transient in TCI. Adult metallic blue-green to green above and white below. Similar to **Bahama Swallow** but Tree Swallow has dark instead of white cheeks, dark underwings with no contrast and slightly forked tail rather than deeply forked. Juvenal Tree Swallow, in fall, is gray-brown above and white below with an indistinct brownish wash across breast. Similar to juvenal Bahama Swallow but juvenal Tree has darker cheeks, pale wash across breast and little contrast on underwing.

Cave Swallow

Petrochelidon fulva

Cave Swallow head

In flight from above

Status and range: Local summer resident on South Andros. Population is low but exact size not known. Not reported from other islands or TCI.

Description: Length: 5.5 ins (14 cm). Small swallow with squared tail. Dark blue crown with chestnut forehead, cheeks and throat. Upperparts have rufous nape or collar, dark blue back, chestnut rump and dark tail. Underparts dull white with pale rufous wash on breast and flanks.

Habits: Pursues insects over open areas such as fields and coppice. Nests on ledges and crevices in limestone caves. Nest is built of mud.

Comments: First discovered breeding on South Andros by divers exploring the caves of inland blue holes. Only found in summer, they are thought to be migratory but their origin and which subspecies they represent are unknown. Overall population is split into two regional groups: one from southwestern USA and Mexico and other from Greater Antilles in the West Indies. Cuba, Jamaica, Hispaniola and Puerto Rico each have their own subspecies but only population on Cuba considered migratory. Assumption is that Cave Swallows on South Andros are from Cuba and thus part of the West Indian population. Colony of Cave Swallows breeding in South Florida also thought to be from Cuba.

Similar species: Cliff Swallow (*Petrochelidon pyrrhonota*) Length: 5.5 ins (14 cm). Probably rare transient through the region. Recorded from only four Bahama islands (three northern and one central) and TCI. Not reported from Andros. Cliff Swallow has white forehead and dark throat whereas Cave Swallow has chestnut forehead and throat. Cliff Swallow also has paler collar and rump color and dull white underparts while Cave Swallow has darker collar and rump color and pale rufous wash on breast and flanks.

Cliff Swallow head

In flight from above

Transient Swallows

Six species of swallows are transients through the region. Tree Swallow and Cliff Swallow have already been described as similar species. The other four species are described below. Will mostly be seen in flight.

Purple Martin   *Progne subis*

Male – May

Female – May

Length: 8 ins (20 cm). Rare to uncommon transient through the region. Early transient with spring records in February and fall records in August. Adult male is large and entirely dark with light purple sheen when seen in good light. Tail relatively broad and slightly forked. Both female and juvenile dark above with gray collar, blotchy dark gray throat and breast and dingy white belly. Soars or glides more than other swallows. Usually silent in region.

Barn Swallow   *Hirundo rustica*

May

Abaco – May

Length: 6.75 ins (17 cm). Uncommon to fairly common transient through the region. Some birds linger into December in fall migration. Barn Swallow has metallic dark blue upperparts and chestnut forehead and throat. Adult male has rich orange underparts while adult female has paler underparts. Deeply forked tail with long and thin outer tail feathers; prominent feature on perched and flying birds. When spread, tail shows small white spots on outer tail feathers. Juvenile in fall similar to adult female but has shorter less forked tail. Aerobatic flight with low swoops. Common call a high *che-det*.

Northern Rough-winged Swallow   *Stelgidopteryx serripennis*

Northern Rough-winged: May

Northern Rough-winged
from below

Bank Swallow   *Riparia riparia*

Bank Swallow from below

Northern Rough-winged Swallow (Length: 5.5 ins (14 cm)) and **Bank Swallow** (Length: 5.25 ins (13.3 cm)). Both species rare to uncommon transients through the region. A few Rough-wingeds have been recorded in winter. Both have uniform brown upperparts but underparts differ. Rough-winged has light brown throat and breast with rest of underparts dingy white. Bank Swallow has white throat and underparts that contrast with well-defined brown breast band that often has small protruding brown stripe in the middle. Both have short buzzy calls.

◆ NUTHATCHES   Family: *Sittidae*

A small world-wide family. Nuthatches from North America are small birds that forage by crawling along tree trunks and large limbs sometimes headfirst down the trunk. Distinctive shape with relatively long bill and short broad tail. Long claws on feet make it well adapted for hanging onto sides of trees. Only representative of the family in the West Indies is Brown-headed Nuthatch on Grand Bahama.

Brown-headed Nuthatch   ⓔ *Sitta pusilla insularis*

Silhouette: Grand Bahama – February   March

Status and range: Permanent resident in pinewoods on Grand Bahama. Population thought to be low and estimated at between a few hundred and maybe a thousand or so birds. Not found on other islands or in TCI.

Description: Length: 4 ins (10 cm). Tiny bird with long bill relative to its size and short tail. Upperparts gray, underparts dull white. Head has brown cap bordered by dark eye-line and white cheek and throat. Pale spot on nape hard to see.

Voice: Vocal but call does not carry far. Series of high but soft single *pit* notes. In addition, researchers in 2004 noted a distinct, rapid and high-pitched 'warble' call. The nasal and squeaky calls (often referred to as the 'rubber ducky' call) given regularly by southeastern USA populations were only heard occasionally by the research team.

Habits: Restricted to pinewoods and not found in any other habitats. Very difficult to find. Forages actively by crawling and creeping along pine branches and trunks, sometimes upside down. Chips away under loose bark for food. Eats insects and seeds. Makes short undulating flights between trees. Excavates nest holes in dead trees.

Comments: Brown-headed Nuthatch in The Bahamas is recognized as an endemic subspecies *S. p. insularis*. Found only in southeastern USA where it is fairly common. Grand Bahama population is only one outside USA. In 2004, a scientific and population survey was done on Grand Bahama by a team of researchers. Their findings included a population estimation (above), a confirmation that this population should be considered vulnerable and threatened and a recommendation (based mainly on longer bill and vocalizations) that Brown-headed Nuthatch on Grand Bahama be elevated from subspecies to full species status.

◆ GNATCATCHERS

Family: *Sylviidae*

The family Sylviidae is made up of mostly Old World species. The small subfamily *Polioptilinae* is made up of mostly gnatcatchers and is restricted to the New World. Gnatcatchers are very small mostly gray birds with long thin bills and long tails. Very active while foraging in trees and bushes.

Blue-gray Gnatcatcher

Polioptila caerulea

Breeding male: Great Inagua – May

Breeding male: Grand Bahama – March

Non-breeding male or female: Grand Bahama – March

Status and range: Permanent resident with an irregular distribution in the region. Common on Grand Bahama, Abaco, Andros, Crooked and Acklins Islands, Mayaguana and Great Inagua. Uncommon on San Salvador, Long Island and Ragged Islands. Rare or unrecorded from other islands in The Bahamas. Common in TCI. Status of winter residents and transients from North America unclear due to difficulty distinguishing from resident birds.

Description: Length: 4.5 ins (11.4 cm). Tiny slim bird with bold white eye-ring, long thin bill and very long tail often cocked or flicked from side to side. Upperparts blue-gray and underparts pale gray. Central tail feathers black with bold white outer tail feathers. From above, folded tail looks black with thin white edge; from below looks mostly white. Breeding adult male has black line over lores and eye; non-breeding male and female lack black line.

Voice: Call note, often repeated, a thin and whining *spee spee*. Song a jumble of high thin warbles, whistles, chips and buzzy notes. Often soft and hard to hear.

Habits: Frequents undergrowth and brushy edges of pinewoods in northern Bahamas; dry thickets and scrub in southern part of region. Actively feeds along limbs and smaller branches of trees. Will fly out to snatch insects. Responsive to pishing.

Comments: The Howard and Moore text recognizes resident Blue-gray Gnatcatcher in the region as an endemic subspecies *P. c. caesiogaster*. Others believe it belongs to the same subspecies as is found in eastern USA *P. c. caerulea*.

◆ THRUSHES   Family: *Turdidae*

Large world-wide family well represented in the West Indies. They are medium-sized birds with an erect posture and long wings and legs. Inhabit wooded areas but often feed and nest on ground. Vocal in breeding season many having beautiful songs. In the region, Red-legged Thrush is permanent resident and is described below. Six other species are transients and are not described. Veery, Gray-cheeked Thrush, Swainson's Thrush and Wood Thrush are all transients (mainly fall) and primarily through northern Bahamas. Numbers vary from year to year. Their overall status is considered rare but if there were more observers at correct time and place during migration, then numbers would most likely increase. Hermit Thrush and American Robin are very rare winter visitors mainly to northern Bahamas.

Red-legged Thrush   ⓔ *Turdus plumbeus plumbeus*

Both Grand Bahama – October

Status and range: Permanent resident. Common on Grand Bahama, Abaco, Andros and New Providence. Uncommon on Berry Islands and Eleuthera and fairly common on Cat Island. Not found on other islands or TCI.

Description: Length: 10.5 ins (27 cm). Large all slate-gray thrush with bold bright orange-red eye-ring, dull dark red bill and orange-red legs. Black throat with small white area at base of bill. Long dark tail with large white tips to outer tail feathers which are most conspicuous when tail is spread in flight or from below.

Voice: Wide repertoire. Call note a catbird-like *mew* and harsh alarm call *wheet-wheet*. Song a series of musical whistles *cheer-up cheer-up* with pauses, low *chips* or *swink* notes in between. Variations include buzzier notes or short trills. Volume of song may be loud or soft. During breeding season, sings from high perch, often before dawn and well into evening. Some singing birds may be difficult to locate.

Habits: Frequents pinewoods, coppice, dense undergrowth and developed areas with ornamental trees and palms. Often seen in gardens and on lawns (where available). Forages mainly on ground for insects, berries and fruit. Often heard scratching through leaf litter in dense habitats. Fairly shy during non-breeding season. Responds to pishing.

Comments: Entire range restricted to the West Indies – mainly in The Bahamas and the large islands of the Greater Antilles. Red-legged Thrush in The Bahamas is recognized as an endemic subspecies *T. p. plumbeus*.

◆ MOCKINGBIRDS AND THRASHERS   Family: *Mimidae*

Small, New World family of birds, many of which have an ability to imitate or mimic other birds' songs. They have fairly long bills and long tails. Plumage is not very colorful. Active and inquisitive birds and sometimes aggressively territorial. Forage mostly on or near ground.

Northern Mockingbird   *Mimus polyglottos*

Grand Bahama – September   Worn plumage: Grand Turk – June

Status and range: Locally common permanent resident in developed areas throughout The Bahamas. Less common on undeveloped islands. Common permanent resident in TCI.

Description: Length: 10 ins (25 cm). Slender long-tailed bird with gray upperparts and white to pale gray underparts. Wings dark with two white wing-bars and large white patch at base of primaries; most visible when wing is spread. Central tail feathers black with bold white outer tail feathers most conspicuous when tail spread. Folded tail, black with white edges when seen from above; white from below. Juvenile similar to adult but has light streaks or spots on breast. In flight, all birds show flashes of white on wings and tail.

Voice: Noisy and vocal. Call note a sharp *check*. Scold note a throaty growling *shkeee*. Song a variety of extended whistled phrases repeated two or three times. Will mimic other birds' songs but quickly returns to its own repertoire. Sings at any time of year and, in breeding season, male may sing all day and sometimes at night. Begging juvenile makes high incessant *szeep szeep* around adults.

Habits: Prefers vegetation and trees around settlements, farms, gardens and other developed areas. Forages both on ground and in trees for insects, seeds and berries. While foraging on ground, sometimes raises wings, apparently to frighten bugs out of hiding. Aggressive when defending breeding and feeding territories. Often cocks tail.

Similar species: See **Bahama Mockingbird**.

Comments: Northern Mockingbird in northern Bahamas is thought to be *M. p. polyglottos*, same subspecies found in southeastern USA. Northern Mockingbird in southern Bahamas and TCI is Greater Antillean subspecies *M. p. orpheus*. Where these two subspecies occur, or overlap, in central Bahamas or elsewhere is unknown.

Bahama Mockingbird · *Mimus gundlachii*

North Andros – May

Worn plumage: Exumas – June

Status and range: Permanent resident throughout the region. Fairly common in northern Bahamas except rare on Bimini and uncommon on Grand Bahama and New Providence. Common in central and southern Bahamas and in TCI.

Description: Length: 11 ins (28 cm). Large long-tailed mockingbird with gray-brown upperparts, inconspicuous, thin, white wing-bars and pale gray to dingy white underparts. In breeding season, adult has white throat with dark 'whisker' mark, breast lightly streaked, flanks and undertail coverts broadly streaked and nape and back lightly streaked. Long tail gray-brown with white tips to outer tail feathers, visible when tail is spread or from below if tail is folded. After breeding season, when feathers become worn and faded, birds show almost no 'whisker' mark and reduced streaking on underparts.

Voice: Call note a sharp *check*, very similar to Northern Mockingbird but slightly harsher. Typical song a series of loud and slightly hoarse phrases *jer-key jer-key jer-key jup jup jup*, with several variations. More abrupt and not as varied or musical as Northern Mockingbird. Does not mimic other birds. At times, jumps in air while singing and returns to same perch.

Habits: Prefers natural habitats along edges and open areas of pinewoods in northern Bahamas and coppice, low bushy scrub and dry woodlands in southern part of range. In some areas, likes to perch or sing from telephone wires and poles. Feeds on insects, berries and, occasionally, on small lizards. Conspicuous when singing and defending territory during breeding season but shy and retiring at other times. Responds to pishing but is often cautious and stays in cover.

Similar species: Northern Mockingbird is smaller and grayer with no streaking above or below. Northern also has white patches on wing and bold white outer tail feathers both traits conspicuous in flight. Bahama Mockingbird lacks these white flashes. Northern is found more often around human settlements and environments, Bahama preferring more natural habitats.

Comments: Found only in the West Indies with an interesting and irregular distribution. Range outside The Bahamas and TCI restricted to a few cays off northern Cuba (not main island) and part of south-central Jamaica. Also rare and irregular visitor to South Florida. Bahama Mockingbird in the region and off Cuba is subspecies *M. g. gundlachii*.

Pearly-eyed Thrasher   *Margarops fuscatus*

Little Inagua – May

Status and range: Fairly common permanent resident on San Salvador, Crooked and Acklins Islands and on both Great and I ittle Inagua. Rare visitor, or unrecorded, from other Bahama islands. In TCI, uncommon permanent resident on Caicos Islands and uncommon visitor to Turks Islands.

Description: Length: 11.5 ins (29 cm). Heavy pale-colored bill and pale yellow (pearly) eye are distinctive. Dark brown upperparts and white underparts with heavy brown streaks on throat and breast becoming 'V'-shaped markings on belly and lower flanks. Long dark brown tail with white tips on outer tail feathers most visible when tail is spread in flight.

Voice: Harsh call note *chook*. Song a series of brief and throaty musical two and three-note phrases with relatively long pauses in between *chur*, *tsee-up*, *see*.

Habits: Found in thick dry scrub or coppice. Usually skulking and secretive but sometimes curious. Feeds on insects, fruit, seeds and small lizards. Known also to prey on eggs and nestlings. Builds nest in cavities or in bushes.

Similar species: Bahama Mockingbird is similar in size, body and tail shape but is grayer overall with a darker eye and bill and fewer streaks to underparts.

Comments: Appears partial to smaller islands with an irregular distribution In the West Indies. Range outside The Bahamas and TCI includes Puerto Rico, northern part of Lesser Antilles and a few islands off Venezuela.

Gray Catbird   *Dumetella carolinensis*

Caymans – March   Grand Bahama – April

Length: 8.5 ins (22 cm). Fairly common winter resident and transient throughout the region. Slender entirely dark gray bird with black cap and tail (sometimes cocked). Rusty undertail coverts. Eyes, bill and legs black. All plumages similar. Several call notes: cat-like harsh *mew*, soft throaty *kwirt*, nasal whiny *whaa* and a number of sharp staccato notes similar to coughing. On occasion, may be heard singing softly and heard only from a short distance referred to as a 'whisper song'. Song includes varied mixture of whistled and squeaky phrases given in series. Fairly shy preferring to stay hidden in all kinds of thick cover, but responds to pishing. Partial to berries.

Grand Bahama: December

STARLINGS   **Family:** *Sturnidae*

Large Old World family of stocky birds with strong bills and squared tails. Social and typically dark with glossy plumage. Many are quite colorful. European Starling has been introduced successfully to North America.

European Starling   *Sturnus vulgaris*

Breeding: May   Non-breeding: December

Status and range: Uncommon to fairly common on Grand Bahama and Bimini. Rare to uncommon elsewhere in northern and central Bahamas. Not recorded in southern Bahamas. Accidental on Grand Turk in TCI. Most starlings in the region are probably winter residents or transients though a few are permanent residents.

Description: Length: 8.5 ins (21.5 cm). Compact black bird with long bill and short tail. Breeding adult has glossy all black plumage with purple sheen on head and neck, spotting on back and conspicuous yellow bill. Legs long and pink. Non-breeding adult has dark bill and heavy spotting above and below. Juvenile gray-brown overall with dark bill and pale throat. In flight, all starlings fly fast and direct with pointed wings.

Voice: Call notes include a sharp *chink* and a chatter. Song a variety of high-pitched whistles, raspy squeaks and warbles. Especially noisy in flocks or going to roost.

Habits: Adaptable and tough, prefers human-altered habitats like towns, settlements, farms, garbage dumps, etc. Usually forages on ground by probing but also takes berries on trees and shrubs. Forms flocks with other starlings and blackbirds during non-breeding season especially at evening roost sites. Likes to sit on telephone wires. Nests in natural cavities or holes in buildings and aggressively competes for them.

Comments: Introduced from Europe to northeastern USA in 1890 and now widespread and abundant throughout North America. Considered a pest and an unwelcome introduction. Competes with other North American cavity nesters for holes and has had a significantly negative impact. First recorded in The Bahamas in 1956 and has had some impact on cavity nesters but to what extent is unknown.

Family: *Motacillidae*

Pipits belong to a small world-wide family of slender birds with thin bills and long tails. They have long legs, feet and toes. Almost always forage on ground in open areas where they walk rather than hop. Three species of pipits breed in North America with American Pipit being the most common and widespread.

American Pipit *Anthus rubescens*

February   March

Length: 6.5 ins (17 cm). Rare to uncommon winter visitor mainly in northern Bahamas. Unrecorded from southern Bahamas and TCI. Numbers vary from year to year. Drab-looking bird with slender bill and body and long tail. Non-breeding plumage has brownish to brownish-gray upperparts and whitish to buffy underparts. Breast and flank streaks vary from light to bold. Head has pale supercilium and eye-ring. Bill mostly dark sometimes pale; dark legs. White on outer tail feathers seen mainly on take-off or landing when tail is spread. Call note, especially in flight or when alarmed on take-off, is high and thin but also a sharp and squeaky *speet* or rapid two-note *speet-tit*; sometimes notes run together. Forages on ground in open areas with little vegetation sometimes near water or puddles. Also golf courses, short grassy areas, livestock farms or garbage dumps. Active and often skittish. Walks rather than hops moving its head back and forth and pumps tail. Formerly called 'Water Pipit'.

WAXWINGS   Family: *Bombycillidae*

Very small family of just three species which are found in North America, Europe and Asia. Sleek birds with short wide bills and prominent crests. Plumage is soft gray and brown with localised areas in wing and tail of red, white and yellow. Vocal and gregarious they are nomadic in non-breeding season searching for berries and fruit, their primary food. The name waxwing refers to the bright red wax-like tips to the secondary feathers. Two species of waxwings breed in North America but only Cedar Waxwing occurs in the region.

Cedar Waxwing   *Bombycilla cedrorum*

Both March

Length: 7.25 ins (18 cm). Rare visitor to northern Bahamas and TCI. Unrecorded from most of central and southern Bahamas. Unpredictable and numbers vary from year to year. Adult has warm brown, crested head with black mask and short black bill. Rest of upperparts brownish-gray; underparts have yellow wash to belly and whitish under-tail coverts. Bright red tips to secondary feathers (sometimes indistinct or absent) and yellow band on tip of tail. Juvenile in fall similar to adult but grayer overall with diffuse streaks on underparts. In flight, fairly distinct shape with short bill, pointed wings and short squared tail. Flight and wing-beats are quick. Quite vocal (but not loud) in flight or perched. Call a high thin *seeee seeee* some notes with slight trill. Usually travels in small groups (occasionally one or two birds) searching for berry-producing trees or shrubs where they congregate until food is gone and then move on to look elsewhere. When not feeding, seem to prefer sitting on highest perches.

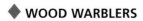

◆ WOOD WARBLERS   Family: *Parulidae*

Large family found only in the New World and popular with birders. Small birds with short thin bills and slender bodies. In many species, adult males can be exceptionally color-ful, especially when compared to females and immatures. Known for quick movements while foraging for insects and larvae which they glean or pick from leaves or branches. They also take small berries and fruits when the opportunity arises and a few species take nectar. Some species feed at medium to high levels in trees and shrubs while oth-ers prefer to feed near or on the ground. In The Bahamas and TCI, warblers use all types of wooded habitats, including tall mangrove stands and gardens with ornamental trees and plants. During migration, or in the winter months, they often form loose mixed-species flocks as they move from one area to another looking for food. Warblers are not known for musical songs as they usually give only simple trills, buzzy notes or high whis-tled notes. Except for resident birds, winter resident and transient warblers rarely sing and, if they do, it is only a partial song. They do, however, give a single call note called a '*chip*' note, which, in some species, can be learned fairly easily, but in others, with dif-ficulty or only with much practice and experience. Despite their size, most warblers migrate long distances between their breeding ranges in North America and their win-tering ranges in Middle America, northern South America and the West Indies. Migration patterns follow those outlined in the Introduction to this book. There are many more war-blers and species (especially immatures) in fall than in spring.

Identification of warblers is mostly straightforward but, at times, can be challenging. Many species have similar plumages with perhaps only slight variations, regardless of age, sex or season. The difficulty arises when males and females of one species, or the sea-sonal adult and immature plumages do not look alike. As an aid to identification, it is impor-tant to have some knowledge of the different plumages and when they occur. This information applies to the migrant warblers of the region. Although the plumage sequences are the same for the resident warblers, they are on a different and/or earlier breeding schedule. Adult male and female warblers have an annual breeding and non-breeding plumage. Most, if not all of the breeding plumage is attained by the time birds start their spring migration and leave the area or pass through from other areas (March–May). Many males, Northern Parula for instance, are at their most colorful at this time. When adults migrate back to, or through, the region in fall (August–October), they will be in non-breed-ing plumage, which they keep until the following spring, when the process begins again. For many species, all these adult plumages are very similar, such as that of Ovenbird and Northern Waterthrush, while for others, Blackpoll and Magnolia Warbler, there are sea-sonal differences. The immatures (warblers have a brief juvenal plumage before they molt to immature plumage) of both male and female birds arrive in the region in fall (September– November). They are in their first-winter plumage, which will be referred to as just the immature or immature male or female. Most of these immature plumages are similar to the non-breeding adults, but the immature female often has the dullest plumage of all, especially within those species that have seasonal variations. It is very difficult to age and sex every individual warbler, so, rather than detail all the plumages, the species accounts concentrate on field marks that identify the species of warbler and discuss briefly only those plumages that may be distinguishable in the field. In the same vein, it is not practical to have photographs of all the various plumages, or to age and sex them all cor-rectly, so, in those cases the photographs are captioned in general, rather than specific terms. This applies to resident species as well.

The species accounts begin with the five warblers (two species and three sub-species) that are permanent residents in the region and end with the 22 species accounts of winter residents and transients. North American Yellow-throated Warbler is included with resident subspecies account.

Yellow Warbler
Dendroica petechia

Breeding male: Little Inagua – May

San Salvador – June

Immature: Grand Bahama – October

Status and range: Resident subspecies is permanent resident. Uncommon in northern Bahamas and fairly common to common in central and southern Bahamas and TCI. Status of migrants from North America unclear, due to difficulty distinguishing them from resident subspecies and the relatively few records available outside habitat of resident subspecies.

Description: Length: 4.75 ins (12 cm). Breeding adult male yellow overall with olive-green tone to upperparts and bright yellow underparts with red streaks on breast and flanks. Breeding female similar but streaks may be missing or slight. Both sexes have prominent dark eye, yellow eye-ring and yellow patches or spots on outer tail feathers. Only warbler with yellow patches on tail. Non-breeding plumage similar but only slightly duller. Immature much duller with varying amounts of gray about head and white eye-ring. Female immature paler below and grayer overall.

Voice: Quite vocal. Call note a loud liquid *chip* often repeated when alarmed. Song a series of *sweet sweet sweet* notes, or a series of *sweet* notes with quick and slightly accented ending or chatter-like ending.

Habits: Preferred habitat is mangrove and buttonwood swamps but also inhabits dry coastal scrub on some islands. Defends feeding territory in winter as well as in summer. Responds actively to pishing.

Comments: Yellow Warbler is widely distributed throughout North, Middle and South America and the West Indies with numerous subspecies. These subspecies are divided into three recognized groups, one each from North America, South America and the West Indies. Birds in the West Indies belong to the 'Golden Warbler' or *petechia* group. Within this group, resident Yellow Warbler in the region is recognized as an endemic subspecies *D. p. flaviceps*. A different subspecies (Cuba) is resident in South Florida and Florida Keys.

Yellow-throated Warbler (e) *Dendroica dominica flavescens*

Male: Grand Bahama – October

Female: Abaco – May

Grand Bahama – February

Status and range: Resident subspecies uncommon to fairly common permanent resident in pinewoods on Grand Bahama and Abaco. Not found on other islands or TCI.

Description: Length: 5 ins (13 cm). Adult male has well-marked black and white facial pattern with long slightly decurved bill (longer on some birds on Abaco). Thin white supercilium with yellow on front part (above lores) and black cheek, bordered by small white patch on sides of neck. Bright yellow throat and breast; yellow wash on belly blending into whitish vent and undertail coverts. Yellow extends into broad black streaks along sides of breast and flanks. Upperparts gray with dark wing and two white wing-bars, upper wing-bar more prominent than lower. Adult female similar to male but has duller yellow on breast and yellow wash on belly. Immature poorly known. Appears similar to adult female but with buffy wash on flanks. This feature, however, may appear on other plumages as well.

Voice: Call note a sharp rich *chip*. Song a series of clear, sweet, whistled notes *sweer sweer sweer sweer* which either just ends or has slight accented ending *swee-up* or a few more notes lower than first part *see see see*.

Habits: Resident subspecies restricted to pinewoods and not found in other habitats. Forages along higher branches and among pine needles like other warblers. In addition, creeps up and down trunks of pine trees, probing under bark for insects with long bill which is well adapted for this behavior. Behavior appears to occur mostly on lower portion of trunk nearer ground. Occasionally seen in understorey in shrubs. Pine and Olive-capped Warblers sometimes feed along trunks but not as extensively as Yellow-throated. Black and White Warbler also feeds along trunks or over and under branches.

Comments: Resident Yellow-throated Warbler in northern Bahamas recognized as an endemic subspecies *D. d. flavescens*. Many authorities believe that it differs enough in appearance, behavior and song from North American Yellow-throated Warbler to be classified as a separate species.

Similar species: Quite similar to North American subspecies of **Yellow-throated Warbler** which is fairly common winter resident on Grand Bahama and Abaco and does occupy pinewoods as well as other habitats. North American bird has shorter bill, broader supercilium and larger white patch behind black cheek. Yellow coloring confined to throat and upper breast and sharply contrasts with white belly. Yellow does not extend into streaks at sides of breast.

Yellow-throated Warbler *Dendroica dominica dominica*

North Andros – November   New Providence – January

Length: 5.5 ins (14 cm). Fairly common to common winter resident and transient in northern and central Bahamas. Uncommon in southern Bahamas and TCI. All seasonal plumages similar. Well-marked black and white facial pattern. Broad white supercilium has yellow spot in front part above lores (sometimes barely visible) and black cheek bordered by white patch on sides of neck. Bright yellow throat and upper breast; rest of underparts white with broad black streaks along sides of breast and flanks. Yellow color does not extend into streaking and contrasts sharply with white underparts. Upperparts gray with dark wing and two white wing-bars. Call note a loud sweet *chip*. Will feed high or low in palm trees, gardens, coppice and pinewoods. North American subspecies in region is *D. d dominica*.

Olive-capped Warbler   *Dendroica pityophila*

Worn adult: Abaco – mid-May

Adult male: Grand Bahama – January   Grand Bahama – October

Status and range: Common permanent resident in pinewoods on Grand Bahama and Abaco. Not found on other islands or TCI.

Description: Length: 5 ins (13 cm). Adult male has bright yellow throat and upper breast bordered by thick or blotchy black streaks; rest of underparts dingy white. Forehead and forecrown olive-yellow; rear of crown, sides of head and upperparts soft gray. Wings slightly darker with indistinct pale gray wing-bars. Adult female similar but has duller forecrown, throat and breast; black breast streaks also duller. Immature plumages poorly known but appear to be duller in these areas than that of adult female.

Voice: Call note a high thin *tsit* or *seep* given in a series when agitated. *Seep* note sounds like flight call note of other warblers. Song a series of high, quick, whistled notes *swee swee swee swee* followed immediately by rapid *chu chu chu chu*. Fast and 'choppy' song when compared to resident subspecies of Yellow-throated Warbler.

Habits: Restricted to pinewoods and not found in other habitats. Usually forages and nests in highest parts of pine trees, infrequently seen lower. Visits century plant flowers when in bloom. Responsive to pishing.

Comments: Found only in the West Indies where entire range restricted to Grand Bahama and Abaco in northern Bahamas and extreme western and eastern ends of Cuba. Bahama birds thought to be an endemic subspecies although no subspecies is currently recognized.

Pine Warbler   (e) *Dendroica pinus achrustera*

Male: North Andros – May

Female or immature male: North Andros – May

Immature female: Grand Bahama – October

Status and range: Resident subspecies is fairly common to common permanent resident in pinewoods on Grand Bahama, Abaco, North Andros and New Providence.

Description: Length: 5.5 ins (14 cm). Large warbler with relatively heavy bill. Adult male has bold yellow eye-crescents and dark lores with yellow line above. Yellow throat, breast and pale yellow belly with rest of underparts dingy white with variable dark streaking along sides of breast. Unstreaked olive upperparts and darker wing with two prominent white wing-bars. Adult female and immature male similar to adult male but slightly browner above and have duller less extensive yellow below with indistinct streaking. Immature female is drab brown overall with pale eye crescents and very pale yellow wash on breast.

Voice: Call note a sharp rich *chip*. Song is simple musical trill, usually given on one pitch. Most often, trill is given rapidly but at other times more slowly. Often sings in non-breeding season.

Habits: Resident subspecies restricted to pinewoods and not found in other habitats. Relatively sluggish feeding behavior for a warbler. Usually forages along upper branches among pine needles but occasionally feeds on trunk and in understorey nearer ground. Often found in family groups shortly after breeding season. Responds to pishing.

Comments: Resident Pine Warbler in northern Bahamas recognized as an endemic subspecies *D. p. achrustera*. Status of migrants from North America unclear because these birds cannot be distinguished from resident subspecies. Furthermore, there are very few records for Pine Warbler in The Bahamas outside range of resident subspecies.

Bahama Yellowthroat   Ⓔ *Geothlypis rostrata*

Adult male

Adult female

Adult male

Possible immature female

All photos from Abaco – January–February

Status and range: Permanent resident in northern Bahamas and Cat Island. Fairly common on Grand Bahama, Abaco and Andros. Rare to uncommon on Eleuthera and uncommon on Cat Island. Rare and threatened on New Providence. Not found on other islands or in TCI.

Description: Length: 5.5 ins (14 cm). Adult male has uniform olive-green upperparts and bright yellow throat and breast with slightly paler yellow belly and yellow under-tail coverts. Sides of breast and flanks gray-olive. Prominent black mask with narrow light-gray or yellowish border along upper edge. Bill relatively long and thick and is black in breeding season but paler on lower mandible at other times. Breeding female head lacks mask but lores and cheek are dusky with incomplete eye-ring and suggestion of pale supercilium. Forehead and forecrown sometimes washed with red-brown. Upperparts and underparts similar to male but sides of breast and flanks washed olive-brown. Non-breeding adults similar to breeding adults but sides of breast and flanks browner and more extensive, obscuring some of belly color.

Immatures not well known but appear similar to adults except immature female which is duller and browner and with paler, less yellow underparts.

Voice: Call note a sharp *tuck* or *chimp*. Also gives chatter-like call. Song is clear and whistled and translates to a slow *wi-chi-ty wi-chi-ty wi-chi-ty*.

Habits: Usually found at low levels. Feeds and moves in deliberate fashion, staying concealed in cover. On islands with pine trees prefers pinewood undergrowth or small mixed coppice areas within pinewoods. Occasionally seen in extensive brushy areas outside pinewoods but still nearby. On other islands, found in low coppice or brushy thickets. Can be difficult to find.

Similar species: Common Yellowthroat (see species account) is common winter resident and transient on those islands inhabited by Bahama Yellowthroat. Common Yellowthroat is smaller, has a shorter and slimmer bill and male has less extensive yellow on underparts, especially belly. Females are more difficult to differentiate except by size, bill structure and more extensive yellow on underparts. Common Yellowthroat's call note has husky sch sound to it which is different than drier call note of Bahama Yellowthroat. Common Yellowthroat is found in same habitats as Bahama Yellowthroat but Bahama Yellowthroat is not found in typical Common Yellowthroat habitats – such as marshes with reeds, thick grassy fields and ornamental plantings.

Comments: Found only in the West Indies and entire range of Bahama Yellowthroat restricted to those islands of The Bahamas listed above. An endemic species with three recognized subspecies: *G. r. tanneri* on Grand Bahama and Abaco, *G. r. rostrata* on Andros and New Providence and *G. r. coryi* on Eleuthera and Cat Island. Some authorities believe yellowthroats on Andros constitute another endemic subspecies *G. r. exigua*. All adult male subspecies differ subtly in forecrown and upperpart coloring, making them difficult to distinguish in the field. However, adult male *G. r. coryi* is suffused with brighter yellow than any of the other subspecies. Female subspecies not distinguishable in the field. **Conservation:** *G. r. rostrata* on New Providence is severely threatened by habitat destruction from development and its future there is doubtful.

Winter Resident and Transient Warblers

Warblers represent a large number of the land birds that migrate from North America to the region. In any given year probably 25–30 warbler species either spend the non-breeding season (August–May) in the region or pass through and continue their migration. The 22 species described below are the most likely to be seen year in and year out. Yellow-throated Warbler has already been described (page 179). Kirtland's Warbler is only rarely seen but since the region is its only known wintering area, it is also described. An additional six species of warblers are mentioned but not described: Blue-winged, Nashville, Chestnut-sided, Blackburnian, Bay-breasted and Wilson's Warbler. Although their numbers vary from year to year, these six species are transients that occur, primarily, during fall rather than spring. Their overall status is considered rare but if there were more observers at the correct time and place, then the numbers would likely increase. Blue-winged, Nashville and Wilson's Warblers are all occasional winter residents but in small numbers.

Tennessee Warbler   *Vermivora peregrina*

Male breeding– May

Immature – November

Immature – October

Length: 4.75 ins (12 cm). Rare to uncommon transient (mainly fall) in northern Bahamas. Rare or mostly unrecorded from rest of region. All seasonal plumages similar except for adult male in spring. All plumages have thin pointed bill, narrow pale supercilium, dark eye-line, dark green to olive-green back and white to whitish undertail coverts. Underparts vary from whitish with tinge of yellow wash to face and breast to entirely yellow (especially immatures). Breeding male in spring has blue-gray crown which contrasts with green back and white underparts. Found in any wooded habitat. Partial to fruit and/or nectar sources. Call note a thin high *tseet*, often repeated and given perched or in flight.

Similar species: Orange-crowned Warbler (*Vermivora celata*) Length: 4.75 ins (12 cm). Rare winter resident (most likely November to March) and transient in northern Bahamas. All plumages with olive-green upperparts and dull yellow underparts; grayish cast to head and neck on some birds in winter. Similar to Tennessee Warbler (except breeding male) but Orange-crowneds have thin yellow or whitish eye-crescents, faint streaks on breast and yellow undertail coverts. Call note a clear sharp *sick*. Subspecies in region is *V. c. celata*.

Orange-crowned:
January

Northern Parula   *Parula americana*

Female: New Providence – May

Immature female: Grand Bahama – December

Male: March

Length: 4.25 ins (11 cm). Common winter resident and transient throughout region. Shows some variation among seasonal plumages. Small compact warbler with thin bill (yellow lower mandible) and short tail. All plumages have white eye-crescents and white wing-bars, blue to blue-gray upperparts with olive-green patch on back and bright yellow throat and breast; rest of underparts white. Breeding adult male has black lores and conspicuous chestnut band on breast sometimes bordered above in black. All other parula plumages lack black lores and have less conspicuous or just tinge of chestnut breast band. However, immature female has greenish wash to upperparts and plain yellow breast. Call note a strong *chip*. Cocks tail occasionally. Prefers secondary growth, coppice and ornamental plantings. Able to forage at tips of plants and branches.

Magnolia Warbler
Dendroica magnolia

Male breeding: May

Possible female: May

Both New Providence – November

Length: 4.75 ins (12 cm). Rare to uncommon winter resident and transient throughout the region. Shows variation among seasonal plumages. All plumages have bright yellow underparts with white vent and undertail coverts, variable breast and flank streaks, yellow rump patch and distinctive white band across dark outer tail feathers (white band visible from below or when tail is spread). Plumage of breeding adult has white supercilium that separates gray crown from black (male) or dull black (female) cheeks, breast and flank streaks (stronger on male) and white patches on wing. Non-breeding adult and immature in fall are different with mostly gray head, distinctive white eye-ring and some side and flank streaks. Immature female has indistinct flank streaks and light gray band below throat. Call note a nasal and squeaky *chewf* unlike chips of other warblers. Feeds actively often in lower parts of habitat.

Cape May Warbler   *Dendroica tigrina*

Breeding male: New Providence –
March

Dull female: Caymans – October

Immature male: Abaco – October

Immature female: New Providence –
November

Length: 4.75 ins (12 cm). Fairly common to common winter resident and transient throughout the region. Numbers vary from year to year. Shows variation among seasonal plumages. Small short-tailed warbler with thin dark bill. All plumages have thin streaks on underparts, yellowish rumps and green edges to primary feathers. Breeding adult male has chestnut cheek, bright yellow patch on sides of neck and white patch on wing. Rump yellow and underparts bright yellow with thin dark streaks on breast. Breeding female similar to male but lacks chestnut cheek and has duller yellow neck patch. Also duller and less extensive yellow underparts with thin wing-bars instead of white patch. Other Cape May plumages are similar to adult female. Significantly different is immature female which is dull gray overall with indistinct streaking below, yellow-green rump and greenish edges to primary feathers; may have trace of yellow on sides of neck. Call note a high thin *seet* sometimes repeated. Feeds on nectar and fruit sources more than other warblers. Congregate at flowering shrubs and trees where they aggressively protect feeding territory chasing other birds away, especially other Cape Mays.

Black-throated Blue Warbler　　　*Dendroica caerulescens*

Male: New Providence – May　　　Female: New Providence – October

Length: 5 ins (13 cm). Fairly common winter resident and transient throughout the region. All males similar in plumage: deep blue upperparts with small white patch on wing at base of primaries; face, throat, sides of breast and flanks black, rest of underparts white. Female very different: uniform olive-brown above and buff-colored below; white patch on wing smaller than male's; pale thin supercilium over slightly darker cheek and white crescent below eye. Immature female often lacks white wing patch. Call note a distinctive dry *tick*. Primarily feeds in wooded areas, brushy undergrowth, mangroves and gardens.

Black-throated Green Warbler　　　*Dendroica virens*

Breeding male: April　　　Female – spring

Length: 4.75 ins (12 cm). Rare to uncommon winter resident and transient throughout the region. Plumages show some variation in color of throat and breast. Breeding adult male has olive-green upperparts, dark wing with bold white wing-bars and several white outer tail feathers. Face yellow with pale green cheeks. Throat and breast black extending to bold streaks along sides of breast and flanks. Rest of underparts whitish with yellow wash on vent and white undertail coverts. Non-breeding male similar. Adult female similar to adult male but black throat missing or very limited; breast mottled with black. Immature female lacks black throat and breast and has light streaking on sides of breast and flanks. Call note a short *chit*. Uses coppice, thickets and secondary growth.

Yellow-rumped Warbler   *Dendroica coronata*

In transition to breeding: April

Immature: Abaco – February

Immature: New Providence – January

Particularly dark and dull immature: Grand Bahama – December

Length: 5.25 ins (13 cm). Uncommon to fairly common winter resident and transient throughout the region. Numbers vary from year to year. Shows variation between seasonal plumages. In fall and winter, all plumages generally have brown upperparts, pale thin superciliums, brown cheek patches and bold white eye-crescents. Throat and breast light buff with variable streaking on breast and flanks. Yellow patch along sides of breast; bright yellow rump best seen in flight. Exceptions include yellow crown patch on both adult male and female and obscure or absent yellow side patch on immature female. In late winter, all adults start molt to breeding plumage – yellow crown more conspicuous, cheeks blacker, upperparts grayer with black streaking and underparts whiter. Call note a loud dry *check* which it gives often. Resilient species found in variety of habitats and using various feeding methods. Sometimes found in single-species flocks. Responsive to pishing. Yellow-rumped Warbler in the region belongs to subspecies *D. c. coronata*. At one time called Myrtle Warbler.

Kirtland's Warbler   *Dendroica kirtlandii*

Breeding male: Eleuthera – March   Immature female: Michigan – September

Length: 5.5 ins (14 cm). Very rare to rare winter resident throughout the region. In TCI, recorded only from North and South Caicos and Grand Turk. Plumages show some seasonal variation. Large warbler with heavy bill and long tail that it pumps up and down, sometimes constantly. Narrow white eye-crescents more prominent in adults and less conspicuous in immatures. Dark streaks on back and along sides of breast and flanks, bolder on adults. Inconspicuous wing-bars and yellow underparts with white undertail coverts. Non-breeding adults and immatures have slightly browner upperparts and duller underparts. Immature female has brownest head and back and thinnest streaks along sides and flanks. Eye-crescents can appear more like thin dull eye-ring. By April, adult males should show full or nearly full breeding plumage – black in lores and face and more blue-gray upperparts. Call note a strong *tchit*. Usually stays low and hidden in high or low coppice, scrublands and pinewoods undergrowth. Usually solitary with slow movements.

Kirtland's Warbler is an endangered species with an approximate population of 2,500 to 3,000 birds. Breeds in selective habitats in northern Michigan (USA) and is known to winter only in The Bahamas and TCI. Birders expecting to see Kirtland's Warbler must remember that it is rare, scattered over many islands and there is not much chance of finding it.

Similar species: Several other species in the region have been misidentified as Kirtland's Warbler. **Prairie Warbler** and **Palm Warbler** also pump their tails but have different facial patterns and are not as secretive. The Bahama subspecies of **Yellow-throated Warbler** has different facial pattern and bill size; feeds along pine trunks and canopy (rarely in understorey) and does not pump tail. Non-breeding adult or immature **Magnolia Warbler** similar but smaller, has bolder wing-bars, yellow rump and different tail pattern. Does not pump tail and is not as secretive. An immature **Pine Warbler** or dull adult is same size with heavy bill but lacks back streaks and has broader wing-bars. Also does not pump tail and only occasionally feeds in pinewoods undergrowth.

Prairie Warbler   *Dendroica discolor*

Immature male: New Providence –
January

Immature: Grand Bahama – October

Male. New Providence – March

Length: 4.5 ins (11.5 cm). Common winter resident and transient throughout the region. Plumages show some seasonal variation. Pumps tail regularly but not as often as Palm Warbler. All plumages have olive green upperparts and yellow underparts with streaks or lines of spots along sides of breast and flanks. Distinctive facial pattern. Breeding adult of both sexes has short yellow supercilium, dark eye line, yellow crescent under eye bordered below by dark stripe that curls down from lores. This stripe is black in adult male and olive green in adult female. Non-breeding adults very similar. Immature of both sexes similar but has duller facial pattern and narrow whitish eye-crescents. In addition, immature female has grayer wash on head and indistinct streaking on sides and flanks. Call note a sharp *tchit*. Prefers secondary growth, overgrown fields, and wooded edges. Forages close to ground or high up in trecs. Responsive to pishing.

Palm Warbler   *Dendroica palmarum*

Mostly breeding: Grand Bahama –
March

Non-breeding: Grand Bahama –
November

Length: 5 ins (12.7 cm). Common winter resident and transient throughout the region. At times, abundant in fall. Some variation between breeding and non-breeding plumages. Pumps tail up and down more than any other warbler. In fall and winter, non-breeding adult and immature have brown crown with pale supercilium over dark eye-line. Upperparts dull brown with pale yellowish-green rump. Underparts pale with thin brown streaks on breast and flanks; yellow undertail coverts. White tips on dark outer tail feathers appear as corners on spread tail. Adult begins molt to breeding plumage in February. Gradually crown turns chestnut, supercilium and throat become yellow and breast and belly have pale yellow wash. Call note a sharp *chick* similar to Prairie Warbler. Also gives a *seep* note in flight. Often forages on ground in a variety of open areas including settlements. Also forages in pinewoods and garbage dumps. Responsive to pishing. Subspecies in region is *D. p. palmarum* referred to as 'Western Palm Warbler'.

Black-and-white Warbler   *Mniotilta varia*

Male molting to breeding plumage:
Grand Bahama – March

Female or immature male: Grand
Bahama – November

Length: 5 ins (12.7 cm). Common winter resident and transient throughout the region. All plumages are black and white with subtle differences. Bill long and thin, bold white wing-bars and dark spots on white undertail coverts. Breeding adult male has black cheek and throat; non-breeding male just black cheek. Adult female and immatures have black eye-line behind eye and pale to dusky cheek with white throat; flanks with various amounts of buff. Dull chip note not often heard but when agitated has quick and loud *chirp-chirp chirp*. Foraging technique unusual for warbler, creeps up and down tree trunks and along large limbs (both top and bottom) probing under pieces of bark for insects. Responsive to pishing.

Blackpoll Warbler

Dendroica striata

Adult male: May

Adult female: – May

Immature: both New Providence – November

Length: 5.25 ins (13.3 cm). Uncommon spring (April–May) and fall (September–November) transient through the region. Generally more common in spring in northern Bahamas and more common in fall in southern Bahamas and TCI. Long distance migrant that breeds in northern regions of North America and winters in South America. Shows variation in seasonal plumages. Breeding adult male has black cap, white face and strong black 'whisker' mark. Back is gray and streaked, bold white wing-bars and legs and feet pale yellowish. Underparts white with dark streaks on sides of breast and flanks. Breeding adult female has upperparts that vary from olive-green to gray-green with bold dark streaks on back and fine streaks on crown. Underparts white with light streaks along sides of breast and flanks. Bold wing-bars and pale-colored legs and feet like those of male. In fall, plumage of both adults and immatures is similar. Dominant feature to head and most of underparts is dull to bright greenish-yellow color. Olive upperparts (streaks on back) and bold wing-bars. Legs usually dark and feet usually pale in color (some birds have orange-yellow legs and feet). Also show narrow supercilium, dark eye-line and light to moderate streaking on underparts with white vent and undertail coverts. *Zeet* call note given in flight.

American Redstart

Setophaga ruticilla

Adult male: Grand Bahama – October   Adult female: New Providence – May

Length: 5 ins (12.7 cm). Common winter resident and transient throughout the region. Adult male and female look different. Distinctive adult male is black with flashy orange patches on sides of breast, base of primaries and base of outer tail feathers. Belly, vent and undertail coverts dull white. Adult female has mostly gray head and olive-gray back and dull white underparts. Yellow patches in same location as male's orange patches. Immature of both sexes similar to adult female. In spring, however, immature male shows black in lores, sometimes with a few black spots about head and breast. Call note a loud rich *chip* similar to call note of Yellow Warbler. Prefers dense growth of coppice, secondary growth and tall mangrove stands. Forages actively, fanning tail, flicking wings and making rapid flights in pursuit of insects. Responsive to pishing.

Prothonotary Warbler

Protonotaria citrea

Male: April   Female: April

Length: 5.25 ins (13.3 cm). Rare to uncommon transient in northern and central Bahamas and in TCI. Not reported from southern Bahamas. Shows little seasonal variation. Adult male has bright golden yellow head with contrasting large black eye and bill. Underparts also yellow with white vent and undertail coverts. Back olive and wings, rump and short tail blue-gray. Adult female similar to male but has olive tinge to crown and nape. Non-breeding adult similar to breeding adult but has paler bill. Immature birds also have paler bills. Immature female has dullest plumage with strong olive tinge to crown, nape and cheeks that does not contrast as much with back color. Also less yellow on belly and grayer flanks. Chip note a sharp *tink*. May occur in any wooded habitat but prefers areas near water.

Worm-eating Warbler

Helmitheros vermivorum

Grand Bahama – October

San Salvador – January

Length: 5.25 ins (13.3 cm). Uncommon winter resident and transient throughout the region. All seasonal plumages similar. Buffy head with two prominent black stripes, one on side of crown and other behind eye. Large pale bill, unmarked olive-brown upperparts and breast pale to rich buff. Common call note a *zeet zeet* given in flight. Loud chip note rarely heard. Prefers wooded habitats and often forages in clumps and tangles of dead leaves. Difficult to see as it usually stays low and remains hidden from view in dense foliage. Sometimes responds to pishing but does not hang around very long.

Swainson's Warbler

Limnothlypsis swainsonii

May

Caymans – October

Length: 5.25 ins (13.3 cm). Rare winter resident and transient in northern and central Bahamas. Not recorded from southern Bahamas or TCI. Plain plumage and skulking behavior make it difficult to find or observe. All seasonal plumages similar. Head has notably long bill, warm brown crown, pale supercilium and dark eye-line. Unmarked brown upperparts and whitish to pale yellow underparts with brown-gray flanks. Strong chip note but hard to differentiate. Prefers wooded and dense habitats. Walks and forages on ground sifting through leaf litter similar to Ovenbird.

Northern Waterthrush   *Seiurus noveboracensis*

Grand Bahama – February   New Providence – November

Louisiana Waterthrush   *Seiurus motacilla*

April

Northern Waterthrush Length: 5.75 ins (14.6 cm). Fairly common to common winter resident and transient throughout the region. **Louisiana Waterthrush** Length: 6 ins (15.2 cm). Rare to uncommon winter resident and transient in The Bahamas and rare in TCI. For both species, all seasonal plumages similar. Keep in mind that Northern Waterthrush is significantly more common than Louisiana Waterthrush. **Comparison:** The two waterthrushes are very similar in appearance and behavior but there are subtle differences. Both are uniformly dark brown above and light below with dark streaking. Northern's underparts, however, can be either white or pale yellow. Louisiana has pink-buff flanks, which contrast with white underparts. Throat usually marked with small dark spots in Northern but usually unmarked in Louisiana. Supercilium conspicuous in both. Northern has either white or pale yellow supercilium and it is of equal width throughout its length, whereas Louisiana has narrow pale buff supercilium in front of eye and broader white supercilium behind eye. Northern has dark pink legs, legs of Louisiana brighter pink. Both give loud metallic *chink* call notes which are difficult to differentiate, but Northern's is sharper. Both occupy shorelines of a variety of wet habitats but Northerns frequent mangrove swamps while Louisianas prefer freshwater ponds. Both walk rather than hop while foraging on ground and have habit of bobbing rear end up and down.

Ovenbird   *Seiurus aurocapilla*

New Providence – May   Grand Bahama – September

Length: 5.75 ins (14.6 cm). Common winter resident and transient throughout the region. All seasonal plumages similar. Large warbler with orange crown bordered by black stripes, prominent white eye-ring and pale-colored lower mandible. Olive-brown above and white below with lines of bold black spots across breast and flanks. Legs long and pink. Call note a loud *chup*. When agitated or responding to pishing, repeats this call note and often raises crest. Walks, rather than hops, while foraging on ground and habitually moves head back and forth, often cocking tail. Prefers dense undergrowth covered with leaf litter.

Hooded Warbler   *Wilsonia citrina*

Male: April   Female: April

Length: 5.25 ins (13.3 cm). Rare to uncommon transient (mainly fall) and rare winter resident throughout the region. Male unmistakable. Black hood surrounds bright yellow face and forehead. Upperparts uniform olive-green, underparts bright yellow. Immature male similar. Adult female similar to male but has only variable amount of black around face. Immature female lacks black in hood. Constantly flicks tail open and shut flashing extensive white outer tail feathers. Call note a sharp *chink*. Usually forages low in shady understorey of dense woods and thickets. Sometimes makes a quick flight to pursue insects.

Common Yellowthroat   *Geothlypis trichas*

Male: Grand Bahama – December

Immature male: Grand Bahama – December

Female: Grand Bahama – November

Immature female: New Providence – March

Length: 5 ins (12.7 cm). Common winter resident and transient throughout the region. Shows some variation in seasonal plumages. Adult male, both breeding and non-breeding, has distinctive black mask with pale gray border along upper edge and unmarked olive-green upperparts with brown tinge. Bright yellow throat and breast, dingy white belly and yellow undertail coverts. Sides of breast and flanks gray-brown. Immature male similar but with only suggestion of mask. Adult female similar to male but lacks black mask and has slightly duller yellow throat and upper breast. Cheeks are dusky with inconspicuous pale eye-ring. Immature female is dullest yellowthroat with browner tones overall, very pale yellow throat and inconspicuous eye-ring. Call note a husky and raspy *schat* or low *chidge*. Habitats include wet brushy areas, marshes with reeds or cattails, weedy fields and brushy tangles. Also understorey along edge or within pinewoods. Stays low and concealed in cover. Responsive to pishing. For similar species see **Bahama Yellowthroat**.

 **BANANAQUIT** **Family:** *Uncertain status*

Formerly considered a single species family but the AOU in 2005 deleted the family classification and placed it under the heading *Genus Incertae Sedis* meaning uncertain status. Only the family name has been removed and everything else remains the same for now. Bananaquit is widespread in the West Indies, southern Caribbean and Middle and South America. A variable species with many distinctive island subspecies and plumages. There are about 40 subspecies recognized throughout its range.

Bananaquit 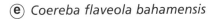 (e) *Coereba flaveola bahamensis*

New Providence – December   Juvenile: South Andros – May

Status and range: Common permanent resident throughout the region except rare to uncommon on Bimini. Can be quite scarce after hurricanes.

Description: Length: 4.5 ins (11.4 cm). Endearing small bird with short, dark, decurved bill with small red spot at base. Adult of both sexes has dark eye-line and broad white supercilium. Upperparts dark with small yellow rump; wings dark with small yellow area at bend of wing and white patch at base of primaries. Underparts pale gray to white with yellowish band across belly. Squared tail short and dark with small white tips to outer tail feathers. In flight, yellow rump and small white tips to tail are more visible. Juvenile has brownish upperparts and dingy olive-yellow underparts with supercilium not as bold as adult.

Voice: Vocal with many variations. Much time has been spent tracking down unfamiliar vocalizations that turn out to be Bananaquits. Call notes include warbler-like *chit* and high thin *seet* similar to call note of Greater Antillean Bullfinch. Song includes a jumbled series of wheezy squeaks, clicks, buzzes and sometimes a gurgling sound. Also a trill-like *tzeeeee*.

Habits: Active and social bird. Prefers both ornamental trees and shrubs of gardens and settled areas and more natural coppice, dense thickets and scrub. Primarily a nectar feeder but also takes insects, fruit and berries. Attracted to flowering vegetation and hummingbird feeders. On large flowers, has habit of piercing base to reach nectar. In some areas, samples sugar or sweet items left on outside tables of restaurants or bars. Known to settle into unused nests for nighttime roost.

Comments: Bananaquit in the region is recognized as an endemic subspecies *C. f. bahamensis*. Common and widespread in the West Indies except for Cuba where it is only a rare visitor. Also rare and irregular visitor to South Florida.

◆ TANAGERS

Family: *Thraupidae*

Large and diverse New World family well represented in the tropics – mostly in South America. Tanagers are generally forest-dwelling colorful birds that specialize in feeding on fruit. Males usually more colorful than females. Most are residents but tanagers that breed in North America are migratory. In the region, resident tanager is described below, followed by a briefer description of migrant Summer and Scarlet Tanager.

Western Spindalis

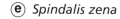

Spindalis zena

Male (green back): Grand Bahama – March

Male (black back): North Andros – May

Both females: Grand Bahama – January

Status and range: Permanent resident in the region. Fairly common to common on Grand Bahama, Abaco, Andros, New Providence and Eleuthera. Less common in central and southern Bahamas. Not found on San Salvador and nearby Rum Cay. In TCI, uncommon on Providenciales and North and Middle Caicos in Caicos Islands. Not reported from Turks Islands.

Description: Length: 6.5 ins (16.5 cm). Adult male has black head with bold white stripes above and below eye and orange-yellow breast with chestnut band or patch in centre. Back color varies from darkish olive-green to black (see comments below). Nape and rump with deep orange-yellow and dark chestnut. Black wing has white edges to flight feathers and prominent white patch on shoulder. Adult female strikingly different with drab brownish-olive upperparts and paler underparts. Also indistinct pale stripe over eye, slightly stronger whitish stripe below eye and small white patch at base of primaries.

Voice: Vocal but calls and song are often weak and difficult to hear. Call note a soft thin *seet*, also given in flight. Song a prolonged gentle and faint series of high-pitched notes, whistles, warbles and buzzes.

Habits: Utilizes habitats such as pinewoods, coppice, tall brushy areas and gardens. Gathers at fruiting trees and shrubs often in small groups. Tends to forage slowly looking for berries, insects or buds.

Comments: Formerly treated as subspecies of Stripe-headed Tanager and formerly called by that name. Recently split into a new species and has been renamed Western Spindalis. The reason for this is that taxonomists are currently not sure if this species is a tanager or not. As a result, tanager was replaced with spindalis in the common name. Some believe it is more finch-like. Also found on Cuba, Cayman Islands and Cozumel Island off Mexico. Also rare visitor to South Florida. Western Spindalis in the region has two recognized endemic subspecies: *S. z. townsendi* found only on Grand Bahama and Abaco has darkish olive green back (some extremes look black) and *S. z. zena*, in remainder of the region, which has black back. Females of both subspecies are similar.

Summer Tanager

Piranga rubra

Male: January

Immature male: April

Female: April

Scarlet Tanager

Piranga olivacea

Male: April

Female: April

Summer Tanager Length: 7.75 ins (20 cm). Rare (mainly fall) transient through the region and rare winter resident in northern Bahamas. All Summer Tanagers have long, thick, pale to dusky-colored bill. Adult male is rosy-red year round. Adult female is brownish-yellow overall but underparts are brighter yellow – some birds are variably washed with red or orange, mainly on throat and tail coverts. Immature of both sexes in fall similar to adult female but, by following spring, immature male will show red head and breast. **Scarlet Tanager** Length: 7 ins (18 cm). Rare (mainly fall) transient through the region. All Scarlet Tanagers have thick pale to dusky-colored bill that is slightly less thick and not as long as Summer Tanager. Breeding adult male in spring has unmistakable, brilliant, scarlet body with black wings and tail. Non-breeding male in fall has black wings and tail but red body plumage molts to darkish olive-green above and greenish-yellow below. Adult and immature female are similar to non-breeding male but wings and tail of female are not as dark as those of male. In the region, greenish plumage of both sexes is the one most often seen. Female and immature Summer Tanager in fall lack olive-green color of upperparts and darker wings and tail of Scarlet Tanager. Call notes also differ; Summer Tanager has a low quick *pit-y-tuck* or *pi-tuck* while Scarlet Tanager has a low and hoarse *chip-burr*.

GRASSQUITS AND SPARROWS   **Family:** *Emberizidae*

Grassquits and sparrows constituite a very large world-wide family (over 300 species) of finch-like birds with conical (cone shaped) bills. Feed mainly on or near ground. Appear like buntings and grosbeaks but are placed in a separate family because of differences in habits, vocalizations and structure.

Cuban Grassquit   *Tiaris canora*

Male: New Providence – November

Female: New Providence – November

Status and range: Introduced species. Fairly common permanent resident on New Providence. Not found on other Bahama islands or TCI.

Description: Length: 4.5 ins (11 cm). Small bird with stubby dark conical bill. Adult male has black face, throat and breast; throat and breast separated by bright yellow band that circles up to eye. Dark gray crown, olive back and gray underparts. Female similar but is duller and lacks black areas of male; face dark red-brown.

Voice: Call note high soft *seet*. Song a high raspy *chit chita-lee* with variations and often repeated. Also jumble of twittering notes or quick *te-dee, te-dee, te-dee*.

Habits: Found in brushy areas and thickets in Nassau and other New Providence settlements. Social and often in small flocks. Comes to seed feeders.

Comments: Formerly called 'Melodious Grassquit'. Endemic to Cuba but declining due to capture for pet trade. In 1963, a plane carrying grassquits and Indigo Buntings from Cuba to Europe was grounded in Nassau and held for repairs. Many birds died but survivors were released and Cuban Grassquits established a viable population. Some Yellow-faced Grassquits were also released but are no longer found on New Providence.

Black-faced Grassquit   *Tiaris bicolor*

Male: New Providence –
May

Female: New Providence
– January

Immature male: Grand
Bahama – December

Status and range: Common permanent resident on major islands throughout The Bahamas. In TCI, common permanent resident on Caicos Islands but not found on Turks Islands.

Description: Length: 4.5 ins (11 cm). Small bird with stubby conical bill. Adult male has dark bill, dark olive upperparts and underparts that are black from face to belly; dark gray vent and undertail coverts. Female has uniformly olive-brown upperparts and gray underparts with thin pale eye-ring. Bill dark with lower mandible pale or partially pale at base. Immature similar to female but immature male shows developing black areas on throat and breast.

Voice: Call note a soft *sip*. Song a *tink tink tink kacheeee* with brief pause after *tink* notes and slightly ringing finish. Sometimes just gives buzzy ringing notes.

Habits: Widely distributed in brushy undergrowth and grassy areas in both natural and developed habitats. Also prefers grassy and brushy areas along roadsides through pinewoods. Not shy but size and habitat make it seem secretive. Found in pairs and/or small groups. Long breeding season. Comes to seed feeders.

Similar species: Female Black-faced Grassquit resembles both female **Indigo Bunting** and female **Painted Bunting** in that they are all small with conical bills and plain-colored with thin pale eye-rings. However, female Indigo is browner with whitish throat and indistinct wing-bars and female Painted is greener to greenish-yellow. Grassquits are also tamer than the two buntings and are almost always found with other grassquits.

Comments: Found throughout the West Indies but only occurs on some isolated cays off Cuba (not main island) and is absent from the Cayman Islands. Range also includes parts of northern South America. Very rare and irregular visitor to South Florida. Black-faced Grassquit in the region and on cays off Cuba is subspecies *T. b. bicolor*.

Greater Antillean Bullfinch   (e) *Loxigilla violacea violacea*

Abaco – January

Immature: Abaco – February

Probable juvenile: Grand Bahama – October

Status and range: Fairly common to common permanent resident on larger Bahama islands. Status unknown on San Salvador, Mayaguana and Ragged Islands. In TCI, common permanent resident on Middle and East Caicos and has recently been reported on North Caicos. Not found on other islands in TCI.

Description: Length: 6.5 ins (17 cm). Slender bird with large head and heavy coni-cal bill. Adult male black with orange-red stripe over eye, on throat and on undertail coverts. Female dark gray with similar orange-red patches of color. Juvenile thought to be brown-olive with smaller and duller-colored patches. Shows some dark blotch-ing as it matures.

Voice: Call note a high soft *seet*. At times, a buzzier *zeet*. Song is like call notes given in a series *seet seet seet seet*, etc.

Habits: Prefers dense thickets, secondary growth and thick coppice. Shy and move-ments secretive. May be difficult to find at times. Feeds on berries, insects and tree buds. Responds to pishing but usually stays hidden.

Comments: Found only in the West Indies and range restricted to The Bahamas, Caicos Islands, Hispaniola and Jamaica. Greater Antillean Bullfinch in the region has two recognized endemic subspecies: *L. v. violacea* from The Bahamas and *L. v. ofella* from Middle and East Caicos Islands. Because of red and black plumage, which resembles the uniform of Bahamian police officers, they are locally known as 'police bird'.

Winter Resident and Transient Sparrows

Six sparrow species migrate annually to or through the region. Three of these are the most widely encountered (usually never more than uncommon) and are described below. Three other species are not described: Chipping Sparrow, Lincoln's Sparrow and White-crowned Sparrow. Numbers vary from year to year but these species are mainly very rare to rare transients in northern Bahamas and occur more often in fall than spring. They are also occasional winter residents but in smaller numbers. Number of records would likely increase with more coverage. Winter resident sparrows generally arrive in the region in October and leave in April.

Clay-colored Sparrow   *Spizella pallida*

July

December

December

Length: 5.5 ins (14 cm). Rare transient (mainly fall) in northern Bahamas and possible winter resident in small numbers. In rest of region, only recorded from San Salvador and Mayaguana. May be more numerous than records indicate. Essentially brown upperparts with streaks on crown (with pale central stripe) and back; underparts clear and unstreaked. Well defined facial pattern with broad pale supercilium, pale lores and brownish cheek outlined by thin dark brown fringe. In fall and winter, more of a buffy wash to head and breast especially immatures. Call note an indistinct high *seep*. Non-breeding and immature **Chipping Sparrow** are similar to Clay-colored but Chipping has dark lores, less of a pale central crown stripe and less of a dark fringe to lower part of brownish cheek.

Grasshopper Sparrow   *Ammodramus savannarum*

Grand Bahama – February   May

Length: 4.5 ins (11 cm). Rare winter resident and rare to uncommon transient in The Bahamas but not recorded from Cat Island, Long Island, Great Inagua or TCI. Regular winter resident on New Providence. Small short-tailed sparrow with flat head and relatively large pale bill. Head has pale thin eye-ring, pale yellow-orange spot in front of eye and dark crown stripe above wide buffy supercilium. Back and wings are mottled and streaked brown, white and chestnut. Unstreaked or slightly streaked buff underparts with white belly. Prefers open areas with dense grass and at times, occupies same habitat as Savannah Sparrow. Call note a soft *tsit*. When flushed, usually flies short distance then plunges back into grass and runs. Difficult to see well. Subspecies in region believed to be *A. s. pratensis*.

Savannah Sparrow   *Passerculus sandwichensis*

April   February

Length: 5.75 ins (15 cm). Rare to uncommon winter resident and transient in northern Bahamas. Regular winter resident on New Providence. Rare in central Bahamas and not found in southern Bahamas or TCI. Upperparts brown with dark streaks on back. Underparts white with heavy streaks on breast and flanks. Face well-marked with wide supercilium (yellow spot in front) and brown cheek bordered above and below by dark line. Bill is pale, legs and feet pink. Call note a thin *seet*. Occupies open habitats with grassy fields, weedy patches and cultivated areas. Often runs rather than flies. When flushed, occasionally perches in view especially if there is a nearby bush.

◆ GROSBEAKS AND BUNTINGS   Family: *Cardinalidae*

Small New World family of finch-like birds with small to large conical bills (cone shaped) that are well adapted for cracking seeds. Their songs are similar. Males are more colorful than females. There is no breeding species in the region, only winter residents or transients. In addition to the four species described below, Dickcissel is a rare fall transient through the region and is not described. The two buntings are covered first followed by the two grosbeaks

Indigo Bunting   *Passerina cyanea*

Male: April

Female: April

Immature male – May

Grand Bahama – December

Length: 5.5 ins (14 cm). Uncommon to fairly common winter resident and transient throughout the region. Adult male in breeding plumage is deep indigo blue, appearing black in poor light. Non-breeding male is browner with uneven patches of blue. Males arrive in fall to region in non-breeding plumage and start molt to breeding plumage in late winter so that by their departure in spring, they are usually all blue. Adult female uniformly brown to warm brown with pale throat and obscure fine streaks on breast and flanks; also faint buffy wing-bars. In fall, immature of both sexes similar to adult female but immature male in late winter starts to acquire blue patches in plumage similar to non-breeding adult male. End result is that you are going to run into a lot of little brown or partially brown jobs. Call note a buzzy *zeet* also given in flight. Second call note a liquid and sharp *spit*. Likes low dense shrubs, thickets and brushy edges usually next to open areas. Shuns unbroken coppice and pinewoods. One of few species that feeds on seeds of introduced Australian Pine (*Casuarina species*). Often in small flocks. Shy and skittish, difficult to approach. Comes to seed feeders.

Painted Bunting

Passerina ciris

Male: April

Female or immature: winter

Female or immature: May

Length: 5.5 ins (14 cm). Rare to uncommon winter resident and transient in northern Bahamas and parts of central Bahamas. Unrecorded or accidental in rest of the region including TCI. Striking adult male has blue head with red eye-ring, red underparts, yellow-green back and wings with red rump and uppertail coverts. Keeps colorful plumage year round. Adult female plain greenish with pale eye-ring, olive-green upperparts and pale yellow-green underparts. Immature of both sexes similar to adult female. Immature male unique in that it does not acquire bright adult plumage for over a year after hatching (It usually takes less than a year for small land birds). Not very vocal. Call note a sharp *chit* that is difficult to identify. Hunts for insects, seeds and berries in dense low growth and edges of open areas. Shy and stays in cover. Occasionally comes to seed feeders. It is believed that Painted Buntings that migrate to the region belong to the population that breeds along Atlantic coast in southeastern USA – subspecies *P. c. ciris*. **Conservation:** Numbers are slowly declining and population considered vulnerable mainly due to habitat destruction on breeding grounds and capture for cage birds on their wintering grounds (mainly Cuba and Mexico).

There are two species of **grosbeaks** that are rare to uncommon transients through the region and are described on the following page. They are found primarily in fall but individuals could occur in spring or winter. In both species, the adult males are stunning and colorful while the adult females and immatures are much less so. Grosbeaks have heavy wide bills.

Rose-breasted Grosbeak   *Pheucticus ludovicianus*

Adult male: April   Adult female: April

Length: 8 ins (20 cm). Breeding adult male has black head and back, black wing with white patches, white rump and black tail; underparts white with rosy red breast. In flight, flashes black and white appearance and rosy red underwing coverts (takes a good look). Non-breeding adult male has more mottled brown on head and back with streaks along flanks. Adult female looks brown and streaky overall. Has bold light and dark stripes on head, brown above and whitish below with extensive streaking on breast and flanks. White in brown wing is much duller than male's and underwing coverts flash yellow in flight. Immature of both sexes similar to adult female except immature male has buffy to light pinkish wash across breast and has rosy red underwing coverts like adult male. Prefers wooded habitats. Call note a sharp squeaky *eek* or *peek*.

Blue Grosbeak   *Passerina caerulea*

Male: May   Female: August

Immature male: April   Immature: North Andros – October

Length: 6.75 ins (17 cm). Adult male is dark blue and adult female brown to warm brown both with prominent rufous or buffy wing-bars. Immature of both sexes in fall similar to adult female but with richer warm brown coloring. Immature most likely plumage to be seen in fall. By following spring, immature male has patches of blue, mainly around head. Habitat and plumage similar to Indigo Bunting but Blue Grosbeak is larger with heavier bill, wider wing-bars and longer tail which it twitches frequently. Call note a sharp and metallic *chink* or *tink* unlike calls of Indigo Bunting.

◆ BLACKBIRDS AND ORIOLES — Family: *Icteridae*

Diverse medium-sized New World family. Most of them have long straight pointed bills and eat insects, fruit and seeds. Blackbirds often feed on or near ground and males are glossy black, often with brightly colored wing patches. Orioles favor trees and have striking patterns of black and orange or yellow. Many oriole species build hanging nests. Resident blackbirds are described first, followed by resident oriole. Descriptions of migrant Bobolink and Baltimore Oriole follow.

Red-winged Blackbird — ⓔ *Agelaius phoeniceus bryanti*

Female: New Providence – May

Male: New Providence – May

Immature male: Grand Bahama – October

Status and range: Resident subspecies is permanent resident. Common on Grand Bahama and Abaco; uncommon to fairly common on Andros, the Berry Islands and New Providence. Not found on other islands in The Bahamas or TCI. Winter resident or transient birds from North America occur and seasonally increase overall red-wing population but status unknown due to difficulty distinguishing them from resident subspecies.

Description: Length: 8.75 ins (22 cm). Breeding adult male is glossy black with bright orange-red shoulder patch on wing bordered below in pale yellow. They can display this colorful patch or obscure it. Non-breeding plumage similar except back feathers lightly edged with rufous. Adult and immature female have white or pale buff superciliium and whitish throat. Upperparts dark brown and pale underparts heavily streaked. Immature male dark brown overall with rufous or buff edges to feathers; sometimes partially developed shoulder patch is visible.

Voice: Call notes include a husky *check* or metallic *tink*. Also gives fairly long scolding 'chatter'. Song a gurgling harsh *onk-a-leee*, last note trill-like.

Habits: Prefers marshes and ponds surrounded with reeds or thick vegetation and mangrove habitats. Also weedy fields and cultivated land around farms. Forages mainly on ground. Forms flocks in winter at night-time roosts in dense thickets or trees with thick foliage.

Comments: Widespread and abundant in North America. Resident Red-winged Blackbird in The Bahamas is recognized as an endemic subspecies *A. p. bryanti*. Resident female has whiter throat and underparts than other female Red-winged Blackbird subspecies but males are not distinguishable by plumage.

Shiny Cowbird   *Molothrus bonariensis*

Male: Grand Bahama – October   Female: Grand Bahama – March

Status and range: Rare to uncommon in northern Bahamas. Not known whether it is permanent resident or summer resident or both. Not reported from other Bahama islands or from TCI but sightings can be anticipated.

Description: Length: 7.5 ins (19 cm). Adult male entirely glossy black with dark purple sheen, mostly on head and back. Appears all black in poor light. Adult female uniformly gray-brown with supercilium slightly paler than face and throat slightly paler than breast. Both sexes have dark, relatively thin-based, pointed bills.

Voice: Call notes include a low *chuck*, a chatter or rattle type call and a high thin whistle given in flight by male. Song consists of several bubbling notes followed by high whistle.

Habits: Feeds mainly on ground in open areas and around farms. Forms small flocks outside breeding season often with Red-winged Blackbirds. Called a 'brood parasite' because of its breeding behavior. Shiny Cowbird does not build a nest or raise its young. Instead female quickly lays its eggs in other birds' nests and then departs. Host parents, not recognizing intruder egg(s), raise young cowbird(s) which usually out-compete young of host species. Results lead to more cowbirds and less breeding success for host species.

Comments: Shiny Cowbird has expanded range from South America to and through the West Indies. It reached Florida in 1985 and was only first recorded in the region on North Andros in 1994. First reported in 1997 on Grand Bahama and New Providence; 1998 on Abaco. Considered a potential threat if cowbird population becomes so high that it begins to reduce breeding success of host population and thereby reducing overall population of host species. It has seriously affected two resident species in Puerto Rico including orioles. Known to parasitize Greater Antillean Oriole on Andros so there is cause for concern and regular monitoring of oriole population.

Similar species: Brown-headed Cowbird (*Molothrus ater*) Length: 7.5 ins (19 cm). Very rare to rare winter visitor to the region. Male has brown head and glossy black body and is readily distinguishable from male Shiny. Female difficult to distinguish from female Shiny Cowbird. Brown-headed has slightly less noticeable supercilium, slightly paler throat and relatively thicker bill at base making bill appear less pointed than that of Shiny Cowbird. However these traits are all relative and some females may not be identifiable as to which species. It is always helpful to have a female Shiny near or next to a male Shiny which is often the case. Brown-headed Cowbird is also a 'brood parasite' and has had a significantly negative effect on certain species in North America.

Brown-headed male and female: May

Greater Antillean Oriole   (e) *Icterus dominicensis northropi*

Adult: North Andros – April

Both same immature: North Andros – October

Status and range: Uncommon to fairly common permanent resident on North and South Andros including Mangrove Cay. Not found elsewhere in The Bahamas or in TCI. Formerly permanent resident on Abaco but no longer found there.

Description: Length: 8 ins (20 cm). Beautiful black and yellow oriole. Adult of both sexes has black upperparts, including breast and tail, and bright yellow underparts, including rump. There is also a yellow panel just above bend of wing. Bill is black and slightly decurved with base of lower mandible silver-blue. Immature has olive-gray back with dark wings and tail, black lores and throat and dull olive-yellow head and breast that blends to yellow underparts.

Voice: Call note a sharp *chec* or nasal *twank*. Song a series of sweet whistled notes (around six) with slightly accented ending.

Habits: Favors coconut palms for foraging and nesting. Also found around taller ornamental trees and shrubs near settlements, sometimes coppice edges and pinewoods. Feeds on insects, fruit and nectar from flowers. Builds hanging nest suspended from palm frond or limb.

Comments: Formerly considered subspecies of Black-cowled Oriole and formerly called by that name. Recently renamed Greater Antillean Oriole and designated a separate species. Also found on Cuba, Hispaniola and Puerto Rico as well as Andros. Greater Antillean Oriole in The Bahamas is recognized as an endemic subspecies *I. d. northropi*. **Conservation:** Oriole population on Andros is cause for concern because reason for disappearance from Abaco is unknown and presence of parasitic Shiny Cowbird threatens future breeding success.

The following two blackbird species occur mainly as transients in the region but some Baltimore Orioles occur in winter.

Bobolink   *Dolichonyx oryzivorus*

Adult/immature: fall

Male breeding: June   Grand Bahama – September

Length: 7 ins (18 cm). Uncommon to fairly common spring and fall transient through the region. Long-distance migrant that breeds in North America and winters in southern South America. Population declining. Most Bobolinks probably overfly the region but strong headwinds or rain may force them down. In spring, breeding adult male entirely black with pale yellow patch on back of head, bold white rump area and white panel on back conspicuous on birds in flight or on ground. Some males, at this time, may still show light brown mottling on head and underparts as part of transition to breeding plumage. Adult female entirely light brown or buff with dark line behind eye and dark stripe on sides of crown. Dark brown streaks on back and light streaks along sides of breast and flanks. In fall migration, all plumages similar to adult female except color is richer yellow-buff. Forages on or near ground in open grassy or weedy fields including golf courses. Usually travels in small to large flocks. Common call note a soft *pink* often given in flight. Spring male occasionally heard singing soft bubbling *bobolink*.

Baltimore Oriole   *Icterus glabula*

Adult male: January

Immature male: May

Adult female: spring

Immature female: February

Length 8.5 ins (21.6 cm). Rare to uncommon winter resident and transient through-out the region. Numbers vary from year to year. Unmistakable adult male has black hood and back, bright orange underparts and rump, dark wings with orange upper wing-bar and white lower wing-bar; orange patches on black tail. Adult female and immature can be variable but both show mainly brownish to olive-brown upperparts with darker wing and two white wing-bars. Underparts dull orange to yellow-orange with color concentrated around breast and undertail coverts. Immature female has dullest plumage of all with brown-gray back, grayish flanks and belly and pale yellow-orange breast and undertail coverts. All these plumages may be encountered in region which sounds complicated (except for adult males) but all Baltimore Orioles will have wing-bars and some orange to yellow-orange on underparts. Forages on insects and larvae but has preference for berries, fruit and nectar from flowers. Common call a dry chatter but also a variable one to two-note whistle.

◆ OLD WORLD SPARROWS   Family: *Passeridae*

This sparrow family is a small family of finch-like birds with stout bills which is wide-spread in the Old World. They are not related to the sparrows of North America although there are some similarities. One species (House Sparrow) has been introduced world-wide and is found in most of the West Indies.

House Sparrow   *Passer domesticus*

Male: New Providence – March

Female: Grand Bahama – September

Status and range: Introduced species. Locally fairly common to common permanent resident in settled areas in northern Bahamas. Uncommon permanent resident in Matthew Town, Great Inagua. Not recorded from other Bahama islands or TCI.

Description: Length: 6.25 ins (16 cm). Breeding adult male has distinctive gray crown, black bill and lores, black throat and breast. Deep chestnut from behind eye to upper back and wings. Underparts plain dingy gray. Non-breeding male duller with paler bill, less chestnut on face and less black on breast. Adult female plain with pale bill, light brown crown and buff-brown stripe behind eye. Back is brownish with buff and dark streaks and underparts light gray-brown with no markings. Juvenile similar to adult female.

Voice: Calls include a single or extended series of *cheep* and *churp* notes. Also chatter-like calls. Vocal in flocks.

Habits: Gregarious around man-made structures in towns, settled areas and farms. Not found in natural habitats away from settlements. Mainly feeds on ground.

Comments: This species was introduced from Europe to northeastern USA in 1850 and is currently widespread and common throughout North America. First reported in Nassau in 1891. Formerly called 'English Sparrow.'

Appendix

Glossary of selected terms

Archipelago: A group of many islands.

Bank: Shallow place in a body of water. All the islands in the region rest on their own bank or are part of a larger bank; the exposed portion of the bank being the island itself, while the rest of the bank is under water (averaging 20 ft (6 m) deep).

Birders/Birding: Terms for people who seek out and observe or watch birds for recreation; considered more serious than general bird watching. Ornithology, the most serious, involves the scientific study of birds and birdlife.

Blue Hole: A mostly circular opening in the limestone with steep sides and filled with water; many with fresh water on top and sea water at the lower depths. Depth of Blue Hole varies from 300 ft (90 m) to 600 ft (180 m).

Buff/Buffy: A color often described on birds. Pale or moderate yellow including moderate orange-yellow to light yellowish-brown; considered a warm tone.

Cay: Low-lying, small island made up of largely coral or sand. Pronounced 'key'.

Cheeks: Patch of feathers below and behind the eye. Also known as an ear patch or the auriculars because these feathers do cover a bird's ears.

Coppice: General term in the region for stands of hardwood or broadleaf trees and shrubs.

Coverts: Feathers that cover and protect the base of the primary and secondary feathers on the wings and the base of the tail feathers from both above and below.

Eye-line:	Linear line, usually dark, that runs continuously through the eye or confined to a line in front of the eye or behind it. Also referred to as an eye-stripe.
Eye-ring:	Ring of contrasting feathers around the eye of a bird. There are different types of eye-rings and an example is given for each.

Ovenbird with complete eye-ring

Northern Parula with eye crescents

Yellow-throated Vireo with spectacles
(eye-ring connected to line above lores)

Thick-billed Vireo with broken or incomplete eye-ring

Ecotourism:	People who travel to an area to observe or participate in that area's specialty environment, i.e. snorkelers, divers, hikers, birders, etc.
Endemic:	In a biological context, plants and animals restricted or native to a certain region. Birds, both species and subspecies, that only breed in the Bahamas, TCI and nowhere else, are the basis for the term in this book.
Feral:	Wild and untamed. Usually referring to domesticated animals which, either purposely or not, are left to fend for themselves. Feral cats and dogs are the best examples.
Introduced:	Refers to birds, intentionally (usually) or unintentionally, released by man in a location outside their native range and that have become established in their new locale. Eurasian Collared-Dove is an introduced species in The Bahamas. Sometimes, the word 'exotic' is used instead of introduced.

Iridescence:	Brilliant colors and only visible at certain angles. Applies to throat color of male hummingbirds and to neck patches on some pigeons and doves.
Lores:	The area just in front of a bird's eye. Lores are not part of the supercilium but may be part of an eye-line.
Nape:	Area at the back of the neck.
New World:	Broad geographic reference to the continents of North, Middle and South America. Also referred to as the 'Americas'.
Metallic:	Refers to a lustrous, sparkling colour – usually hummingbirds. Less intense and visible in all directions as opposed to iridescence.
Mottled:	General term for markings, streaks, spots or blotches of different shades or colour. Antillean Nighthawk has an overall, mottled plumage.
Old World:	Broad geographic reference to the continents of Europe, Asia, Africa and Australia.
Pelagic:	The open sea; oceanic.
Pishing:	A sound made with the mouth by birders in the field to entice birds to come out of cover and provide a better look. Thought to resemble a general alarm call for birds or to stimulate their curiosity. Does not always work and some species are more 'pishable' than others. Also called spishing. See squeaking.
Scalloped:	Term for the appearance of a plumage. Many female ducks have a scalloped appearance to the back and flanks made by darker feathers with a wide, lighter border to the left side. Appears fan-shaped or like a scallop.
Scaly:	Term for the appearance of a plumage. Most often used in reference to shorebirds. Dark feathers to the back and scapulars with lighter edges creating an overall scaly appearance.
Scapulars:	Feathers of the upperparts that cover the area between the back and where the wing joins the body. Most noticeable on shorebirds.
Squeaking:	A sound (like kissing back of hand) made by birders to lure birds from cover for a better look. Along with pishing, can be quite effective but not always.

Supercilium: A horizontal area or stripe (usually pale) on the side of the head immediately above the eye. Also known as an eyebrow, superciliary line or stripe. Varies among some species in width and length.

Underparts: The lower surface of a bird's body, including the throat, breast, sides of breast, flanks, belly and undertail coverts.

Upperparts: The upper surface of a bird's body, including the crown, nape, back, rump and uppertail coverts. Sometimes the upper surface of the tail.

Whisker mark: Narrow dark or colored stripe running from the base of the bill down along the side of the throat. Also know as whisker stripe, lateral throat stripe or malar stripe.

The following list features species and subspecies that are endemic to the region. Biologists refer to the word endemic to mean restricted to a particular geographic area and nowhere else. In this case, these species and subspecies breed only in The Bahamas and Turks and Caicos Islands. The subspecies listed here are based on the information from the Howard and Moore text. The only exception is the subspecies of Bahama Yellowthroat from Andros which is shown in parentheses.

Endemic species Ⓔ with subspecies

Common Name	Scientific Name	Range in Region
Bahama Woodstar	C. e. evelynae	Throughout except Inaguas
	C. e. lyrura	Great and Little Inagua
Bahama Swallow	T. cyaneoviridis	Breeds on Grand Bahama, Abaco and Andros
Bahama Yellowthroat	G. r. rostrata	New Providence
	G. r. tanneri	Grand Bahama/Abaco
	G. r. coryi	Eleuthera/Cat Island
	(G. r. exigua)	Andros

Endemic subspecies ⓔ

Common Name	Scientific Name	Range in Region
Green Heron	B. v. bahamensis	Throughout region
Clapper Rail	R. l. coryi	Throughout region
Cuban Parrot	A. l. bahamensis	Abaco/Great Inagua
Great Lizard Cuckoo	S. m. bahamensis	Andros, New Providence, Eleuthera
West Indian Woodpecker	M. s. blakei	Abaco
	M. s. nyeanus	San Salvador
Hairy Woodpecker	P. v. piger	Grand Bahama/Abaco
	P. v. maynardi	Andros/New Providence
Cuban Pewee	C. c. bahamensis	Northern Bahamas/Cat Island
La Sagra's Flycatcher	M. s. lucaysiencis	Northern Bahamas/Great Inagua
Loggerhead Kingbird	T. c. bahamensis	Grand Bahamas, Abaco, Andros, New Providence
Thick-billed Vireo	V. c. crassirostris	The Bahamas
	V. c. stalagmium	Caicos Islands

Brown-headed Nuthatch	*S. p. insularis*	Grand Bahama
Blue-gray Gnatcatcher	*P. c. caesiogaster*	Throughout region except Berry Is., Exumas and Cat Is.
Red-legged Thrush	*T. p. plumbeus*	Northern Bahamas/Cat Island
Yellow Warbler	*D. p. flaviceps*	Throughout region
Yellow-throated Warbler	*D. d. flavescens*	Grand Bahama/Abaco
Pine Warbler	*D. p. achrustera*	Northern Bahamas except Eleuthera
Bananaquit	*C. f. bahamensis*	Throughout region
Western Spindalis	*S. z. townsendi*	Grand Bahama/Abaco
	S. z. zena	Remainder of region
Greater Antillean Bullfinch	*L. v. violacea*	Throughout region
	L. v. ofella	Middle/East Caicos
Red-winged Blackbird	*A. p. bryanti*	Northern Bahamas
Greater Antillean Oriole	*I. d. northropi*	Andros

Photography notes

It has been over a dozen years since I first took an interest in photographing birds. The same seductive pull that got me interested in birds over twenty-five years ago also got me started with a camera. I enjoy all aspects of the process of taking a photograph, but I also like the fact that it has increased my perceptions about birds and given me a deeper appreciation of the subtleties of their behavior and identification.

I have to admit, however, that equipment technology has had a lot to do with improving my interest and skills. It wasn't until Canon came out with a really useable auto focus system in the early 1990s that the ball got rolling. Add to that advances in metering systems, film, through the lens flash, lenses, image stabilization (IS) etc. and what was only a hope and a prayer ten years ago, is now more hope than prayer. The current system that I use is responsible for almost all of the photographs in the book. The equipment is all Canon – EOS 3 body, 100–400 zoom (IS) lens with a 1.4x extender and the 550 TTL flash. Film is Fujichrome Sensia 100 pushed to 200. Of course, my 'gone digital' friends chuckle or sneer at this system at every opportunity.

One of my preferences in the field is to make sure that birding and photography are in balance. If I carried one of those magnificent, large lenses with an accompanying tripod, it might improve my images but it would drastically interfere with my process of birding and I fear I don't have the all-day drive or patience for that method not to mention strength. So, as a trade-off, I sling the camera and 100–400 lens over my shoulder and off I go. If the opportunity arises, I let the binos fall and put up the camera. Without a tripod, I rely on the image stabilization feature of the lens and the flash, when applicable. There are still plenty of 'throw aways' just not as many as before.

My original objective was to have all the photos for the book taken in The Bahamas and the Turks and Caicos Islands. Most of the time that objective was met (about 85%) but in some cases, either I was unable to get the photograph from the region or the one I had was either not good enough or what I wanted. In other cases, I had no photograph of certain birds, or they were not worthy of publication, so I had to rely on the outside help of photographer friends.

The following people contributed their images and they are listed in alphabetical order along with their photo and the page number of where it appears.

Bob Abrams (McLean, VA)
Juvenal Semipalmated Sandpiper, page 92
Adult Western Sandpiper, page 93

Ailene Bainton (Nassau)
Female Hooded Mergansers, page 34
Common Terns Mayaguana, page 114
Cuban Parrots Great Inagua, page 134
Adult Barn Owl, page 138
Adult male Kirtland's Warbler in hand, page 190

Giff Beaton (Marietta, GA)
Male Green-winged Teal, page 31
Female Lesser Scaup, page 33
Glossy Ibis in flight (digital) page 62
Sora, page 66
Stilt Sandpiper in transition, page 89
Juvenal Least Sandpiper, page 94
Adult White-rumped Sandpiper, page 95
Red-tailed Hawk in flight, page 121
Chuck-will's-widow, page 142
Rough-winged Swallow perched, page 165
Both American Pipits, page 174
Immature Tennessee Warbler (November) (digital), page 184
Orange-crowned Warbler (digital), page 184
Adult male Northern Parula, page 185
Worm-eating Warbler (October) (digital), page 195
Louisiana Waterthrush, page 196
Female Scarlet Tanager, page 202
Grasshopper Sparrow (USA), page 207
Savannah Sparrow (February), page 207
Adult female Baltimore Oriole, page 216

Shawneen Finnegan (Tucson, AZ)
Non-breeding Bobolink on ground, page 215

Ed Greaves (Carmichael, CA)
Adult Peregrine Falcon, page 124
Adult male Painted Bunting, page 209
Adult male Blue Grosbeak, page 210

Ed Harper (Sacramento, CA)
Juvenal Spotted Sandpiper, page 85
First-winter Western Sandpiper, page 93
Western Kingbird (June), page 156
Second photo Red-eyed Vireo, page 158
First photo immature White-eyed Vireo, page 159
Adult male breeding Tennessee Warbler, page 184
Male American Redstart, page 194
Clay-colored Sparrow (July), page 206
Female Brown-headed Cowbird, page 213
Female Painted Bunting on ground, page 209
Adult male Baltimore Oriole, page 216

Kevin Karlson (Rio Grande, NJ)
Adult breeding Stilt Sandpiper, page 89
Second Eastern Phoebe, page 152
First Swainson's Warbler, page 195
Female Indigo Bunting, page 208
Female/immature Painted Bunting (May), page 209
Female Blue Grosbeak (August), page 210
Adult male Bobolink, page 215

Greg Lasley (Austin, Tx)
Two Clay-colored Sparrows (December), page 206

David Lee (Raleigh, NC)
Bahama Woodstar Great Inagua, page 145

Allan Sander (Trabuco Canyon, CA)
Non-breeding Gull-billed Tern, page 104
Back view Eastern Phoebe, page 152

Paul Sykes (Athens, GA)
Immature female Kirtland's Warbler in hand, page 190

Checklist of the Birds of The Bahamas and the Turks and Caicos Islands

The following is an unofficial list of all the birds that have occurred from The Bahamas and Turks and Caicos Islands – commonly referred to as a checklist. (The Bahamas Avian Records Committee is responsible for the official checklist of birds from The Bahamas. There is currently no committee for TCI.) It covers the birds from the text together with other rare, very rare and accidental species which were not mentioned. The sequence follows that of *The Checklist of North American Birds* (AOU, 7th ed 1998) and its supplements up through 2005. Those species marked with an asterisk (*) mean there has been only one record and a plus sign (+) indicates that there have been less than five records.

Black-bellied Whistling-Duck +
West Indian Whistling-Duck
Fulvous Whistling-Duck
Snow Goose
Canada Goose
Wood Duck
Gadwall
Eurasian Wigeon*
American Wigeon
American Black Duck *
Mallard
Blue-winged Teal
Cinnamon Teal *
Northern Shoveler
White-cheeked Pintail
Northern Pintail
Green-winged Teal
Canvasback *
Redhead
Ring-necked Duck
Greater Scaup *
Lesser Scaup
Hooded Merganser
Red-breasted Merganser

Ruddy Duck
Ring-necked Pheasant
Common Peafowl
Northern Bobwhite
Least Grebe
Pied-billed Grebe
Northern Fulmar *
Black-capped Petrel +
Cory's Shearwater
Greater Shearwater +
Sooty Shearwater +
Manx Shearwater *
Audubon's Shearwater
Wilson's Storm-Petrel
Leach's Storm-Petrel +
Band-rumped Storm-Petrel +
White-tailed Tropicbird
Masked Booby
Brown Booby
Red-footed Booby
Northern Gannet
American White Pelican +
Brown Pelican
Neotropic Cormorant

Double-crested Cormorant
Anhinga +
Magnificent Frigatebird
American Bittern
Least Bittern
Great Blue Heron
Great Egret
Snowy Egret
Little Blue Heron
Tricolored Heron
Reddish Egret
Cattle Egret
Green Heron
Black-crowned Night-Heron
Yellow-crowned Night-Heron
White Ibis
Glossy Ibis
Roseate Spoonbill
Black Vulture +
Turkey Vulture
Greater Flamingo
Osprey
Swallow-tailed Kite
Bald Eagle +
Northern Harrier
Sharp-shinned Hawk
Broad-winged Hawk *
Red-tailed Hawk
American Kestrel
Merlin
Peregrine Falcon
Black Rail +
Clapper Rail
Virginia Rail +
Sora
Purple Gallinule
Common Moorhen
American Coot
Limpkin
Sandhill Crane*
Double-striped Thick-knee*

Northern Lapwing *
Black-bellied Plover
American Golden-Plover +
Pacific Golden-Plover *
Snowy Plover
Wilson's Plover
Semipalmated Plover
Piping Plover
Killdeer
American Oystercatcher
Black-necked Stilt
American Avocet
Greater Yellowlegs
Lesser Yellowlegs
Solitary Sandpiper
Willet
Spotted Sandpiper
Upland Sandpiper
Whimbrel
Hudsonian Godwit +
Ruddy Turnstone
Red Knot
Sanderling
Semipalmated Sandpiper
Western Sandpiper
Least Sandpiper
White-rumped Sandpiper
Pectoral Sandpiper
Dunlin
Stilt Sandpiper
Buff-breasted Sandpiper +
Short-billed Dowitcher
Long-billed Dowitcher +
Wilson's Snipe
Wilson's Phalarope +
Red Phalarope *
South Polar Skua *
Pomarine Jaeger
Parasitic Jaeger
Laughing Gull
Black-headed Gull +

Bonaparte's Gull
Ring-billed Gull
Herring Gull
Lesser Black-backed Gull
Great Black-backed Gull
Black-legged Kittiwake *
Gull-billed Tern
Caspian Tern
Royal Tern
Sandwich Tern
Roseate Tern
Common Tern
Arctic Tern*
Forster's Tern
Least Tern
Bridled Tern
Sooty Tern
White-winged Tern *
Whiskered Tern *
Black Tern
Brown Noddy
Black Skimmer
Dovekie *
Rock Pigeon
White-crowned Pigeon
Eurasian Collared Dove
White-winged Dove
Zenaida Dove
Mourning Dove
Common Ground-Dove
Caribbean Dove
Key West Quail-Dove
Cuban Parrot
Yellow-billed Cuckoo
Mangrove Cuckoo
Great Lizard-Cuckoo
Smooth-billed Ani
Barn Owl
Burrowing Owl
Short-eared Owl *
Common Nighthawk

Antillean Nighthawk
Chuck-will's-widow
Chimney Swift
Cuban Emerald
Bahama Woodstar
Ruby-throated Hummingbird
Belted Kingfisher
Red-bellied Woodpecker +
West Indian Woodpecker
Yellow-bellied Sapsucker
Hairy Woodpecker
Cuban Pewee
Eastern Wood-Pewee
Acadian Flycatcher +
Least Flycatcher *
Eastern Phoebe
Great Crested Flycatcher
La Sagra's Flycatcher
Western Kingbird
Eastern Kingbird
Gray Kingbird
Loggerhead Kingbird
Giant Kingbird *
Scissor-tailed Flycatcher
Fork-tailed Flycatcher *
White-eyed Vireo
Thick-billed Vireo
Yellow-throated Vireo
Blue-headed Vireo
Philadelphia Vireo
Red-eyed Vireo
Black-whiskered Vireo
Cuban Crow
Fish Crow *
Purple Martin
Cuban/Caribbean Martin *
Tree Swallow
Bahama Swallow
N. Rough-winged Swallow
Bank Swallow
Cliff Swallow

Cave Swallow
Barn Swallow
Brown-headed Nuthatch
House Wren
Ruby-crowned Kinglet
Blue-gray Gnatcatcher
Veery
Gray-cheeked Thrush
Bicknells Thrush *
Swainson's Thrush
Hermit Thrush
Wood Thrush
American Robin
Red-legged Thrush
Gray Catbird
Northern Mockingbird
Bahama Mockingbird
Brown Thrasher +
Pearly-eyed Thrasher
European Starling
American Pipit
Sprague's Pipit *
Cedar Waxwing
Blue-winged Warbler
Golden-winged Warbler +
Tennessee Warbler
Orange-crowned Warbler
Nashville Warbler
Virginia's Warbler *
Northern Parula
Yellow Warbler
Chestnut-sided Warbler
Magnolia Warbler
Cape May Warbler
Black-throated Blue Warbler
Yellow-rumped Warbler
Black-throated Green Warbler
Townsend's Warbler *
Blackburnian Warbler
Yellow-throated Warbler
Olive-capped Warbler

Pine Warbler
Kirtland's Warbler
Prairie Warbler
Palm Warbler
Bay-breasted Warbler
Blackpoll Warbler
Cerulean Warbler +
Black-and-White Warbler
American Redstart
Prothonotary Warbler
Worm-eating Warbler
Swainson's Warbler
Ovenbird
Northern Waterthrush
Louisiana Waterthrush
Kentucky Warbler
Connecticut Warbler
Mourning Warbler +
Common Yellowthroat
Bahama Yellowthroat
Hooded Warbler
Wilson's Warbler
Canada Warbler +
Yellow-breasted Chat
Bananaquit
Summer Tanager
Scarlet Tanager
Western Spindalis
Cuban Grassquit
Black-faced Grassquit
Greater Antillean Bullfinch
Chipping Sparrow
Clay-colored Sparrow
Lark Sparrow +
Savannah Sparrow
Grasshopper Sparrow
Lincoln's Sparrow
Swamp Sparrow *
White-throated Sparrow *
White-crowned Sparrow
Dark-eyed Junco *

Snow Bunting *
Rose-breasted Grosbeak
Blue Grosbeak
Indigo Bunting
Painted Bunting
Dickcissel
Bobolink
Red-winged Blackbird

Yellow-headed Blackbird
Shiny Cowbird
Brown-headed Cowbird
Greater Antillean Oriole
Orchard Oriole +
Baltimore Oriole
House Sparrow

Bibliography

Allen, P. E. (1996) 'Breeding Biology and Natural History of the Bahama Swallow', *Wilson Bulletin* 108 (3): 480–495.

American Ornithologists' Union (1998) *Checklist of North American Birds*, 7th ed, American Ornithologists' Union, Washington DC.

Baltz, M. E. (1996) 'The Distribution and Status of Shiny Cowbirds on North Andros Island', *Bahamas Journal of Science* 3 (2): 2–6.

Baltz, M. E. (1997) 'Shiny Cowbirds in the Bahamas: A Threat to the Archipelago's Avifauna?' *El Pitirre* 10 (1): 21.

Baltz, M. E. (1997) 'Is the Bahama Yellowthroat a Threatened Species?' *Bahamas Journal of Science* 4 (3): 2–5.

Bancroft, G. T. (1992) 'A Closer Look: White-crowned Pigeon', *Birding* 24 (1): 21–24.

Beaman, M. and Madge, S. (1998) *The Handbook of Bird Identification for Europe and the Western Palearctic*, Princeton University Press.

Bond, J. (1993) *A Field Guide to the Birds of the West Indies*, 5th ed., Houghton Mifflin Company.

Bradley, P. (1995) *Birds of the Cayman Islands*, rev. ed., Caerulea Press, Italy.

Bradley, P. (1995) *The Birds of the Turks and Caicos Islands, The Official Checklist*, National Trust of the Turks and Caicos Islands.

Browning, M. R. (1994) 'A Taxonomic Review of Dendroica Petechia (Yellow Warbler) (Aves: Parulinae)', *Proceedings of the Biological Society of Washington* 107: 27–51.

Brudenell-Bruce, P.G.C. (1975) *The Birds of New Providence and The Bahama Islands*, Collins, London.

Buden, D. W. (1987) *The Birds of the Southern Bahamas*, The British Ornithologist Union.

Buden, D. W. (1985) 'New subspecies of Thick-billed Vireo (Aves: Vireoniidae) from the Caicos Islands with remarks on taxonomic status of other Populations', *Proceedings of the Biological Society of Washington* 98: 591–597.

Buden, D. W. (1986) 'A New Subspecies of Greater Antillean Bullfinch Loxigilla Violacea from the Caicos Islands with notes on other Populations', *Bulletin of the British Ornithologist Club* 106: 156–161.

Clements, J. (2000) *Birds of the World: A Checklist*, 5th ed.

Dickinson, E. C. (ed) (2003) *The Howard and Moore Complete Checklist of the Birds of the World*, revised and enlarged, 3rd ed., Princeton University Press.

Downer, A. and Sutton, R. (1990) *Birds of Jamaica: A Photographic Field Guide*, Cambridge University Press.

Dunn, J. and Garrett, K. (1997) *A Field Guide to Warblers of North Americal*, Houghton Mifflin Company.

Garrido, O. H., Parks, K. C., Reynard, G. B., Kirkconnell, A, and Sutton, R. (1997) 'Taxonomy of the Stripe-headed Tanager, Genus Spindalis (Aves: Thraupidae) of the West Indies', *Wilson Bulletin* 109 (4): 561–594.

Garrido, O.H. and Kirkconnell, A. (2000) *Field Guide to the Birds of Cuba*, Comstock Publishing Associates.

Gibbs, D., Barnes, E. and Cox, J. (2001) *Pigeons and Doves* Yale University Press.

Gorman, L. R. and Haig, S. M. (2002) 'Distribution and Abundance of Snowy Plovers in Eastern North America, the Caribbean, and The Bahamas', *Journal of Field Ornithology* 73 (1): 38–52.

Ground, R. (2001) *The Birds of the Turks and Caicos Islands*, Turks and Caicos National Trust.

Hancock, J. and Kushlan, J. (1984) *The Herons Handbook*, Harper and Row, Publishers.

Hayes, W. K., Barry, R. X., McKenzie, Z. and Barry, P. (2004) 'Grand Bahama's Brown-headed Nuthatch: a taxonomically distinct and endangered species', *Bahamas Journal of Science* 12 (1): 21–28.

Jaramillo, A. and Burke, P. (1999) *New World Blackbirds: The Icterids*, Princeton University Press.

Kaufman, K. (2000) *Birds of North America*, Houghton Mifflin Company.

Murphy, M. T., Zysik, J. and Pierce, A. (2004) 'Biogeography of the birds of The Bahamas with special reference to the island of San Salvador', *Journal of Field Ornithology* 75 (1): 18–30.

National Geographical Society (2002) *Field Guide to the Birds of North America*, 4th ed.

Lee, D. S. (1996) 'Winter avifauna of the Abaco National Park', *Bahamas Journal of Science* 3 (3): 7-15, 4 (1): 29–34.

Lee, D. S., and Clark, M. K. (1994) 'Seabirds of the Exuma Land and Sea Park', *Bahamas Journal of Science* 2 (1): 2–9, 2 (2): 15–21.

Oberle, M.W. (1999) *Puerto Rico's Birds in Photographs*, Editorial Humanitas, San Juan, Puerto Rico.

Olsen, K.M. and Larsson, H. (1995) *Terns of Europe and North America*, Princeton University Press.

Paterson, A. (1972) *Birds of The Bahamas*, Durrell Publications.

Paulson, D. (1993) *Shorebirds of the Pacific Northwest*, University of Washington Press.

Raffaele, H., Wiley, J., Garrido, O., Keith, A., and Raffaele, J. (1998) *A Guide to the Birds of the West Indies*, Princeton University Press.

Reynard, G. B., Garrido, O. H., and Sutton, R. L. (1993) 'Taxonomic revision of the Greater Antillean Pewee', *Wilson Bulletin* 105 (2): 217–227.

Robertson, Jr., W.B. and Woolfenden, G.E. (1992) *Florida Bird Species, An Annotated List*, Florida Ornithological Society, Special Publication No. 6.

Schreiber, E.A. and Lee, D.S. (eds) (2000) *Status and Conservation of West Indian Sea birds*, Society of Caribbean Ornithology, Special Publication No.1.

Schwartz, A. (1970) 'Subspecific variation in two species of Antillean birds', *Quarterly Journal of the Florida Academy of Sciences* 33: 221–236.

Short, L.L. (1982) *Woodpeckers of the World*, Delaware Museum of Natural History.

Sibley, David Allen (2000) *The Sibley Guide to Birds*, Alfred A. Knopf.

Smith, P. W., and Evered, D. S. (1992) 'La Sagra's Flycatcher', *Birding* 24: 294–297.

Smith, P. W., and Evered, D. S., Messick, L. R., and Wheeler, M. C. (1990) 'First verifiable records of the Thick-billed Vireo from the United States', *American Birds* 44: 372–376.

Smith, P. W., and Smith, S. A. (1990) 'The identification and status of the Bahama Swallow in Florida', *Birding* 22: 264–271.

Smith, P. W., Woolfenden, G. E., and Sprunt iv, A. (2000) 'The Loggerhead Kingbird in Florida: The evidence revisited', *North American Birds* 54: 235–240.

Svensson, L. and Grant, P.J. (1999) *Collins Bird Guide*, Harper Collins Publishers, London.

Taylor, B. (1998) Rails, *A Guide to the Rails, Crakes, Gallinules and Coots of the World*, Yale University Press.

White, Anthony (1998) *A Birder's Guide to the Bahama Islands (Including Turks and Caicos)* American Birding Association.

White, Anthony et al (2005) 'Preliminary Checklist of the Birds of the Bahamas', *Bahamas Journal of Science* 12 (2): 26–30

Winkler, H., Christie, D.A. and Nurney (1995) Woodpeckers, *A Guide to the Woodpeckers of the World*, Houghton Mifflin Company.

Wotzkow, C. (1998) 'Comments on the American Kestrel Falco Sparverius (Aves Falconidae) in the West Indies', *El Pitirre* 11 (1): 7–10.

Index of common names

ani, smooth-billed 137

bananaquit 199
bittern
    American 48
    least 48
blackbird, red-winged 211–212
bobolink 215
bobwhite, northern 118
booby
    brown 40–41
    red-footed 42. *See also*
    gannet.
bullfinch, Greater Antillean
    205
bunting
    indigo 208
    painted 209

catbird, gray 172
chuck-will's-widow 142
collared-dove, Eurasian
    127–128
coot, American 68
cormorant
    double-crested 45
    neotropic 44
cowbird
    brown-headed 213
    shiny 212–213
crow, Cuban 160
cuckoo
    mangrove 135

yellow-billed 135. *See also*
    lizard-cuckoo.

dove
    Caribbean 132
    mourning 130
    white-winged 128
    Zenaida 129. *See also*
    collared-dove; ground-
    dove; quail-dove.
dowitcher
    long-billed 88
    short-billed 88
duck
    ring-necked 33
    ruddy 29. *See also* pintail;
    scaup; shoveler; teal;
    wigeon and whistling-
    duck.
dunlin 87

egret
    cattle 56
    great 50
    reddish 54–55
    snowy 51
emerald, Cuban 143–144
falcon
    peregrine 124. *See also*
    kestel; merlin.
flamingo, greater 63–64
flycatcher
    Acadian 151

La Sagra's 153
scissor tailed 151. *See also* kingbird; peewee; phoebe.
frigatebird, magnificent 46

gallinule, purple 69
gannet, northern 41
gnatcatcher, blue-gray 167
golden-plover, American 75
goose
    Canada 126
    Snow 126
grassquit
    black-faced 204
    Cuban 203
grebe
    least 35
    pied-billed 36
grosbeak
    blue 210
    rose-breasted 210
ground-dove, common 131
gull
    black-headed 99
    Bonaparte's 99
    great black-backed 102
    herring 100
    laughing 97–98
    lesser black-backed 101
    ring-billed 99

harrier, northern 120
hawk
    red-tailed 121
    sharp-shinned 120. *See also* osprey.
heron
    great blue 49
    green 57
    little blue 52

tricolored 53. *See also* night-heron.
hummingbird
    ruby-throated 146. *See also* emerald; woodstar.

ibis
    glossy 62
    white 61

kestrel, American 122–123
killdeer 74
kingbird
    eastern 156
    gray 154
    loggerhead 155
    western 156
kingfisher, belted 147
kite, swallow-tailed 120
knot, red 87

limpkin 70
lizard-cuckoo, great 136

martin, purple 164
merganser
    hooded 34
    red-breasted 34
merlin 123
mockingbird
    Bahama 170
    northern 169
moorhen, common 67

night-heron
    black-crowned 58
    yellow-crowned 59
nighthawk
    Antillean 140–141
    common 141
noddy, brown 113

nuthatch, brown-headed 166

oriole
  Baltimore 216
  Greater Antillean 214
osprey 120
ovenbird 197
owl
  barn 138
  burrowing 139
oystercatcher, American 78

parrot, Cuban 134
parula, northern 185
pelican, brown 43
petrel, black-capped 37
pewee
  Cuban 151–152. See also
    wood-pewee.
Phoebe, Eastern 152
pigeon
  rock 125
  white-crowned 126
pintail
  northern 32
  white-cheeked 28
pipit, American 174
plover
  black-bellied 75
  piping 77
  semipalmated 76
  snowy 72
  Wilson's 73. See also
    golden-plover; killdeer.

quail-dove, Key West 133

rail
  black 66
  clapper 65
  virginia 66. See also sora.
redstart, American 194

robin, American 168

sanderling 91
sandpiper
  least 94
  pectoral 90
  semipalmated 92
  solitary 84
  spotted 85
  stilt 89
  western 93
  white-rumped 95
sapsucker, yellow-bellied 149
scaup, lesser 33
shearwater
  Audubon's 37
  Cory's 37
  greater 37
  sooty 37
shorebirds 71–95
shoveler, northern 32
skimmer, black 116
snipe, Wilson's 90
sora 66
sparrow
  chipping 206
  clay-colored 206
  grasshopper 207
  house 217
  Lincoln's 206
  savannah 207
  white-crowned 206
spindalis, western 200–201
spoonbill, roseate 60
starling, European 173
stilt, black-necked 79
storm-petrel
  band-rumped 38
  Leach's 38
  Wilson's 38
swallow
  Bahama 161–162

bank 165
barn 164
cave 163
cliff 163
northern rough-winged 165
tree 162. *See also* martin.

tanager
scarlet 202
summer 202. *See also* spindalis.
teal
blue-winged 31
green-winged 31
tern
black 115
bridled 110–111
Caspian 106
common 114
Forster's 116
gull-billed 104
least 109
roseate 108
royal 105–106
sandwich 107
sooty 112. *See also* noddy.
thrasher, pearly-eyed 171
thrush
red-legged 168. *See also* thrush family 168.
tropicbird, white-tailed 39
turnstone, ruddy 86
tyrant flycatchers 151–156

vireo 157–159
black-whiskered 158
blue-headed 159
Philadelphia 159
red-eyed 158
thick-billed 157
white-eyed 159

yellow-throated 159
vulture
black 119
turkey 119

warbler
bay-breasted 184
black-and-white 192
blackburnian 184
black-throated blue 188
black-throated green 188
blackpoll 193
blue-winged 184
Cape May 187
chestnut-sided 184
hooded 197
Kirtland's 190
magnolia 186
Nashville 184
olive-capped 180
orange-crowned 184
palm 192
pine 181
prairie 191
prothonotary 194
Swainson's 195
Tennessee 184
Wilson's 184
worm-eating 195
yellow 177
yellow-rumped 189
yellow-throated 178–179
waterthrush
Louisiana 196
northern 196
waxwing, cedar 175
whimbrel 86
whistling-duck
black-bellied 26
fulvous 26
West Indian 27
wigeon, American 30

willet 80–81
wood-pewee, Eastern 152
woodpecker
    hairy 150
    West Indian 148–149. *See
    also* sapsucker.
woodstar, Bahama 145–146
wood warblers 176–198

yellowlegs
    greater 83–84
    lesser 83–84
yellowthroat
    Bahama 182–183
    common 198

Index of scientific names

Accipitridae 120–121
Actitus macularius 85
Agelaius phoeniceus bryanti 211–212
Alcedinidae 147
Amazona leucocephala bahamensis 134
Ammodramus savannarum 207
Anas acuta 32
Anas americana 30
Anas bahamensis 28
Anas clypeata 32
Anas crecca 31
Anas discors 31
Anatidae 26–34
Anous stolidus 113
Anthus rubescens 174
Aramidae 70
Aramus guarauna 70
Archilochus colubris 146
Ardea alba 50
Ardea herodias 49
Ardeidae 47–59
Arenaria interpes 86
Athene cunicularia 139
Aythya affinis 33
Aythya collaris 33

Bombycilla cedrorum 175
Bombycillidae 175
Botaurus lentiginosus 48
Bubulcus ibis 56

Buteo jamaicensis 121
Butorides virescens bahamensis 57

Calidris alba 91
Calidris alpina 87
Calidris canutus 87
Calidris fuscicollis 95
Calidris himantopus 89
Calidris mauri 93
Calidris melanotos 90
Calidris minutilla 94
Calidris pusilla 92
Calliphlox evelynae 145–146
Caprimulgidae 140–142
Caprimulgus carolinensis 142
Cardinalidae 208
Cathartes aura 119
Cathartidae 119
Catoptrophorus semipalmatus 80–81
Ceryle alcyon 147
Charadriidae 72–77
Charadrius alexandrinus 72
Charadrius melodus 77
Charadrius semipalmatus 76
Charadrius vociferus 74
Charadrius wilsonia 73
Chlidonias niger surinamensis 115
Chlorostilbon ricordii 143–144

Chordeiles gundlachii
  140–141
Chordeiles minor 141
Coccyzus americanus 135
Coccyzus minor 135
Coereba flaveola
  bahamensis 199
Colinus virginianus 118
Columba livia 125
Columbidae 125–133
Columbina passerina 131
Contopus caribaeus
  bahamensis 151–152
Contopus virens 152
Coragyps atratus 119
Corvidae 160
Corvus nasicus 160
Crotophaga ani 137
Cuculidae 135–137

Dendrocygna arborea 27
Dendroica caerulescens 188
Dendroica coronata 189
Dendroica discolor 191
Dendroica dominica
  dominica 179
Dendroica dominica
  flavescens 178
Dendroica kirtlandii 190
Dendroica magnolia 186
Dendroica palmarum 192
Dendroica petechia flaviceps
  177
Dendroica pinus achrustera
  181
Dendroica pityophila 180
Dendroica striata 193
Dendroica tigrina 187
Dendroica virens 188
Dolichonyx oryzivorus 215
Dumetella carolinensis 172

Egretta caerulea 52
Egretta rufescens 54–55
Egretta thula 51
Egretta tricolor 53
Emberizidae 203–207
Eudocimus albus 61

Falco columbarius 123
Falco peregrinus 124
Falco sparverius 122–123
Falconidae 122–124
Fregata magnificens 46
Fregatidae 46
Fulica americana 68

Gallinago dclicata 90
Gallinula chloropus 67
Geothlypis rostrata 182–183
Geothlypis trichas 198
Geotrygon chrysia 133

Haematopodidae 78
Haematopus palliatus 78
Helmitheros vermivorum 195
Himantopus mexicanus 79
Hirundinidae 161–165
Hirundo rustica 164
Hydrobatidae 38

Icteridae 211
Icterus dominicensis
  northropi 214
Icterus glabula 216
Ixobrychus exilis 48

Laridae 96–116
Larus argentatus
  smithsonianus 100
Larus atricilla 97–98
Larus delawarensis 99
Larus fuscus graellsii 101

Larus marinus 102
Laterallus jamaicensis 66
Leptotila jamaicensis 132
Limnodromus griseus 88
Limnodromus scolopaceus 88
Limnothlypsis swainsonii 195
Lophodytes cucullatus 34
Loxigilla violacea violacea 205

Margarops fuscatus 171
Melanerpes superciliaris 148–149
Mergus serrator 34
Mimidae 169–172
Mimus gundlachii 170
Mimus polyglottos 169
Mniotilta varia 192
Molothrus ater 213
Molothrus bonariensis 212–213
Morus bassanus 41
Motacillidae 174
Myiarchus sagrae lucaysiensis 153

Numenius phaeopus 86
Nyctanassa violacea 59
Nycticorax nycticorax 58

Oceanites oceanicus 38
Odontophoridae 118
Oxyura jamaicensis 29

Pandion haliaetus 120
Parula americana 185
Parulidae 176
Passer domesticus 217
Passerculus sandwichensis 207
Passeridae 217

Passerina caerulea 210
Passerina ciris 209
Passerina cyanea 208
Patagioenas leucocephala 126
Pelecanidae 43
Pelecanus occidentalis 43
Petrochelidon fulva 163
Petrochelidon pyrrhonota 163
Phaethon aethereus 39
Phaethon lepturus 39
Phaethontidae 39
Phalacrocoracidae 44–45
Phalacrocorax auritus 45
Phalacrocorax brasilianus 44
Pheucticus ludovicianus 210
Phoenicopteridae 63–64
Phoenicopterus ruber 63–64
Picidae 148–150
Picoides villosus 150
Piranga olivacea 202
Piranga rubra 202
Platalea ajaja 60
Plegadis falcinellus 62
Pluvialis dominica 75
Pluvialis squatarola 75
Podicipedidae 35–36
Podilymbus podiceps 36
Polioptila caerulea 167
Porphyrio martinica 69
Porzana carolina 66
Procellariidae 37
Progne subis 164
Protonotaria citrea 194
Psittacidae 134
Puffinus lherminieri 37

Rallidae 65–69
Rallus limicola 66
Rallus longirostris coryi 65
Recurvirostridae 79
Riparia riparia 165

Rynchops niger 116

Saurothera merlini
  bahamensis 136
Sayornis phoebe 152
Scolopacidae 80–95
Seiurus aurocapilla 197
Seiurus motacilla 196
Seiurus noveboracensis 196
Setophaga ruticilla 194
Sitta pusilla insularis 166
Sittidae 166
Sphyrapicus varius 149
Spindalis zena 200–201
Spizella pallida 206
Stelgidopteryx serripennis
  165
Sterna anaethetus 110–111
Sterna antillarum 109
Sterna caspia 106
Sterna dougallii 108
Sterna forsteri 116
Sterna fuscata 111, 112
Sterna hirundo 114
Sterna maxima 105–106
Sterna nilotica 104
Sterna sandvicensis 107
Streptopelia decaocto
  127–128
Strigidae 139
Sturnidae 173
Sturnus vulgaris 173
Sula leucogaster 40–41
Sula sula 42
Sulidae 40–42
Sylviidae 167

Tachybaptus dominicus 35
Tachycineta bicolor 162
Tachycineta cyaneoviridis
  161–162
Thraupidae 200

Threskiornithidae 60–62
Tiaris bicolor 204
Tiaris canora 203
Tringa flavipes 83–84
Tringa melanoleuca 83–84
Tringa solitaria 84
Trochilidae 143–146
Turdidae 168
Turdus plumbeus plumbeus
  168
Tyrannidae 151–156
Tyrannus caudifasciatus
  bahamensis 155
Tyrannus dominicensis 154
Tyrannus tyrannus 156
Tyrannus verticalis 156
Tyto alba 138
Tytonidae 138

Vermivora celata celata 184
Vermivora peregrina 184
Vireo altiloquus 158
Vireo crassirostris 157
Vireo flavifrons 159
Vireo griseus 159
Vireo olivaceus 158
Vireonidae 157–159

Wilsonia citrina 197

Zenaida asiatica 128
Zenaida aurita 129
Zenaida macroura 130